GOSPEL STUDY SERIES

Your Study of the
Pearl of Great Price
Made Easier

David J. Ridges

Springville, Utah

© 2009 David J. Ridges

All rights reserved.

No part of this book may be reproduced in any form whatsoever, whether by graphic, visual, electronic, film, microfilm, tape recording, or any other means, without prior written permission of the author, except in the case of brief passages embodied in critical reviews and articles.

ISBN 13: 978-1-59955-344-3

Published by CFI, an imprint of Cedar Fort, Inc.
2373 W. 700 S., Springville, UT, 84663
Distributed by Cedar Fort, Inc., www.cedarfort.com

   Library of Congress Cataloging-in-Publication Data

   Ridges, David J.
   The Pearl of Great Price made easier / David J. Ridges.
      p. cm.
   Includes bibliographical references.
   ISBN 978-1-59955-344-3 (acid-free paper)
   1. Pearl of Great Price--Criticism, interpretation, etc. I. Title.

   BX8629.P5R64 2009
   289.3'2--dc22

                               2009016618

Cover design by Jen Boss
Cover design © 2009 by Lyle Mortimer
Edited by Heidi Doxey

Printed in the United States of America

10 9 8 7 6 5 4 3 2 1

Printed on acid-free paper

Your Study of the
Pearl of Great Price
Made Easier

Books
by David J. Ridges

The *Gospel Study Series:*

- *Isaiah Made Easier*
- *The New Testament Made Easier, Part 1*
- *The New Testament Made Easier, Part 2*
- *Your Study of The Book of Mormon Made Easier, Part 1*
- *Your Study of The Book of Mormon Made Easier, Part 2*
- *Your Study of The Book of Mormon Made Easier, Part 3*
- *Your Study of The Doctrine and Covenants Made Easier, Part 1*
- *Your Study of The Doctrine and Covenants Made Easier, Part 2*
- *Your Study of The Doctrine and Covenants Made Easier, Part 3*
- *The Old Testament Made Easier—Selections from the Old Testament, Part 1*
- *The Old Testament Made Easier—Selections from the Old Testament, Part 2*
- *The Old Testament Made Easier—Selections from the Old Testament, Part 3*
- *Your Study of the Pearl of Great Price Made Easier*

Additional titles by David J. Ridges:

- *Our Savior, Jesus Christ: His Life and Mission to Cleanse and Heal*
- *Mormon Beliefs and Doctrines Made Easier*
- *The Proclamation on the Family: The Word of the Lord on More Than 30 Current Issues*
- *50 Signs of the Times and the Second Coming*
- *Doctrinal Details of the Plan of Salvation: From Premortality to Exaltation*

Watch for these titles to also become available through Cedar Fort as e-books and on CD.

The Gospel Studies Series

Welcome to this volume of the Gospel Studies Series, which will take you through the Pearl of Great Price verses with brief notes and commentary designed to keep you in the scripture while providing instruction and help along the way.

As with other study guides in the Gospel Studies Series, this work is intended to be a user-friendly, introductory study of the Pearl of Great Price as well as a refresher course for more advanced students of the scriptures. It is also designed and formatted to be a quick-reference resource that will enable readers to easily look up a particular verse or set of verses and gain additional understanding regarding them. It is hoped by the author that readers will write in the margins of their own scriptures some of the notes given in this study guide in order to assist them as they read and study the Pearl of Great Price in the future.

—David J. Ridges

The JST References in Study Guides by David J. Ridges

Note that some of the JST (The Joseph Smith Translation of the Bible) references I use in my study guides are not found in our LDS Bible in the footnotes or in the Joseph Smith Translation section in the reference section in the back. The reason for this, as explained to me while writing curriculum materials for the Church, is simply that there is not enough room to include all of the JST additions and changes to the King James Version of the Bible (the one we use in the English speaking part of the Church). As you can imagine, as was likewise explained to me, there were difficult decisions that had to be made by the Scriptures Committee of the Church as to which JST contributions were included and which were not.

The Joseph Smith Translation of the Bible in its entirety can generally be found in or ordered through LDS bookstores. It was originally published under the auspices of the Reorganized Church of Jesus Christ of Latter Day Saints in Independence, Missouri. The version of the JST I prefer to use is a parallel column version, *Joseph Smith's "New Translation" of the Bible*, published by Herald Publishing House, Independence, Missouri, in 1970. This parallel column version compares the King James Bible with the JST side by side and includes only the verses that have changes, additions, or deletions made by the Prophet Joseph Smith.

By the way, some members of the Church have wondered if we can trust the JST since it was published by a breakaway faction from our Church. They worry that some changes from Joseph Smith's original manuscript might have been made to support doctrinal differences between us and the RLDS Church. This is not the case. Many years ago, Robert J. Matthews of the Brigham Young University Religion Department was given permission by leaders of the RLDS Church to come to their Independence, Missouri, headquarters and personally compare the original JST document word for word with their publication of the JST. Brother Matthews was thus able to verify that they had been meticulously true to the Prophet's original work.

Contents

Foreword xi
Introduction xiii
Introduction to the Pearl of Great Price xv
The Book of Moses 1
The Book of Abraham 119
The Facsimiles in the Book of Abraham 163
Joseph Smith—Matthew 173
Joseph Smith—Matthew and Matthew 24
    Parallel Column Comparison 186
Joseph Smith—History 195
Articles of Faith 243
Sources 253
About the Author 256

Foreword

There is great value in studying the word of the Lord in the scriptures themselves. The Holy Ghost bears witness and teaches our minds and hearts as we do so. In over forty years of teaching in the Church, including thirty-five years of teaching seminary and institute of religion classes, I found that my students had an inspired hunger to understand the scriptures themselves. They developed an eagerness to mark their own scriptures and make brief notes in the margins as we studied blocks of scripture, verse by verse. Time and again, students from years past have approached me and expressed appreciation for this approach to scripture study, showing me their marked up scriptures and saying that the notes bring back to their minds the discussions and lessons of past classes as they continue to study their scriptures today.

With this in mind, this study guide for the Pearl of Great Price is designed to help you study this precious "pearl" of scripture verse by verse, as if you were in a class with the teacher giving brief background and commentary as you go along. It is designed to help readers:

- Quickly gain a basic understanding of the Pearl of Great Price as they read and study, through the use of brief explanatory notes in brackets within the verses as well as some notes between the verses.

- Better understand the beautiful language of the scriptures.

- Mark their own scriptures and put brief notes in the margins that will help them understand now and remember later some of the things that a particular passage of scripture teaches.

It is hoped by the author that this book will serve effectively as a "teacher in your hand" to members of the Church as they seek to increase their understanding and testimony of the Pearl of Great Price.

A special thanks goes to my wife, Janette, and to my sons and daughters who have encouraged and supported me every step of the way.

—David J. Ridges

Introduction

The Pearl of Great Price is a compilation of five books:

- Selections from the Book of Moses

- The Book of Abraham

- Joseph Smith—Matthew

- Joseph Smith—History

- The Articles of Faith of The Church of Jesus Christ of Latter-day Saints

Though it is a comparatively short book of scripture, the Pearl of Great Price is very concentrated. It is not unusual for individuals and classes who undertake a careful study of this standard work of the Church to find that it takes far longer than they originally planned. It seems that almost every verse or set of related verses leads to rich discussion of doctrines of the plan of salvation and consideration of related passages in other volumes of scripture.

The style of this study guide is somewhat conversational to help you feel as if a teacher were guiding you through the Pearl of Great Price. The true teacher is the Holy Ghost. It is the desire and hope of the author that the helps provided in this book will be of some value in setting the stage for the reader to have a rich experience in being taught by the Spirit.

Introduction to the Pearl of Great Price

The Pearl of Great Price has five books:

Selections from the Book of Moses

The Book of Moses was given to the Prophet Joseph Smith by direct revelation between June of 1830 and February of 1831, as he worked on what we now know as the Joseph Smith Translation of the Bible (JST).

The Book of Abraham

The Book of Abraham came to us as a result of the Prophet Joseph Smith's translation of some ancient Egyptian papyri which came into the hands of the Church in Kirtland, Ohio, in July 1835.

Joseph Smith—Matthew

Joseph Smith—Matthew is an extract from the Joseph Smith Translation of the Bible (JST) and was given by revelation to the Prophet in 1831. It deals with many of the signs of the times, in other words, prophecies that will be fulfilled before the Savior's Second Coming. It is Matthew 23:39 and Matthew chapter 24 of the King James Version of the Bible, with about 450 words added by Joseph Smith under inspiration. He also rearranged the order of some of the verses.

Joseph Smith—History

Joseph Smith's account of his life given in 1838, including the First Vision, the coming forth of the Book of Mormon, and the restoration of the Aaronic Priesthood.

The Articles of Faith

An extract from the Wentworth Letter, written by the Prophet Joseph Smith at the request of John Wentworth, the editor of the Chicago Democrat newspaper, in 1842. In it, the Prophet included thirteen brief statements or "articles" that explain some of the major beliefs of The Church of Jesus Christ of Latter-day Saints. The letter was published in the Church's newspaper, *Times and Seasons*, in March, 1842.

The origin of the name "Pearl of Great Price"

The Pearl of Great Price gets its name from a parable about a "pearl of great price" given by the Savior as recorded in Matthew 13:45–46. We will quote the parable here using **bold** for emphasis.

> 45 Again, the kingdom of heaven is like unto a merchant man, seeking goodly pearls:
>
> 46 Who, when he had found one **pearl of great price**, went and sold all that he had, and bought it.

As you can see from the parable, the "pearl" of great value represents the gospel of Jesus Christ. The merchant considered the pearl to be of such value that he gave up everything else he had in order to obtain it. In other words, it is worth sacrificing whatever is necessary in order to possess the gospel in our lives.

The first publishing of the Pearl of Great Price

In 1851, Elder Franklin D. Richards, a member of the Quorum of the Twelve Apostles who was then presiding over the missionary work of the Church in England, compiled several revelations and teachings of the Prophet Joseph Smith, including Moses and Abraham, for the Saints in England to read and study. He titled the publication "The Pearl of Great Price." The contents of the book were revised somewhat over the next several years, and it eventually became a "Standard Work" of the Church in 1880 (in other words, it was officially canonized, that is, accepted by the Church as scripture).

THE BOOK OF MOSES

General Background

As mentioned above, the Book of Moses was given to the Prophet Joseph Smith by direct revelation between June 1830 and February 1831. You may wish to underline or highlight this fact in your own scriptures in the heading to the Book of Moses.

Moses, which consists of eight chapters in the Pearl of Great Price, was given to the Prophet during the time he was working on Genesis in his inspired translation of the King James Bible, which is now referred to as the Joseph Smith Translation of the Bible, or the JST. During these months, the Prophet completed his translation of Genesis 1:1 through 6:13, which now appears in the Pearl of Great Price as Moses, chapters 1–8.

As you can see, by comparing the Book of Moses with corresponding chapters in Genesis, a great deal has been left out of this part of the Bible. The information found in Moses 1 is not found in Genesis at all. Moses 2–8 add much to the account found in Genesis up to the Flood.

By way of reminder, it was Moses who wrote the books of Genesis, Exodus, Leviticus, Numbers, and Deuteronomy in the Bible. These five books are sometimes referred to as the Pentateuch, or the five books of Moses.

MOSES, CHAPTER 1
(Revealed to Joseph Smith in June 1830)

Background

The events spoken of in Moses, chapter 1, take place after the "burning bush" and before Moses returns to Egypt to lead the children of Israel out of Egyptian bondage. See verses 17, 25–26. Thus, we are given to understand that the Lord gave Moses tremendous strength and perspective, not recorded in the Bible, before sending him to accomplish the extremely difficult task of leading the Israelites into the wilderness and toward the promised land. We will proceed now with our verse-by-verse study of Moses, chapter 1, using bold for teaching emphasis.

As we do so, we will be introduced to many gospel concepts and doctrines. Indeed, the Book of Moses is filled with understanding and facts, in concentrated form, that can greatly enhance our understanding of other scriptures and how God operates.

Beginning with verse 1, we see God, who, in this case is Jehovah, the premortal Jesus Christ, taking Moses to a "high mountain," which, among other things, is symbolic of a place where one can be privileged to see as God sees. Thus, Moses is given perspective and enabled to lead his people, many of whom are rebellious and crude, with the patience of God, who sees all things from a "high mountain" perspective and knows our potential to become like Him. We will say more about this as we continue.

1 The words of God [*Jehovah, the premortal Jesus Christ*], which he spake unto Moses at a time when Moses was **caught up into an exceedingly high mountain** [*symbolic of being given the perspectives that God has*],

> We do not know whether the "high mountain" in verse 1, above, is literal or symbolic. Suffice it to say that it represents a place of instruction, strengthening and being given the perspectives of God, in order to see as He sees and do His work as He would do it in leading people toward exaltation.
>
> Next, we are told that Moses saw the premortal Christ face to face. We understand that Jesus Christ is the God of the Old Testament, working under the direction of His Father. Joseph Fielding Smith explained this. He said:
>
> "All revelation since the fall has come through Jesus Christ, who is the Jehovah of the Old Testament. . . . He is the God of Israel, the Holy One of Israel; the one who led that nation out of Egyptian bondage, and who gave and fulfilled the Law of Moses. The Father has never dealt with man directly and personally since the fall, and he has never appeared except to introduce and bear record of the Son" (*Doctrines of Salvation,* Vol. 1, page 27).

2 And **he saw God face to face**, and **he talked with him**, and the glory of God was upon Moses; therefore Moses could endure his presence.

> Did you notice the brief explanation, in verse 2, above, as to why Moses could survive being in the direct presence of God, even though he was only a mortal? It said that Moses had the glory of God upon him. Verses 11 and 14 give us a gospel vocabulary word for this. The word is "transfigured." A mortal can be transfigured by the power of the Holy Ghost in order to survive the direct glory and presence of God. Elder Bruce R. McConkie explained this. He said:

"Transfiguration is a special change in appearance and nature which is wrought upon a person or thing by the power of God. This divine transformation is from a lower to a higher state; it results in a more exalted, impressive, and glorious condition. . . .

"By the power of the Holy Ghost many prophets have been transfigured so as to stand in the presence of God and view the visions of eternity" (*Mormon Doctrine,* page 803).

In fact, the righteous Saints who are living upon the earth at the time of the Savior's Second Coming will be transfigured and caught up to meet Him (see D&C 88:96). If they were not transfigured, their mortal bodies would be burned by the glory that will accompany Him as He comes to cleanse the world of wickedness and to rule and reign on earth for a thousand years.

In verse 3, next, the Savior formally introduces Himself to Moses.

3 And God spake unto Moses, saying: Behold, **I am the Lord God Almighty**, and **Endless is my name**; for **I am without beginning of days or end of years**; and is not this endless?

Perhaps you have noticed that often in the scriptures, the Savior speaks directly for the Father, without formally notifying us that He is going to do so. This is called "divine investiture." We see an example of this next, in verses 4–7 (especially verse 6), where Jesus Christ speaks directly for the Father.

4 And, behold, **thou art my son**; wherefore look, and I will show thee the workmanship of mine hands; but not all, for my works are without end [*including worlds without number*], and also my words, for they never cease [*the doctrine of continuous revelation*].

5 Wherefore, no man [*no mortal*] can behold [*see*] all my works, except he behold all my glory; and no man can behold all my glory, and afterwards remain in the flesh on the earth.

In verse 6, next, the Savior, speaking for the Father, informs Moses that he has a role that is symbolic of the Savior's role. Moses is to be a savior to his people, just as Jesus Christ is the Savior of all. Moses is to free his people, the children of Israel, from the spiritual darkness and wickedness that has overcome them during many generations in the bondage of Egyptian slavery. He will lead them through the waters of the Red Sea (symbolic of baptism) and into the promised land (symbolic of heaven). This is similar to the Savior's role of leading us from a world of sin to the cleansing waters of baptism and, through our obedience to His commandments and leadership thereafter, on to the promised land (celestial exaltation).

Watch, now, as Moses is tenderly told that his role is symbolic of the Savior's.

6 And I have a work for thee, Moses, my son; and thou art in the similitude of mine Only Begotten [*Moses' role is symbolic of the Savior's role*]; **and mine Only Begotten is and shall be the Savior, for he is full of grace** [*He is filled with the ability to help us*] **and truth; but there is no God beside me** [*Heavenly Father is the Supreme God—see Ephesians 4:6*], **and all things are present with me, for I know them all.**

You can see another example of such divine investiture, in which Jesus speaks for the Father, in D&C 29:42, 46. In Moses 5:9, there is even an example of divine investiture in which the Holy Ghost speaks directly for the Savior.

Just a quick additional comment about the phrase "there is no God beside me" in verse 6, above. Remember that Moses was raised in Egypt, a culture where the people considered their many idols to be gods. In fact, the Pharaoh was considered by his people to be a god. Thus the statement "there is no God beside me" could be a simple reminder to Moses that idols are not gods, that Pharaoh is not a god, and that there is one true God, Heavenly Father, who rules and reigns supreme.

Next, Moses is told that he will be shown details about this earth upon which we live.

7 And now, behold, this one thing [*our earth*] **I show unto thee, Moses, my son**, **for thou art in the world, and now I show it unto thee.**

In verse 8, next, by the power of the Holy Ghost, Moses is enabled to comprehend and understand far more than a mortal would otherwise be capable of. One of the lessons we can learn from this verse is that through the power of the Holy Ghost, we can be enabled to know and understand far beyond our mortal capabilities and limitations. We will continue to use **bold** for teaching emphasis.

8 And it came to pass that Moses looked, and beheld the world upon which he was created; and **Moses beheld the world and the ends thereof, and all the children of men** [*all the people*] **which are,**

and which were created; of the same he greatly marveled and wondered [*he was astonished*].

> Beginning with verse 9, next, the stage is set for Satan's coming onto the scene and attempting to persuade Moses to worship him, taking advantage of the fact that Moses is no longer in the direct presence of God. Certainly there is symbolism in this. Having come to earth, we are no longer in the direct presence of God, and Lucifer does everything he can to take advantage of that fact.
>
> Before Satan enters the scene in verse 12, we are given additional perspective and doctrine in verses 9–11. For instance, a lesson for us in verse 9 might be that when left to ourselves, without the power of God in our lives, we are basically helpless.

9 And the presence of God withdrew from Moses, that his glory was not upon Moses; and **Moses was left unto himself**. And as he was left unto himself, he **fell unto the earth**.

> In verse 10, next, one lesson or perspective for us is the power of God compared to that of man. For Moses, this apparently came as a surprise. He had been reared for forty years as an Egyptian prince and was a mighty man in that culture (see Acts 7:22). Among other things, according to the Jewish historian Flavius Josephus, he had gained great fame as a successful military leader (see *Antiquities of the Jews*, book 2, chapters 9 and 10). In light of this background of being a "mighty" man associated with great and powerful leaders and being accustomed to commanding and being obeyed for the first forty years of his life, no wonder Moses was startled, as expressed at the end of verse 10 and the beginning of verse 11.

10 And it came to pass that it was for the space of many hours before Moses did again receive his natural strength like unto man; and **he said unto himself**: Now, for this cause **I know that man is nothing, which thing I never had supposed.**

> Over my years of teaching, students have often asked how the observation that "man is nothing" can be reconciled with the great "worth of souls" taught in D&C 18:10. The answer is simple. It deals with context. Moses had discovered that "man is nothing" when compared to God, not that man has no worth. In fact, he will express his faith in the value and worth of souls shortly, in verse 13, as he bears witness of his great worth as a "son of God."
>
> Continuing, verse 11 explains how Moses could survive in

the direct presence of God. As quoted previously, he was transfigured by the Holy Ghost, which enabled him to be in the direct presence of God without withering and dying.

11 **But now mine own eyes have beheld God**; but not my natural, but my spiritual eyes, for my natural eyes could not have beheld; for **I should have** [*would have*] **withered and died in his presence; but his glory was upon me**; and I beheld his face, for **I was transfigured** before him.

Once in a while, students get a bit confused between the words "transfigured" and "translated" in reference to people. We will briefly define each of these gospel vocabulary words:

Transfigured
To be temporarily changed and enabled by the power of the Holy Ghost to be in the direct presence of God while still in a mortal body. This is what happened to Moses.

Translated
To be changed for a longer period of time in order to remain on earth and fulfill a special mission, such as is the case with John the Apostle and the Three Nephites. In Third Nephi, chapter 28, we read that the mortal bodies of the Three Nephites were changed such that they could remain on earth, were no longer subject to physical pain, and were no longer subject to the power of Satan. These four translated beings (John and the Three Nephites) will continue ministering on earth until the Second Coming of the Savior, at which time they will "be changed in the twinkling of an eye from mortality to immortality" (3 Nephi 28:8).

Shifting our attention now to verse 12, next, we see Satan approaching Moses to tempt him. Remember, in verse 6, that Moses was told that God had a "work" for him to do and that his mission was symbolic of the mission of Jesus Christ. In conjunction with this, it is interesting to note that as the Savior embarked on His mission to save His people, Satan approached Him and attempted to detour Him by tempting Him, among other things, to "fall down and worship me" (Matthew 4:3–10).

So, likewise, as Moses was about to return to Egypt to save his people, Lucifer approached him in an attempt to stop him from fulfilling his mission. As seems to be quite typical of Satan, he starts out somewhat suave and mild in verse 12, inviting Moses to worship him, but as things move along, he will show his true nature as he yells and rants in verse 19.

12 And it came to pass that when Moses had said these words, behold, **Satan came tempting him, saying: Moses, son of man, worship me.**

By the way, did you notice the put-down used by the devil in verse 12? Satan addresses Moses as "son of man" rather than as a "son of God," implying that Moses does not have a divine nature or eternal worth. Moses will set the record straight in verses 13–15, next.

13 And it came to pass that **Moses looked upon Satan and said: Who art thou?** [*perhaps meaning "Who do you think you are?"*] For behold, **I am a son of God**, in the similitude of his Only Begotten; and **where is thy glory, that I should worship thee?**

14 For behold, **I could not look upon God, except his glory should come upon me, and I were transfigured before him. But I can look upon thee in the natural man** [*in other words, Moses could look upon Satan without needing to be transfigured*]. Is it not so, surely?

15 Blessed be the name of my God, for his Spirit hath not altogether withdrawn from me, or else **where is thy glory, for it is darkness unto me?** And I can judge [*discern*] between thee and God; for God said unto me: Worship God, for him only shalt thou serve.

Among the vital lessons we can learn from verses 16–22 is the fact that we cannot overcome the devil by ourselves. We must have the help of the Savior. As you will see, it is not until his fourth attempt to have Lucifer depart that Moses commands in the name of Jesus Christ (verse 21). Then Satan departs.

It appears that perhaps at first, Moses felt that he could handle the situation by himself, so he commanded Lucifer to leave, much the same perhaps as he had done as a crown prince and military leader in Egypt. It didn't work. The attempts in verses 16, 18, and 20 were unsuccessful. We will number these attempts as we proceed. We will also deal with other subjects and add notes about them as we go along.

As stated above, Moses makes his first attempt to command the devil to depart in verse 16.

16 **Get thee hence, Satan [1]**; deceive me not; for God said unto me: Thou art after the similitude of mine Only Begotten [*the fact that Moses knows that he is a child of God and has eternal worth is a*

great source of strength to him in his quest to overcome the devil].

Verse 17, next, provides the timing of this event in the life of Moses. As you can see, the interview with Jehovah (JST Exodus 3:2) at the "burning bush" had already taken place (Exodus 3:1–10). Moses uses this as part of his defense against the devil here.

17 And he [*the Lord, Jehovah, Jesus Christ, speaking for the Father through divine investiture*] also gave me commandments **when he called unto me out of the burning bush**, saying: Call upon God in the name of mine Only Begotten, and worship me.

Another great lesson for us here is that Moses emphasizes his determination to keep the commandments of God, including calling "upon God in the name of mine Only Begotten" and worshipping the Father. You can feel the determination of Moses to do so in verse 18, next.

Yet another lesson for us is that keeping the commandments opens up additional opportunities for us to inquire of him and thus continue our celestial education.

18 And again Moses said: **I will not cease to call upon God, I have other things to inquire of him**: for his glory has been upon me, wherefore I can judge between him and thee. **Depart hence, Satan [2]**.

Satan will still not depart from Moses. As mentioned earlier, Lucifer started out somewhat calm and sophisticated as he began his initial temptation of Moses (verse 12). Now, however, as he sees that he is failing, his true vicious nature comes out, and he desperately yells and rants against him, even commanding him—an attempt to counterfeit God!

19 And now, **when Moses had said these words, Satan cried with a loud voice, and ranted** upon the earth, **and commanded**, saying: I am the Only Begotten, worship me [*this, of course, is an outright lie; one of Satan's titles might well be "the Great Counterfeiter"*].

It appears that at this point, Moses begins to realize that it is not so easy to get rid of Satan, and fear enters his heart as he sees the devil and his evil kingdom in their awful reality. Moses will attempt yet a third time to make Lucifer depart. He will still not succeed.

20 And it came to pass that **Moses began to fear exceedingly; and as he began to fear, he saw the bitterness of hell**. Nevertheless, calling upon God, he received

strength, and he commanded, saying: **Depart from me, Satan [3]**, for this one God only will I worship, which is the God of glory [*Satan has no glory at all*].

Next, we are clearly taught that "there is none other name given under heaven save it be this Jesus Christ, of which I have spoken, whereby man can be saved" (2 Nephi 25:20. It is a simple fact that it is only through the Savior that we can overcome the devil.

21 And now Satan began to tremble, and the earth shook; and Moses received strength, and called upon God, saying: **In the name of the Only Begotten, depart hence, Satan [4]**.

This time, because of the power of Christ, Satan departs (verse 22, next). In so doing, he displays great frustration and anger at being obligated by God's power to obey such a command. One of the important and comforting lessons we learn from this scene is that God does have power over Lucifer.

22 And it came to pass that **Satan** cried with a loud voice, with weeping, and wailing, and gnashing of teeth [*this sounds very much like a tantrum*]; and he **departed** hence, even from the presence of Moses, that he beheld him not.

As mentioned in the introduction to this chapter, many things were left out of Genesis over the centuries, and this chapter of the writings of Moses, as revealed to the Prophet Joseph Smith, restores some of them. The fact that precious things were left out is confirmed by verse 23, next.

23 **And now of this thing** [*Satan's tempting Moses and being commanded in the name of Jesus Christ to depart*] **Moses bore record; but because of wickedness it is not had among the children of men**.

We might wonder why Satan would want this left out of the Bible. One of the obvious answers is that he is a loser here.

We are now about to be taught another important lesson. It is that obeying the commandments we have already received from God opens the door for additional light and knowledge from above.

Moses had been commanded that he should only worship God (verses 15 and 17, above). Then Satan came along and commanded Moses to worship him (verses 12 and 19). Moses remained faithful to God, refusing to give in to the devil's temptations. As a result, he was "filled with the Holy Ghost" (verse 24, next) and was taught many more things, as recorded in the next verses, including the following:

1. He learned prophetic details about his mission to free the children of Israel from Egypt (Egypt is often symbolic of Satan's kingdom in biblical symbolism), in verses 25–26.

2. He was taught more about the inhabitants of this earth, in verses 27–29.

3. He was privileged to again be transfigured and speak with Jehovah face-to-face, asking questions and receiving answers, in verses 30–41.

4. He was taught that there are other planets with people on them that exist now, in verses 33 and 35.

5. He learned that many earths have already "passed away," in verse 35.

6. He was taught that there is no limit to the number of worlds that the Father has created, in verses 33, 35, and 38.

7. He was shown that the highest satisfaction and glory of the Father consists in sending His spirit children to earths and helping them gain immortality (gaining a resurrected body of flesh and bones, thus living forever with physical bodies) and eternal life (exaltation), in verses 37–39.

8. He was told that many of his writings would be lost but that in the last days a prophet (Joseph Smith) would restore much of what he wrote (in Genesis through Deuteronomy).

Having seen the brief summary above of the rewards Moses received for obedience, is there any doubt that it is worth obeying the commandments in order to qualify for additional light and knowledge? We will now go through verses 24–41, using **bold** to point out the light and knowledge that Moses gained as a result of his obedience.

24 And it came to pass that when Satan had departed from the presence of **Moses, that Moses** lifted up his eyes unto heaven, being **filled with the Holy Ghost**, which beareth record of the Father and the Son [*the Holy Ghost testifies to us of the reality of Heavenly Father and Jesus Christ*];

25 And calling upon the name of God, **he beheld his glory again**, for it was upon him; and **he heard a voice**, saying: Blessed art thou, Moses, for I, the Almighty, have

chosen thee, and thou shalt be made stronger than many waters [*Moses will part the Red Sea—see Exodus 14:21*]; for **they shall obey thy command as if thou wert God.**

26 And lo, I am with thee, even unto the end of thy days; for **thou shalt deliver my people from bondage**, even Israel my chosen.

27 And it came to pass, as the voice was still speaking, **Moses cast his eyes** [*looked*] and **beheld the earth**, yea, even **all of it**; and **there was not a particle of it which he did not behold, discerning it by the spirit of God** [*seeing and comprehending by the power of the Holy Ghost far beyond the capacity of a mortal man*].

28 And he beheld also the inhabitants thereof, and **there was not a soul which he beheld not**; and **he discerned them by the Spirit of God**; and their numbers were great, even numberless as the sand upon the sea shore.

29 **And he beheld many lands**; and each land was called earth, and there were inhabitants on the face thereof.

The fact that the Holy Ghost was with Moses, enabling him to see and comprehend the things in verses 27–29, above, answers a question that sometimes comes up in gospel discussions. The question is whether the Holy Ghost was upon the earth before the time of Christ. As you can see, the answer is yes. You may wish to read more on this subject in the Bible Dictionary (in the back of the LDS Bible), under "Holy Ghost."

Next, Moses asks Jehovah a broad question.

30 And it came to pass that Moses called upon God, saying: **Tell me, I pray thee, why these things are so, and by what thou madest them?**

31 And behold, **the glory of the Lord was upon Moses** [*he was transfigured; compare with verse 11*], so that **Moses stood in the presence of God, and talked with him face to face**. And the Lord God said unto Moses: For mine own purpose have I made these things. Here is wisdom and it remaineth in me.

You will no doubt notice, in verses 32–35, that Jesus Christ is speaking here by way of divine investiture (see note following verse 3, above). In other words, He is speaking directly for the Father, as if He were the Father, without formally announcing that He is speaking the words of the Father. He is answering Moses' question, posed in verse 30.

32 And **by the word of my power** [*in other words, by Jesus Christ; Christ is the "Word"; see John 1:1–3*], **have I created them, which is mine Only Begotten Son**, who is full of grace and truth.

33 And **worlds without number have I created**; and I also created them for mine own purpose [*which is explained in verse 39*]; and **by the Son I created them**, which is mine Only Begotten.

34 And **the first man** of all men have I called **Adam**, which is many.

> From Moses 3:7 we understand that verse 34, above, is referring to Adam being the first of all people on this earth (see Moses 1:34, footnote 34a; see also Bible Dictionary, under "Adam").
>
> Next, the Lord informs Moses that He will limit their discussion to this earth and its inhabitants, giving him just a bit more information about other earths and the people belonging to them.

35 But **only an account of this earth, and the inhabitants thereof, give I unto you**. For behold, **there are many worlds that have passed away by the word of my power** [*many worlds have already been created and have become celestialized, having been created and redeemed by the power of Jesus Christ—compare with D&C 76:24*]. And **there are many that now stand** [*there are many planets now, in outer space, that have people like us on them; they too are children of God*], and **innumerable are they unto man; but all things are numbered unto me, for they are mine and I know them.**

> The last part of verse 35, above, contains a sweet and comforting insight into the power of God. We may sometimes feel tiny and insignificant among all His creations, but we are reminded above that even though it appears impossible to us, He does know us individually. The same message is found at the end of verse 37.
>
> Next, in verse 36, Moses humbly responds to the Savior's statement at the beginning of verse 35 that He wishes to limit His instructions to Moses to this earth.

36 And it came to pass that **Moses spake unto the Lord**, saying: Be merciful unto thy servant, O God, and **tell me concerning this earth, and the inhabitants thereof, and also the heavens, and then thy servant will be content.**

37 And the Lord God spake unto Moses, saying: The heavens, they are many, and they cannot be

numbered unto man; but **they are numbered unto me, for they are mine.**

38 And **as one earth shall pass away, and the heavens thereof even so shall another come,** and there is no end to my works, neither to my words.

> Verse 39, next, is one of the most often-quoted verses in all of the scriptures. You may wish to make sure it is marked in your own scriptures. It is a brief and powerful statement of the Father's mission and goals for us.

39 **For behold, this is my work and my glory—to bring to pass the immortality** [*resurrection and living forever in a physical body of flesh and bones*] **and eternal life** [*exaltation, becoming like our Father in Heaven, becoming gods and living in family units forever*] **of man.**

> Next, the Lord assigns Moses to record what he has been taught and will yet be taught. His writings are found today in the Bible, in Genesis, Exodus, Leviticus, Numbers, and Deuteronomy. However, as explained in verse 41, many of the "plain and precious things" (1 Nephi 13:28) he records will eventually be deleted by wicked men (see Moses 1:23).

40 And now, Moses, my son, **I will speak unto thee concerning this earth** upon which thou standest; and **thou shalt write the things which I shall speak.**

41 And **in a day when the children of men shall esteem my words as naught** [*do not consider the Bible to be of any value*] and **take many of them from the book** [*the book of Moses, known today as Genesis through Deuteronomy, in the Old Testament*] **which thou shalt write,** behold, I will raise up another [*the Prophet Joseph Smith*] like unto thee; and **they shall be had again among the children of men—among as many as shall believe** [*in other words, among members of the Church; perhaps you've noticed that we don't generally give the Pearl of Great Price to anyone other than members, who have the capacity to appreciate and respect it; this is in harmony with the instructions given in verse 42*].

> The taking of words "from the book," spoken of in verse 41, above, in addition to being literal, can mean ignoring the Bible, considering it to be outdated and of no relevancy to modern society, even though it still exists and many people have copies of it.
>
> As you are no doubt aware, many of the marvelous doctrines and insights given to us in this chapter

would not be appropriate to share during a "first discussion" given by missionaries. Obviously, it would cause overload in people who do not already have a good foundation in the gospel. With this in mind, we see in verse 42, next, counsel from the Lord not to show these things to any except those who already believe and have a testimony of the restored gospel.

42 (These words were spoken unto Moses in the mount, the name of which shall not be known among the children of men. And now they are spoken unto you. **Show them not unto any except them that believe**. Even so. Amen.)

MOSES, CHAPTER 2

(Revealed to Joseph Smith, June–October 1830)

Background

In Moses 1:30, Moses asked the Lord about the creation of this earth. In answering his question, the premortal Christ (Jehovah) briefly explained a number of things to His newly called prophet, including that this earth is one of "worlds without number" that He had created for the Father, under the Father's direction. Then, in verse 40, Moses was commanded to write an account of the creation of this earth. His account of the earth's physical creation is found mainly in Moses 2:1–25, 31.

In Moses 3:1–7, among other things, he writes briefly about the creation of all things, in spirit form, in preparation for placing them on earth. His account of the creation of Adam and Eve and their placement in the Garden of Eden is found in Moses 2:26–30 and 3:8–25.

The information given above may help you avoid confusion between the spirit creation (often referred to as the "spiritual creation") and the actual physical creation of all things. It is worth repeating. Moses 2:1–25, 31 contains an account of the actual physical creation of the earth and its ecosystem in preparation for placing Adam and Eve in the Garden of Eden and eventually bringing us to our mortal schooling. Moses 3:1, 4–7 contains a brief but informative account of the spiritual creation of all things before they were given physical form and placed upon the earth (see heading to Moses, chapter 3, in your Pearl of Great Price).

Joseph Fielding Smith said the following about the accounts of the Creation that we have:

"The account of the creation of the earth as given in Genesis, and the Book of Moses, and as given in the temple, is the creation of the physical earth, and of physical animals and plants" (*Doctrines of Salvation,* Vol. 1, page 75).

We will now proceed with chapter 2 of Moses, which deals with the physical creation. First, in verse 1, Moses records that he was commanded by the Lord (Jesus Christ) to write what he was told about this subject. We will continue to use **bold** to point things out for teaching purposes.

1 And it came to pass that **the Lord spake unto Moses,** saying: Behold, **I reveal unto you concerning this heaven, and this earth** [*as promised in Moses 1:35*]; **write the words which I speak.** I am the Beginning and the End [*a phrase that often means "I am the Creator"*], the Almighty God; [*next, the Savior speaks directly for the Father as if the Father Himself were speaking; as explained in the notes for Moses 1:3, this is often called divine investiture*] **by mine Only Begotten I created these things**; yea, in the beginning I created the heaven, and the earth upon which thou standest.

As you know, many people do not believe that God created the earth. They believe and teach that it was some sort of accidental happening. With Moses, chapter 2, as well as with Genesis, chapter 1, we are blessed with the Lord's own testimony that He, indeed, created the earth. In fact, if you read these chapters carefully, you will find more than forty ways in which He says, in effect, "I did it." Thus, although we do not have much detail about the "how" of creation, we do have the "who." According to D&C 101:32–34, we will be given the details of the Creation by the Savior at the time of His Second Coming.

We will use underlining and bold together (**bold**) to point out several of the words and phrases in this chapter that Moses used to say to us, one way or another, that the Lord created the earth. We will repeat verse 1, above, and then proceed through the rest of the chapter. You will likely find some that we miss.

1 And it came to pass that the Lord spake unto Moses, saying: Behold, I reveal unto you concerning this heaven, and this earth; write the words which I speak. I am the Beginning and the End, the Almighty God; by mine Only Begotten **I created these things**; yea, in the beginning **I created the heaven, and the earth** upon which thou standest.

2 And the earth was without form, and void; and **I caused** darkness to come up upon the face of the deep; and **my Spirit** moved upon the

face of the water; for I am God.

3 And **I, God**, said: Let there be light; and there was light.

4 And **I, God**, saw the light; and that light was good. And **I, God**, divided the light from the darkness.

5 And **I, God**, called the light Day; and the darkness, I called Night; and **this I did** by the word of my power, and **it was done as I spake**; and the evening and the morning were the first day.

6 And again, **I, God**, said: Let there be a firmament in the midst of the water, and **it was so, even as I spake**; and **I said**: Let it divide the waters from the waters; and it was done;

7 And **I, God**, made the firmament and divided the waters, yea, the great waters under the firmament from the waters which were above the firmament, and **it was so even as I spake**.

8 And **I, God**, called the firmament Heaven; and the evening and the morning were the second day.

9 And **I, God**, said: Let the waters under the heaven be gathered together unto one place, and it was so; and **I, God**, said: Let there be dry land; and it was so.

10 And **I, God**, called the dry land Earth; and the gathering together of the waters, called I the Sea; and **I, God**, saw that all things which I had made were good.

11 And **I, God**, said: Let the earth bring forth grass, the herb yielding seed, the fruit tree yielding fruit, after his kind, and the tree yielding fruit, whose seed should be in itself upon the earth, and **it was so even as I spake**.

12 And the earth brought forth grass, every herb yielding seed after his kind, and the tree yielding fruit, whose seed should be in itself, after his kind; and **I, God, saw that all things which I had made were good**;

13 And the evening and the morning were the third day.

14 And **I, God**, said: Let there be lights in the firmament of the heaven, to divide the day from the night, and let them be for signs, and for seasons, and for days, and for years;

15 And let them be for lights in the firmament of the heaven to give light upon the earth; and it was so.

16 And **I, God**, made two great lights; the greater light to rule the day, and the lesser light to rule the night, and the greater light was the sun, and the lesser light was the moon; and the stars also

were **made even according to my word**.

17 And **I, God**, set them in the firmament of the heaven to give light upon the earth,

18 And the sun to rule over the day, and the moon to rule over the night, and to divide the light from the darkness; and **I, God, saw that all things which I had made were good**;

19 And the evening and the morning were the fourth day.

20 And **I, God**, said: Let the waters bring forth abundantly the moving creature that hath life, and fowl which may fly above the earth in the open firmament of heaven.

21 And **I, God**, created great whales, and every living creature that moveth, which the waters brought forth abundantly, after their kind, and every winged fowl after his kind; and **I, God, saw that all things which I had created were good**.

22 And **I, God**, blessed them, saying: Be fruitful, and multiply, and fill the waters in the sea; and let fowl multiply in the earth;

23 And the evening and the morning were the fifth day.

24 And **I, God**, said: Let the earth bring forth the living creature after his kind, cattle, and creeping things, and beasts of the earth after their kind, and it was so;

25 And **I, God**, made the beasts of the earth after their kind, and cattle after their kind, and everything which creepeth upon the earth after his kind; and **I, God, saw that all these things were good**.

26 And **I, God**, said unto mine Only Begotten, which was with me from the beginning: **Let us** make man in our image, after our likeness; and it was so. And **I, God**, said: Let them have dominion over the fishes of the sea, and over the fowl of the air, and over the cattle, and over all the earth, and over every creeping thing that creepeth upon the earth.

27 And **I, God**, created man in mine own image, in the image of mine Only Begotten **created I** him; male and female **created I them**.

28 And **I, God**, blessed them, and said unto them: Be fruitful, and multiply, and replenish the earth, and subdue it, and have dominion over the fish of the sea, and over the fowl of the air, and over every living thing that moveth upon the earth.

29 And **I, God**, said unto man: Behold, **I have** given you every herb bearing seed, which is upon

the face of all the earth, and every tree in the which shall be the fruit of a tree yielding seed; to you it shall be for meat.

30 And to every beast of the earth, and to every fowl of the air, and to everything that creepeth upon the earth, wherein **I grant life**, there shall be given every clean herb for meat; and **it was so, even as I spake**.

31 And **I, God, saw everything that I had made**, and, behold, all things which **I had made** were very good; and the evening and the morning were the sixth day.

As you can see in verses 1–31, above, there are almost fifty ways in which we are assured that God created the earth and everything in it. Thus, we know that it is not an accident of nature, nor is it a chance evolutionary happening. Elder John A. Widtsoe, of the Twelve, said:

"The earth came into being by the will and power of God.... Chance is ruled out. Latter-day Saints believe that the earth and the heavens and the manifold operations within the universe are products of intelligent action, of the mind of God" (*Evidences and Reconciliations,* page 150).

We will now repeat verses 1–31, adding notes and commentary as we go. As mentioned previously, verse 1 is the Lord's answer to Moses' question in Moses 1:30, in which he asked the Lord to tell him how He had created the earth.

1 And it came to pass that the Lord spake unto Moses, saying: **Behold, I reveal unto you concerning this heaven, and this earth**; write the words which I speak. I am the Beginning and the End, the Almighty God; **by mine Only Begotten I created these things** [*our heaven and our earth; in other words, Heavenly Father initiated the creation, and Jesus carried it out*]; yea, **in the beginning I created the heaven, and the earth upon which thou standest.**

The phrase "in the beginning," as used near the end of verse 1, clearly refers to the beginning of our world because other worlds have already become celestialized (see Moses 1:35).

Also, the word "create," as used here, is sometimes understood to mean to "create something out of nothing." Such is not the case (see Genesis 1:1, footnote c, in your Bible). Also, the Prophet Joseph Smith taught:

"You ask the learned doctors why they say the world was made out of nothing: and they will answer, 'Doesn't the Bible say He created the world?' And they infer, from the word create, that it must have been made out of nothing. Now, the word create came from the word *baurau*, which does not mean to create out of nothing; it means to organize; the same as a man would organize materials and build a ship. Hence, we infer that God had materials to organize the world out of chaos—chaotic matter, which is element, and in which dwells all the glory. Element had an existence from the time he had. The pure principles of element are principles which can never be destroyed; they may be organized and reorganized, but not destroyed. They had no beginning, and can have no end" (*Teachings of the Prophet Joseph Smith,* pp. 350–52).

2 And **the earth was without form, and void** [*"empty and desolate because they had not formed anything but the earth"* (see Abraham 4:2)]; and **I caused darkness to come up upon the face of the deep** [*the water; see* Old Testament Student Manual: Genesis through 2 Samuel, *page 30*]; and **my Spirit moved** [*Hebrew: "brooded," much like a mother hen does when sitting on her nest, protecting her eggs, or guarding and protecting her chicks after they have hatched*] **upon the face of the water; for I am God.**

Elder John Taylor, who later became president of the Church, taught that the light spoken of in verses 3–4, next, was not the sun. The sun will be created in verses 14–18. He said that God "caused light to shine upon [the earth] before the sun appeared in the firmament [see Moses 2:3–4, 14–19]; for God is light, and in him there is no darkness. He is the light of the sun and the power thereof by which it was made; he is also the light of the moon and the power by which it was made; he is the light of the stars and the power by which they are made" (*Journal of Discourses,* Vol. 18, page 327; see also Revelation 21:23–25; D&C 88:7–13).

There may be important symbolism here, namely, that the most important light of all is the light that comes into our lives from God—a light that enables us to distinguish between light from God and spiritual darkness.

3 And I, God, said: **Let there be light; and there was light.**

4 And I, God, saw the light; **and that light was good.** And I, God, divided the light from the darkness.

The phrase "and that light was good" is important. Eight times in Moses' account of the Creation, we read, in one form or another, that "it was good" (Moses 2:4, 10, 12, 18, 21, 25, 31; 3:2). The fact that the Creation was good, in addition to being a statement of doctrine, offers, no doubt, a message for us, namely, that there is great satisfaction in being a creator.

5 And I, God, called the light Day; and the darkness, I called Night; and this I did by the word of my power, and it was done as I spake; and the evening and the morning were **the first day**.

The word "day," at the end of verse 5, brings up the topic of how long it took to create the earth. There are many opinions as to how long it took. The fact is that we do not know. It has not yet been revealed. In the gospel doctrine manual for Old Testament classes, we read:

"The length of time required for the Creation is not known" (*Old Testament Gospel Doctrine Teacher's Manual,* page 11).

Speaking of the "six days" required for creating the earth, President Brigham Young said that it "is a mere term, but it matters not whether it took six days, six months, six years, or six thousand years. The creation occupied certain periods of time. **We are not authorized to say what the duration of these days was** (bold added for emphasis), whether Moses penned these words as we have them, or whether the translators of the Bible have given the words their intended meaning. However, God created the world. God brought forth material out of which he formed this little terra firma upon which we roam. How long had this material been in existence? Forever and forever, in some shape, in some condition" (*Discourses of Brigham Young,* page 100).

Furthermore, Elder Bruce R. McConkie taught that a day, as used in the creation accounts, "is a specified time period; it is an age, an eon, a division of eternity; it is the time between two identifiable events. And each day, of whatever length, has the duration needed for its purposes. . . . There is no revealed recitation specifying that each of the 'six days' involved in the Creation was of the same duration" ("Christ and the Creation," *Ensign,* June 1982, page 11).

Next, in verses 6–8, we find the word "firmament." One simple definition of it would be "the atmosphere" or the "sky." Another way it is used is to mean the stars in the night sky, or the "heavens." You can see these definitions in the Bible Dictionary (at the back of your LDS Bible), under "Firmament."

Thus, in these verses, we see that the waters on the surface of the earth separated from the waters contained in clouds, dew, humidity, and so forth, which provide moisture to sustain life on earth.

6 And again, I, God, said: **Let there be a firmament** [*the atmosphere surrounding the earth, the sky, the heavens we see as we look up from the earth*] in the midst of the water, and it was so, even as I spake; and I said: **Let it divide the waters** [*upon the surface of the earth*] **from the waters** [*in the sky, the clouds, the dew*]; and it was done;

Verse 7, next, basically repeats the information given in verse 6 and adds a bit more detail.

7 And I, **God, made the firmament and divided** [*separated*] the waters, yea, **the great waters under the firmament** [*the waters on the earth's surface*] **from the waters which were above the firmament** [*the clouds and moisture in the atmosphere above us*], and it was so even as I spake.

Joseph Fielding Smith taught:

"The waters above the firmament is a reference to the clouds and the waters which exist in the atmosphere above the earth" (*Answers to Gospel Questions,* Vol. 4, pp. 116–17).

Bruce R. McConkie taught:

"'The waters' were 'divided' between the surface of the earth and the atmospheric heavens that surround it. A 'firmament' or an 'expanse' called 'Heaven' was created to divide 'the waters which were under the expanse from the waters which were above the expanse.' Thus, as the creative events unfold, provision seems to be made for clouds and rain and storms to give life to that which will yet grow and dwell upon the earth. (See Moses 2:6–8; Abr. 4:6–8.)" ("Christ and the Creation," *Ensign,* June 1982, page 11).

8 And I, **God, called the firmament Heaven** [*the sky, what we see when we look up from the earth*]; and the evening and the morning were **the second day** [*the second time period of the creation of our earth*].

As the third "day," or period of creation begins, we see preparation of the earth to host all living things. First, the waters are gathered into one place, and dry, solid land appears. Genesis 10:25 informs us that the continent formed at this point in the Creation was divided in the days of Peleg. We now have many continents, islands, and oceans, and we understand that the oceans will "be driven back into the north countries, and the islands [*continents*] shall become one land" again, at the time of the Second Coming (D&C 133:23).

9 And I, God, said: **Let the waters under the heaven** [*the waters on the surface of the earth; see verse 7*] **be gathered together unto one place**, and it was so; and I, God, said: **Let there be dry land**; and it was so.

10 And **I, God, called the dry land Earth**; and the gathering together of **the waters, called I the Sea**; and I, God, saw that **all things which I had made were good.**

Next, as the third "day" continues in verses 11–12, the ecosystem that was needed to support all forms of life on earth is prepared. Note that the phrase "after his kind" is repeated three times in these verses. We will say more about that at the end of verse 12.

11 And I, God, said: Let the earth bring forth **grass**, the **herb** yielding seed, the **fruit tree** yielding fruit, **after his kind**, and the tree yielding fruit, whose seed should be in itself upon the earth, and it was so even as I spake.

12 And the earth brought forth grass, every herb yielding seed **after his kind**, and the tree yielding fruit, whose seed should be in itself, **after his kind**; and I, God, saw that all things which I had made were good;

Regarding the phrase "after his kind," Elder Boyd K. Packer taught:

"No lesson is more manifest in nature than that all living things do as the Lord commanded in the Creation. They reproduce 'after their own kind.' (See Moses 2:12, 24.) They follow the pattern of their parentage. . . . A bird will not become an animal nor a fish. A mammal will not beget reptiles, nor 'do men gather . . . figs of thistles' (Matt. 7:16.)" (in Conference Report, October 1984, page 83; or "The Pattern of Our Parentage," *Ensign,* November 1984, page 67).

Elder Mark E. Petersen, of the Twelve, likewise taught the doctrinal significance of these words. He said:

"He commanded them to reproduce themselves. They too would bring forth only 'after their kind.' It could be in no other way. Each form of life was destined to bring forth after its own kind so that it would be perpetuated in the earth and avoid confusion.

"Man was always man, and always will be, for we are the

offspring of God. The fact that we know of our own form and image and the further fact that we are God's offspring give us positive knowledge of the form and image of God, after whom we are made and of whom we are born as his children.

"God would not violate his own laws. When he decreed that all reproduction was to be 'after its kind,' he obeyed the same law. We are therefore of the race of God. To follow an opposite philosophy is to lead us into atheism" (*Moses: Man of Miracles,* page 163).

13 And the evening and the morning were **the third day** [*the third time period of the creation of our earth*].

As we begin the fourth "day" of the creation of our earth (verses 14–19), we see the creation and placement of the sun and moon into our solar system, as well as the creation of the stars in our night sky. Among other things, these were arranged and given laws that would provide the order and reliability needed for navigation and calendars.

14 And I, God, said: **Let there be lights in the firmament of the heaven** [*in the sky*], **to divide the day from the night**, and let them be **for signs** [*including that God exists and organized for our benefit; also, for purposes of navigation, and so forth*], **and for seasons, and for days, and for years**;

15 And let them be for lights in the firmament of the heaven to give light upon the earth; and it was so.

16 And I, God, made two great lights; **the greater light to rule the day, and the lesser light to rule the night**, and the greater light was **the sun**, and the lesser light was **the moon**; and **the stars** also were made even according to my word.

17 And I, God, set them in the firmament of the heaven **to give light upon the earth**,

18 And the sun to rule over the day, and the moon to rule over the night, and to divide the light from the darkness; and I, God, saw that all things which I had made were good;

We will again quote from an *Ensign* article in which Elder Bruce R. McConkie taught about the fourth day:

"The Fourth Day—After seeds in all their varieties had been planted on the earth; after these had sprouted and grown; after each variety was prepared to bring forth fruit and seed after its own kind—the Creators organized all things in such a way as to make their earthly garden a productive and beautiful place. They then 'organized the lights in the expanse of the heaven' so there would be 'seasons' and a way of measuring 'days' and 'years.' We have no way of knowing what changes then took place in either the atmospheric or the sidereal heavens, but during this period the sun, moon, and stars assumed the relationship to the earth that now is theirs. At least the light of each of them began to shine through the lifting hazes that enshrouded the newly created earth so they could play their parts with reference to life in all its forms as it soon would be upon the new orb. (See Moses 2:14–19; Abraham 4:14–19.)" ("Christ and the Creation," *Ensign,* June 1982, page 12).

19 And the evening and the morning were **the fourth day**.

The Prophet Joseph Smith summarized the third and fourth "days" of creation, bearing witness that the things created follow the laws of God, for the benefit of mankind. He said:

"God has made certain decrees which are fixed and immovable: for instance, God set the sun, the moon, and the stars in the heavens, and gave them their laws, conditions and bounds, which they cannot pass, except by His commandments; they all move in perfect harmony in their sphere and order, and are as lights, wonders and signs unto us. The sea also has its bounds which it cannot pass. God has set many signs on the earth, as well as in the heavens; for instance, the oak of the forest, the fruit of the tree, the herb of the field, all bear a sign that seed hath been planted there; for it is a decree of the Lord that every tree, plant, and herb bearing seed should bring forth of its kind, and cannot come forth after any other law or principle" (*Teachings,* pp. 197–98).

The fifth "day" of creation is briefly explained in verses 20–23. It appears that creatures which live in the water, as well as birds of all kinds, were created during this period. Once again, Moses emphasizes "after their kind," an important doctrinal reminder that the earth and all things upon it were organized and placed here by God and operate according to His laws for the benefit of His children. The Creation did not just happen as a chance accident of nature.

20 And I, God, said: **Let the waters bring forth abundantly** the moving creature that hath life, and fowl [*birds, probably including all water fowl*] which may fly above the earth in the open firmament of heaven [*the sky*].

21 And I, **God, created great whales, and every living creature that moveth, which the waters brought forth** abundantly, **after their kind**, and every winged fowl **after his kind**; and I, God, saw that all things which I had created were good.

22 And I, God, blessed them, saying: **Be fruitful, and multiply** [*produce offspring*], and fill the waters in the sea; and let fowl multiply in the earth;

23 And the evening and the morning were **the fifth day.**

> Verses 24–25 inform us that the first portion of the sixth "day" involved the creation of all creatures that live on land. Yet again, Moses says "after their kind," emphasizing that each type of creature was created as such in the beginning by God, rather than developing from one form to another.

24 And I, God, said: **Let the earth bring forth the living creature after his kind, cattle** [*animals that are commonly domesticated*], and **creeping things**, and **beasts of the earth** [*generally speaking, wild animals*] **after their kind**, and it was so;

25 And I, God, made the beasts of the earth **after their kind**, and cattle **after their kind**, and everything which creepeth upon the earth **after his kind**; and I, God, saw that all these things were good.

Have you noticed that when it comes to placing mankind on earth, there is a change in creators? Up to now, Jesus, assisted by "many of the noble and great ones," has done the creating (see Abraham 3:22, 24). But as we see at the beginning of verse 26, next, Heavenly Father takes over now.

This is doctrinally significant since we are the literal "offspring of God" (Acts 17:29) rather than "creations," as is the case with all else.

The First Presidency and the Quorum of the Twelve Apostles made this clear. They taught (**bold** added for emphasis):

"All human beings—male and female—are created in the image of God. **Each is a beloved spirit son or daughter of heavenly parents**, and, as such, each has a divine nature and destiny. Gender is an essential characteristic of individual premortal, mortal, and eternal identity and purpose" ("The Family: A Proclamation to the World," *Ensign*, November 1995, page 102).

26 And **I, God** [*Heavenly Father*], **said unto mine Only Begotten** [*Jesus Christ*], which was with me

from the beginning: **Let us make man in our image, after our likeness**; and it was so. And I, God, said: Let them have dominion over the fishes of the sea, and over the fowl of the air, and over the cattle, and over all the earth, and over every creeping thing that creepeth upon the earth.

Elder McConkie clearly taught that the Father took over when it came to the placement of man upon the earth. He said:

"We know that Jehovah-Christ, assisted by 'many of the noble and great ones' (Abraham 3:22), of whom Michael is but the illustration, did in fact create the earth and all forms of plant and animal life on the face thereof. But when it came to placing man on earth, there was a change in Creators. That is, the Father himself became personally involved. All things were created by the Son, using the power delegated by the Father, except man. In the spirit and again in the flesh, man was created by the Father. There was no delegation of authority where the crowning creature of creation was concerned" (*The Promised Messiah,* page 62; see also *Doctrines of the Gospel Student Manual,* page 18).

27 And **I, God** [*the Father*], **created man in mine own image, in the image of mine Only Begotten created I him; male and female created I them.**

Concerning the creation of man and woman, the First Presidency taught (**bold** added for emphasis):

"**All men and women are in the similitude of the universal Father and Mother**, and are literally the sons and daughters of Deity.

"'God created man in His own image.' This is just as true of the spirit as it is of the body, which is only the clothing of the spirit, its complement; the two together constituting the soul. The spirit of man is in the form of man, and the spirits of all creatures are in the likeness of their bodies. This was plainly taught by the Prophet Joseph Smith (D&C 77:2)" (the First Presidency [Joseph F. Smith, John R. Winder, and Anthon H. Lund], in James R. Clark, *Messages of the First Presidency of The Church of Jesus Christ of Latter-day Saints,* Vol. 4, page 203).

Concerning how the physical bodies of Adam and Eve were formed, President Spencer W. Kimball taught.

"Man became a living soul—mankind, male and female. The Creators breathed into their nostrils the breath of life, and man and woman became living souls. **We don't know exactly how their coming into this world happened**, and when we're able to understand it the Lord will tell us" ("The Blessings and Responsibilities of Womanhood," *Ensign*, March 1976, page 72).

Our stewardship and responsibility for taking proper care of the earth and all things in it are summarized in verse 28, next.

28 And I, God, blessed them, and said unto them: **Be fruitful** [*have children*], and **multiply**, and **replenish the earth** [*fill the earth—see Genesis 1, footnote 28c*], and **subdue it**, and **have dominion** over the fish of the sea, and over the fowl of the air, and over every living thing that moveth upon the earth.

> The word "replenish," in verse 28, above, has led some to speculate that the earth had been full of people before Adam and Eve came on the scene and that they were to refill it. As used here, the word "replenish" means to "fill." In Joseph Smith's day, one of the common definitions of "replenish" was "to stock with numbers or abundance" (see Noah Webster's 1828 *American Dictionary of the English Language*, under "Replenish").
>
> Adam and Eve were the first people on earth, according to the following statement from the First Presidency:
>
> "It is held by some that Adam was not the first man upon this earth, and that the original human being was a development from lower orders of the animal creation. These, however, are the theories of men. The word of the Lord declares that Adam was 'the first man of all men' (Moses 1:34), and we are therefore in duty bound to regard him as the primal parent of our race" (The First Presidency [Joseph F. Smith, John R. Winder, and Anthon H. Lund], in *Messages of the First Presidency of The Church of Jesus Christ of Latter-day Saints,* Vol. 4, pp. 205–6).
>
> President Kimball summarized the things taught in the above verses as follows:
>
> "'And I, God, created man in mine own image, in the image of mine Only Begotten created I him; male and female created I them. [The story of the rib, of course, is figurative.]
>
> "'And I, God, blessed them [Man here is always in the plural. It was plural from the beginning] and said unto them: Be fruitful, and multiply, and replenish the earth, and subdue it, and have dominion over [it]' (Moses 2:27–28).

"And the scripture says, "'And I, God, said unto mine Only Begotten, which was with me from the beginning: Let us make man [not a separate man, but a complete man, which is husband and wife] in our image, after our likeness; and it was so.' (Moses 2:26.) What a beautiful partnership! Adam and Eve were married for eternity by the Lord. . . .

"'Male and female created he them; and blessed them, and called their name Adam [Mr. and Mrs. Adam, I suppose, or Brother and Sister Adam], in the day when they were created.' (Gen. 5:1–2.)

"This is a partnership. Then when they had created them in the image of God, to them was given the eternal command, 'Be fruitful, and multiply, and replenish the earth, and subdue it' (Gen. 1:28), and as they completed this magnificent creation, they looked it over and pronounced it 'good, very good'—something that isn't to be improved upon by our modern intellectuals; the male to till the ground, to support the family, to give proper leadership; the woman to cooperate, to bear the children, and to rear and teach them. It was 'good, very good.'

"And that's the way the Lord organized it. This wasn't an experiment. He knew what he was doing" ("The Blessings and Responsibilities of Womanhood," *Ensign,* March 1976, page 71).

In verses 29–30, Moses gives a brief account of instructions given to Adam and Eve as far as food for them and for the creatures on earth is concerned.

29 And I, God, said unto man [*Adam and Eve—see President Kimball's talk, quoted above*]: Behold, I have given you every herb bearing seed, which is upon the face of all the earth, and every tree in the which shall be the fruit of a tree yielding seed; to you it shall be for meat [*food*].

When you study the scriptures, it is helpful to know that, in ancient times, "meat" was a general term for "food." If the writer was referring to what we call meat in our day, he used the word "flesh."

30 And to every beast of the earth, and to every fowl of the air, and to everything that creepeth upon the earth, wherein I grant life, there shall be given every clean herb for meat [*food*]; and it was so, even as I spake.

Finally, in verse 31, next, God expresses satisfaction with the creation.

31 And **I, God, saw everything that I had made, and, behold, all things which I had made were**

very good; and the evening and the morning were **the sixth day**.

MOSES, CHAPTER 3

(Revealed to Joseph Smith, June–October 1830)

Background

This chapter is a continuation of Moses' account of the Creation, which he was commanded to write (see Moses 1:40). Verse 1 is a summary of the fact that all things and all people belonging to this earth were created in spirit form before the earth was created physically. Verses 2–3 deal with the seventh day, the Sabbath, following the physical creation of the earth. Verse 4 is a transition between the account of the physical creation in chapter 2 and the spirit creation that preceded it, as spoken of briefly in verses 5–7 of this chapter. This spirit creation is sometimes referred to as the "spiritual creation."

The remaining verses in this chapter teach us about the Garden of Eden and the placing of Adam and Eve in it.

1 Thus **the heaven and the earth were finished, and all the host of them**.

Joseph Fielding Smith explained verse 1, above. He taught:

"'Thus the heaven and the earth were finished, and all the host of them.' [Moses 3:1] That is, the physical creation was completed. Then the account explains, by way of interpolation, that nevertheless all things had been created spiritually before this physical creation. But hosts of the earth were not on the earth, although they had been created preparatory to coming to the earth" (*Man: His Origin and Destiny*, page 284).

He also taught:

"It is reasonable to believe that in the beginning, before the earth was prepared, the Lord would have all things organized from the beginning to the end of time. It is written in the scriptures: 'Thus the heaven and the earth were finished, and all the host of them' [Moses 3:1]. This is equivalent to the Lord's saying that everything was in preparation to be placed on the earth in its due course when mankind should be placed upon it" (*Answers to Gospel Questions,* Vol. 5, page 182).

Next, in verses 2–3, we see that the Sabbath is to be a holy day.

2 And on the **seventh day** I, God, ended my work, and all things which I had made; and **I rested on the seventh day from all my work**, and all things which I had

made were finished, and I, God, saw that they were good;

3 And **I, God, blessed the seventh day, and sanctified it** [*made it holy*]; because that in it I had rested from all my work which I, God, had created and made.

As stated previously, verse 4, next, is a transition verse between the account of the physical creation of the earth, given in Moses 2, and a brief review of the creation of all things in spirit form, prior to the physical creation, briefly touched upon in verses 5–7.

4 And now, behold, I say unto you, **that these are the generations of** [*the story of, the account of*] **the heaven and of the earth, when they were created**, in the day that I, the Lord God, made the heaven and the earth,

As you are probably aware, very little is written in the scriptures about our premortal existence. And most Christian churches do not even teach the premortal life as a doctrine. Therefore, although brief, verses 5–7, next, are significant!

5 And every plant of the field before it was in the earth, and every herb of the field before it grew. For **I, the Lord God, created all things, of which I have spoken, spiritually** [*in spirit form*], **before they were naturally** [*in physical form*] **upon the face of the earth.** For I, the Lord God, had not caused it to rain upon the face of the earth. And **I, the Lord God, had created all the children of men** [*those of us who were to come to this earth had all been born as spirit children of our Heavenly Parents*]; and **not yet a man to till the ground**; for **in heaven created I them**; and there was not yet flesh upon the earth, neither in the water, neither in the air;

We inserted a note, in verse 5, above, indicating that our group of spirits had all been born as spirit children to our Heavenly Parents before the physical creation of our earth. Elder James E. Talmage taught that there is a certain number of spirits assigned to this earth. He said:

"The population of the earth is fixed according to the number of spirits appointed to take tabernacles of flesh upon this planet; when these have all come forth in the order and time appointed, then, and not till then, shall the end come" (*Articles of Faith*, page 175).

Obviously, since our Heavenly Parents are exalted beings and have "a continuation of the seeds forever and ever" (D&C 132:19), they will continue to have and rear spirit offspring forever, just as they did us, and will continue to create worlds to which these spirit offspring will be sent for their mortal experience and progression. Thus, this account of the creation which we are reading, written for us by Moses, is "only an account of this earth" (Moses 1:35) and our group of spirits.

Concerning the creating of all things in spirit form before they were given their physical existence, Joseph Fielding Smith said:

"There is no account of the creation of man or other forms of life when they were created as spirits. There is just the simple statement that they were so created before the physical creation. The statements in Moses 3:5 and Genesis 2:5 are interpolations [parenthetical explanations] thrown into the account of the physical creation, explaining that all things were first created in the spirit existence in heaven before they were placed upon this earth.

"We were all created untold ages before we were placed on this earth. We discover from Abraham 3:22–28, that it was before the earth was formed that the plan of salvation was presented to the spirits, or 'intelligences.' This being true, then man, animals and plants were not created in the spirit at the time of the creation of the earth, but long before" (*Doctrines of Salvation,* Vol. 1:75–76).

Specifically, concerning the creation of men and women, the First Presidency in 1925 taught:

"Man, as a spirit, was begotten and born of heavenly parents, and reared to maturity in the eternal mansions of the Father, prior to coming upon the earth in a temporal body to undergo an experience in mortality" ("'Mormon' View of Evolution," *Improvement Era,* September 1925, page 1090; see also D&C 77:2; *Pearl of Great Price Student Manual,* page 9).

In verses 6–7, next, the Lord speaks of the physical creation but then reminds us that all things were first created in spirit form (last of verse 7).

6 But I, the Lord God, spake, and **there went up a mist from the earth, and watered the whole face of the ground.**

7 And **I, the Lord God, formed man from the dust** [*the physical elements of the earth*] **of the ground** [*the physical creation*], and breathed into his nostrils the breath of life; and **man became a living soul** [*a spirit in a physical body; compare with D&C 88:15*], **the first flesh upon the earth, the**

first man also; nevertheless, all things were before created; but spiritually were they created and made according to my word.

In verse 7, above, we are taught that Adam was the "first man." The First Presidency explained this as follows:

"It is held by some that Adam was not the first man upon this earth, and that the original human being was a development from lower orders of the animal creation. These, however, are the theories of men. The word of the Lord declares that Adam was 'the first man of all men' (Moses 1:34), and we are therefore in duty bound to regard him as the primal [original] parent of our race" ("The Origin of Man," *Improvement Era,* November 1909, page 80).

Next, verses 8–25 teach us of the formation of the Garden of Eden and the placing of Adam and Eve in it. First, Adam was placed in it.

8 And I, the Lord God, planted a garden eastward in Eden, and there I put the man whom I had formed.

The following two quotes tell us the location of the Garden of Eden (**bold** added for emphasis):

Brigham Young

"In the beginning, after this earth was prepared for man, the Lord commenced his work upon what is now called **the American continent, where the Garden of Eden was made**" (*Discourses of Brigham Young,* page 102).

Heber C. Kimball,

"The spot chosen for the Garden of Eden was **Jackson County**, in the State of **Missouri**, where [the city of] **Independence** now stands; it was occupied in the morn of creation by Adam" (*Journal of Discourses,* Vol. 10, page 235).

Among other things, we learn from verse 9, next, that trees are also living souls. In other words, trees and plants have spirits too. From this and what we are taught in verse 19, we are given to understand that all living things have spirits and are thus "souls." Joseph Fielding Smith taught us about this. He said:

"The idea prevails in general, I believe, in the religious world where the gospel truth is misunderstood, that man is the only being on the earth that has what is called a soul or a spirit. We know this is not the case, for the Lord has said that not only has man a spirit, and is thereby a living soul, but likewise the beasts of the field, the fowl of the air, and the fish of the sea have spirits, and hence are living souls" (*Doctrines of Salvation,* Vol. 1, page 63).

We can learn from D&C 88:15 that a "soul" is a spirit and a physical body combined.

D&C 88:15

15 And the spirit and the body are the soul of man.

9 And out of the ground made I, the Lord God, to grow **every tree**, naturally, that is pleasant to the sight of man; and man could behold it. And it **became also a living soul**. For it was spiritual [*in spirit form*] in the day that I created it; for it remaineth in the sphere in which I, God, created it, yea, even all things which I prepared for the use of man; and man saw that it was good for food. And I, the Lord God, planted **the tree of life** also **in the midst of the garden**, and also **the tree of knowledge of good and evil**.

Did you notice in verse 9 where the Lord placed the tree of knowledge of good and evil? It was in the "midst of the garden" (see also Moses 4:9). Since Adam and Eve were commanded not to partake of it (see verse 17 as well as Moses 4:9,) we might find ourselves wondering why it was not placed out of sight in an obscure corner of the garden.

Perhaps Lehi can help with this. He taught that "it must needs be, that there is an opposition in all things. If not so, . . . righteousness could not be brought to pass, neither wickedness, neither holiness nor misery, neither good nor bad" (2 Nephi 2:11).

Knowing as we do that agency and choice are vital components of our continuing education toward exaltation, we understand that it was essential that Adam and Eve be faced with opposition. Perhaps that is why the tree was placed in the midst of the Garden of Eden.

One more thing before we move on. Elder Bruce R. McConkie gave a brief insight about the two trees specifically mentioned in verse 9. He said (**bold** added for emphasis):

"The scriptures set forth that there were in the Garden of Eden two trees. One was **the tree of life**, which figuratively refers to eternal life; the other was **the tree of knowledge of good and evil**, which figuratively refers to how and why and in what manner mortality and all that appertains to it came into being" (*A New Witness for the Articles of Faith,* page 86).

We will not attempt to do anything with the geography described in verses 10–14, next, other than to suggest that there may be symbolic meaning in the fact that the four great rivers mentioned had their origin in the river that came out of the Garden of Eden. Symbolically, one message might be that all the world has greatly benefited from that which started in the Garden of Eden (Adam and Eve and the Fall).

10 And I, the Lord God, caused **a river** to go **out of Eden** to water the garden; and from thence it was **parted, and became into four heads** [*became the source of four rivers*].

11 And I, the Lord God, called the name of **the first** Pison, and it compasseth the whole land of Havilah, where I, the Lord God, created much gold;

12 And the gold of that land was good, and there was bdellium and the onyx stone.

13 And the name of **the second** river was called Gihon; the same that compasseth the whole land of Ethiopia.

14 And the name of **the third** river was Hiddekel; that which goeth toward the east of Assyria. And **the fourth** river was the Euphrates.

Next, we are taught more of the placement of Adam in the Garden of Eden and of the commandment not to partake of the tree of knowledge of good and evil.

15 And **I, the Lord God, took the man** [*Adam, also known as Michael; see Bible Dictionary, under "Adam"*], **and put him into the Garden of Eden**, to dress it, and to keep it.

Remember that in Moses 2:28, we were informed that Adam and Eve were commanded to "be fruitful, and multiply, and replenish [*fill*] the earth." In other words, they were to have children and begin the process of bringing Heavenly Father's spirit children to earth for their mortal probation and education.

However, in verses 16–17, next, Adam is commanded not to eat of the fruit of the tree of the knowledge of good and evil. Partaking of this fruit will enable Adam and Eve to have children (see Moses 5:2). These two commandments are often referred to as the two "conflicting commandments." As we proceed, we will get help on this seeming dilemma.

16 And **I, the Lord God, commanded** the man, saying: **Of every tree of the garden thou mayest freely eat**,

17 **But of the tree of the knowledge of good and evil, thou shalt not eat of it**, nevertheless, thou

mayest choose for thyself, for it is given unto thee; but, remember that I forbid it, for in the day thou eatest thereof thou shalt surely die.

We underlined the portion of verse 17, above, which has been lost from the Bible and which has been restored here by Moses in the Pearl of Great Price. It is important in helping us see that perhaps the two "conflicting commandments" did not conflict.

We will include a quote from Joseph Fielding Smith, in which he helps us understand the significance of the underlined portion of verse 17, above (**bold** added for emphasis):

"Just why the Lord would say to Adam that he forbade him to partake of the fruit of that tree is not made clear in the Bible account, but in the original as it comes to us in the Book of Moses it is made definitely clear. It is that **the Lord said to Adam that if he wished to remain as he was in the garden, then he was not to eat the fruit, but if he desired to eat it and partake of death, he was at liberty to do so**. So really it was not in the true sense a transgression of a divine commandment. Adam made the wise decision, in fact the only decision he could make" (*Answers to Gospel Questions*, Vol. 4, page 81).

Next, the topic changes to the creation of Eve. Many people misread this verse. The mistake they make is seeing, in their mind's eye, "helpmeet" rather than "help meet" (two separate words). We will say more about this in a moment.

18 And I, the Lord God, said unto mine Only Begotten, that **it was not good that the man should be alone**; wherefore, I will make an **help meet** for him.

The distinction between "help meet" and "helpmeet" (or "helpmate," as it is sometimes referred to) is crucial to a proper understanding of the roles of husband and wife. "Helpmeet" means "helper" or "assistant" and is often interpolated to mean "servant," whereas "help meet" means "help that is vital for him." "Meet" means "necessary," "vital," "required" (see D&C 58:26).

Thus, God created a vital help for Adam, a companion of equal status to work with him and he with her. The equality of husband and wife is clearly taught in the Proclamation on the Family. The First Presidency and the Quorum of the Twelve stated (**bold** added for emphasis):

"By divine design, fathers are to preside over their families in love and righteousness and are responsible to provide the necessities of life and protection for their families. Mothers are primarily responsible for the nurture of their children. In these sacred responsibilities, **fathers and mothers are** obligated to help one another as **equal partners**" (*Ensign,* November 1995, page 102).

President Howard W. Hunter taught the following about the proper relationship between husband and wife (**bold** added for emphasis):

"A man who holds the priesthood accepts his wife as a partner in the leadership of the home and family with full knowledge of and full participation in all decisions relating thereto. . . . The Lord intended that the wife be a help meet for man (**meet means equal**)—that is, **a companion equal and necessary in full partner**ship" ("Being a Righteous Husband and Father," *Ensign,* November 1994, 50–51).

Verse 19, next, and the first half of verse 20 inform us that Adam was given the responsibility to name the creatures. This was a tremendous task and would require much inspiration. It also shows us the high intelligence and capability of Adam.

Also, emphasis is again given to the fact that, upon their physical creation, these also became "living souls." No doubt this knowledge is given to us, among other things, to enable us to have more respect for the living things around us upon our earth.

19 And out of the ground [*symbolic of the physical creation*] I, the Lord God, formed **every beast of the field, and every fowl of the air**; and commanded that they should come unto Adam, to see what he would call them; and they **were also living souls**; for I, God, breathed into them the breath of life, and commanded that whatsoever Adam called every living creature, that should be the name thereof.

Did you notice that the creatures obeyed God and came to Adam to see what he would name them. Adam didn't have to chase down each one and name it.

20 And **Adam gave names to all cattle, and to the fowl of the air, and to every beast of the field**; but as for Adam, there was not found an help meet for him.

Verses 21–24, next, contain beautiful symbolism concerning the placement of Eve on earth. Most people consider the taking of one of Adam's ribs and creating Eve to be literal. It is not. It is symbolic. Ancient culture and writing created intensity of feeling to drive home a message. The message here is that Adam and Eve are a team, working together as one part of a body does with another part, with deep loyalty to each other as family ("bone of my bones and flesh of my flesh"), cleaving to each other more than to any others (verse 24). President Spencer W. Kimball taught that the story of the rib is symbolic. He said:

"The story of the rib, of course, is figurative" ("The Blessings and Responsibilities of Womanhood, Ensign, March 1976, page 71).

We will go through these verses now and then make a few more comments. Remember, the taking of Adam's rib is symbolic, even though it appears literal.

21 And I, the Lord God, caused a deep sleep to fall upon Adam; and he slept, and **I took one of his ribs** and closed up the flesh in the stead thereof;

22 **And the rib which I, the Lord God, had taken from man, made I a woman**, and brought her unto the man.

23 And **Adam said: This I know now is bone of my bones, and flesh of my flesh** [*a Near Eastern phrase for "family, belonging to each other"*]; she shall be called Woman, because she was taken out of man.

24 **Therefore shall a man leave his father and his mother, and shall cleave unto his wife**; and they shall be one flesh.

Regarding the "rib" that President Kimball reminds us is symbolic, students sometimes wonder why the scriptures make it sound so literal. We "Westerners" (residents of the western hemisphere, especially of the United States and Canada) tend to want things to be literal, and much of our writing and culture tend to reflect this. However, such is not the case with many other cultures, including biblical and other "Eastern" cultures. Thus, much of their writing is highly symbolic, transferring emotion and feeling, as well as fact, to the reader.

So it is that the scriptural accounts of the creation of Eve give much more than the fact that she came on the scene. They provide drama and feeling, warmth and tenderness, belonging and protectiveness, unity and purpose to the account far beyond the fact of Adam and Eve's coming forth to fulfill their role in the great "plan of happiness."

Verse 25, next, reminds us that, at this point in the Creation, Adam and Eve were still in a state of innocence, not being embarrassed at being naked. Those feelings will come after the Fall.

25 And they were both naked, the man and his wife, and were not ashamed.

MOSES, CHAPTER 4

(Revealed to Joseph Smith, June–October 1830)

Background

In this chapter we will be told how Lucifer became the devil. We will then be taken through the scene in the Garden of Eden where Satan tempts Eve and then to the Fall of Adam and Eve. Then we will be taught the consequences and blessings of the Fall.

Verses 1–4 are not found in the Bible. This is an example of the great value of Moses in the Pearl of Great Price. In fact, the "equivalent" of this chapter (Moses 4) is Genesis 3 in the Bible, which has twenty-four verses as compared to the thirty-two verses in this chapter.

The first four verses give us insights about premortality and the Grand Council in Heaven that we all attended. We will be taught many important doctrines as we study these four verses.

In verse 1, we are informed that Lucifer wanted to be the Redeemer. (By the way, Lucifer means "the Shining One" or "Light bringer"; see Bible Dictionary, under "Lucifer.") At the beginning of the verse, the Lord reminds Moses that he is already acquainted with Satan because of the confrontation he had with him in Moses 1:12–22. At the end of that tense confrontation, Lucifer was forced to depart after Moses commanded him to do so in the name of Jesus Christ. Now, the Lord tells Moses, in effect, that He is going to tell him how Lucifer became the devil. Pay close attention to how Lucifer proposed to carry out our redemption.

1 And I, the Lord God, spake unto Moses, saying: **That Satan, whom thou hast commanded in the name of mine Only Begotten** [*in Moses 1:21*], **is the same which was from the beginning** [*perhaps meaning that he is the same character who caused trouble in the premortal councils*], and **he came before me** [*the Father*], **saying—Behold, here am I, send me** [*to be the Redeemer*], **I will be thy son, and I will redeem all mankind, that one soul shall not be lost,** and surely **I will do it**; wherefore **give me thine honor.**

Did you notice in verse 1 that Lucifer has "I" trouble? His focus is on himself. Not only that, but he claimed that he would "redeem all mankind," which means that no one would have had agency. Such would be impossible. Satan could not have delivered on that promise because compulsion in place of agency cannot lead to redemption and exaltation.

Did you also notice what Lucifer wanted in return for his proposed service? He wanted to replace the Father (Isaiah 14:14; see also Moses 4:3) and take the Father's "honor" for himself. In other words, he wanted the Father's power. We read this in the Doctrine and Covenants as follows (**bold** added for emphasis):

D&C 29:36

36 And it came to pass that Adam, being tempted of the devil—for, behold, the devil was before Adam, for he rebelled against me [*in premortality*], saying, **Give me thine honor, which is my power**; and also a third part of the hosts of heaven turned he away from me because of their agency;

Next, in verse 2, Jesus Christ humbly volunteers to be the Redeemer and to carry out the Father's plan, giving the Father the honor and glory.

2 But, behold, **my Beloved Son**, which was my Beloved and Chosen from the beginning, **said** unto me—**Father, thy will be done, and the glory be thine forever.**

Some people wonder whether it is permissible for members of the Church to think and come up with their own ideas about things as far as the gospel is concerned. Of course it is. The Lord encourages us to use our capacity to think and analyze (see D&C 58:26–28). However, if we eventually find that our thinking goes against the revealed word and will of God, we would be wise to quickly change our thinking and to follow and support Him. Otherwise, we will find ourselves in the same situation as the devil—in open rebellion against God and the laws that govern the universe.

In summary, it is not a sin to think. But it is a sin to rebel. We learn this from verse 3, next, as Moses is told what Lucifer did that led him to become the devil.

3 Wherefore, because that **Satan rebelled** against me, and **sought to destroy the agency of man**, which I, the Lord God, had given him [*in the premortal realm*], and **also, that I should give unto him mine own power**; by the power of mine Only Begotten, I caused that he should be cast

down [see Revelation 12:4, 7–9];

There is an important issue to consider before we leave verses 1–3, above. It is whether there were two plans presented in the Council in Heaven. We often hear that Jesus Christ presented his plan and Lucifer presented his plan. This is not true. Christ did not propose a separate plan of His own. The plan was already in place. It was the Father's plan, used countless times already on many worlds that had already become celestialized (see Moses 1:35) before our great premortal Council in Heaven was even held.

Jesus supported the Father's plan. Lucifer proposed to change it—in effect, corrupting it. In a sense, it could be said that Lucifer came up with his own plan, but it is more accurate to say that he wanted to be the Savior in the Father's plan, proposing to eliminate agency so that all would be saved and desiring the glory for himself.

Guidelines for Church curriculum writers, reaffirmed in 2001 by the First Presidency and the Twelve, state that only one plan was presented, not two, that Jehovah (the premortal Jesus Christ) sustained Heavenly Father's plan, that Satan attempted to amend the Father's plan, and that Lucifer did not propose a separate plan of his own. Elder Bruce R. McConkie explained this. He taught:

"Although we sometimes hear it said that there were two plans—Christ's plan of freedom and agency, and Lucifer's plan of slavery and compulsion—such teaching does not conform to the revealed word. Christ did not present a plan of redemption and salvation, nor did Lucifer. There were not two plans up for consideration; there was only one; and that was the plan of the Father: originated, developed, presented, and put in force by him. Christ, however, made the Father's plan his own by his willing obedience to its terms and provisions" (Bruce R. McConkie, *Improvement Era,* May 1953, page 322).

Elder Neal A. Maxwell spoke of this. He said that it is "extremely important to get straight what happened in that premortal council. It was not an unstructured meeting, nor was it a discussion between plans, nor an idea-producing session, as to how to formulate the plan for salvation and carry it out. Our Father's plan was known, and the actual question put was whom the Father should send to carry out the plan" (*Deposition of a Disciple,* 11; see also John 7:16–18).

Verse 4, next, gives us a brief

summary of Lucifer's motives and goals after he rebelled and became the devil.

4 And he became Satan, yea, even **the devil**, the **father** [*author*] **of all lies**, to **deceive** and to **blind** men, and to **lead** them **captive** at his will, even as many as would not hearken unto my voice.

Beginning with verse 5, next, the stage is set for the Fall of Adam and Eve. Remember that the Fall was good. It was an essential part of the Father's plan. There was no Plan B (see 2 Nephi 2:24). Both President Joseph Fielding Smith and President Brigham Young taught that there was no alternative plan in case the first one failed. We will use **bold** for emphasis as we quote them:

Joseph Fielding Smith

"We came into this world to die. That was understood before we came here. It is part of the plan, all discussed and arranged long before men were placed upon the earth. **When Adam was sent into this world, it was with the understanding that he would violate a law, transgress a law, in order to bring to pass this mortal condition** which we find ourselves in today" (*Doctrines of Salvation,* Vol. 1, page 66; quoted in *Doctrines of the Gospel Student Manual*, page 21).

Brigham Young

"Did they [Adam and Eve] come out in direct opposition to God and to his government? No. But they transgressed a command of the Lord, and through that transgression sin came into the world. **The Lord knew they would do this, and he had designed that they should**" (*Discourses of Brigham Young,* page 103; quoted in the *Doctrines of the Gospel Student Manual*, 2000 edition, page 21).

As mentioned above, verse 5 sets the stage for Moses' account of Satan's tempting Eve. Before we continue, we will point out an important item. According to the heading to Genesis 3, it was Satan who was doing the talking. The image of a serpent is used symbolically to remind the reader of the fact that Satan is subtle and sly, cunning and quiet as he sneaks up on us to afflict us with his venom of deception. We will provide a quote here that helps make this clear:

"In the Genesis account the serpent speaks to Eve and tempts her to partake of the fruit. The more complete account in the book of Moses points out that Satan is the one speaking, although he does so through the serpent (see Moses 4:6–7). Satan is also symbolized elsewhere by the image of a serpent (see Revelation 12:9; D&C 76:28; 84:72; 88:110)" (*Old Testament Student Manual*, page 40).

5 And now **the serpent** [*Satan*] **was more subtle than any beast of the field** which I, the Lord God, had made.

6 And **Satan** put it into the heart of the serpent (for he had drawn away many after him [*perhaps a reference to the "third part" (D&C 29:36) of the premortal spirits who had followed him in his rebellion against the Father*]) and **he sought also to beguile Eve,** for **he knew not the mind of God,** wherefore **he sought to destroy the world.**

Let's back up to verse 6 and consider three things before we move on.

First

The wording "he sought also to beguile Eve" bears looking at closely. Is there perhaps a hint that he didn't succeed in deceiving her completely? We will give a quote that helps answer this:

"Satan was present to tempt Adam and Eve, much as he would try to thwart others in their divine missions: 'and he sought also to beguile Eve, for he knew not the mind of God, wherefore he sought to destroy the world' (Moses 4:6). **Eve faced the choice between selfish ease and unselfishly facing tribulation and death** (*Evidences and Reconciliations*, John A. Widtsoe, page 193). As befit her calling, she realized that there was no other way and **deliberately chose mortal life so as to further the purpose of God and bring children into the world**" (*The Encyclopedia of Mormonism*, under "Eve").

Question: How could Eve "deliberately" choose, as indicated by Elder Widtsoe in the above quote, when she and Adam were "innocent" in the Garden of Eden? Where would she get the knowledge with which to make such an informed decision?

Elder Widtsoe answers this question in the following quote. He said:

"Such was the problem before our first parents: to remain forever at selfish ease in the Garden of Eden, or to face unselfishly tribulation and death, in bringing to pass the purposes of the Lord for a host of waiting spirit children. They chose the latter. . . . **This they did with open eyes and minds as to consequences**. The memory of their former estates [*including their premortal spirit existence*] may have been dimmed, **but the gospel had been taught them during their sojourn in** the Garden of Eden.... The choice that they made raises Adam and Even to preeminence among all who have come on earth" (*Evidences and Reconciliations*, pp. 193–94).

Elder George Albert Smith, who later became president of the Church, also taught on this subject. He said:

"When God created the earth and placed our first parents upon it, **He did not leave them without knowledge concerning Himself**. It is true that there had been taken from them the remembrance of their pre-existent life, but in His tender mercy **He talked with** them and later He sent His choice servants to instruct them in the things pertaining to eternal life (George Albert Smith, in Conference Report, October 1928, pp. 90–91).

One last question before we move on. Why does Paul say that Eve was deceived? (See 1 Timothy 2:14.) No doubt she was, in some ways. But in the most important matters, she made an intelligent and wise choice. We will probably have to wait until we get a chance to talk to Eve, perhaps during the Millennium, for the complete account. If you listen carefully to what she said in the account as given in holy places, you will be reminded that she asked important and intelligent questions before partaking of the fruit and responded with unselfishness. Yet, there could be many ways in which she was deceived—perhaps in the sense of not believing that mortality would be so difficult at times. Perhaps she had no idea what it would be like to care for twenty or thirty sick children when they all had the flu! Maybe she was deceived into thinking that old age with its attendant pains and disabilities would not be difficult. Actually, she couldn't have understood these physical struggles because she had no basis on which to judge, because she and her husband were not yet mortal, even though they had physical bodies at this point.

Second

It is insightful to be made aware that Satan "knew not the mind of God." In other words, he does not know all things, as do members of the Godhead. He apparently did not realize that his tempting of Adam and Eve would further the work of the Father. One other example of Satan's not knowing all things is that he does not know the "thoughts and the intents of [our] heart" (D&C 6:16).

Third

Satan's ultimate goal is "to destroy the world," fair warning to us not to succumb to his wiles.

As we move on, watch as Satan plies his trade as the master of deception and subtlety. Can you hear his smooth voice as he cunningly implies that God is holding out on Adam and Eve, trying to keep them in the dark, up to old tricks again?

7 And he said unto the woman: Yea, **hath God said—Ye shall not eat of every tree of the garden?** (And he spake by the mouth of the serpent.)

Eve's answer is clear and to the point.

8 And the woman said unto the serpent: **We may eat of the fruit of the trees of the garden;**

9 **But of the fruit of the tree which thou beholdest in the midst of the garden, God hath said—Ye shall not eat of it, neither shall ye touch it, lest ye die.**

In this whole temptation scene, Satan only told one lie. We find it next, in verse 10. Everything he says in verse 11 is true. He still uses the same subtle approach to deception today as an effective tool, mixing truth with falsehood and lies.

10 And the serpent said unto the woman: **Ye shall not surely die** [*a lie, in direct opposition to the word of God wherein He had said "in the day thou eatest thereof thou shalt surely die" (Moses 3:17)*];

11 For God doth know that in the day ye eat thereof, then **your eyes shall be opened** [*true*], and **ye shall be as gods, knowing good and evil** [*true*].

The words "became pleasant" in verse 12, next, implying that it took some time for Eve to make her final decision regarding partaking of the fruit. Ultimately, she made the choice, as did Adam, which would allow all of us to be born on earth.

12 And when the woman saw that the tree was good for food, and that it **became pleasant** to the eyes, and a tree to be desired to make her wise, **she took of the fruit thereof, and did eat, and also gave unto her husband with her, and he did eat.**

There may be an important lesson for husbands and wives in verse 12, combined with other scriptures. We know that Adam led out in offering sacrifices after they had been cast out of the Garden of Eden (see Moses 5:5–6). We also know that Eve led out in the decision to leave the comforts of the Garden of

Eden and become mortal so that mortality and its attendant blessings could be gained. Thus, a marriage creates a husband-wife team in which both take turns leading out in things of value, according to their sensitivities, talents, skills, and so forth.

13 And **the eyes of them both were opened**, and they knew that they had been naked. And they sewed fig-leaves together and made themselves aprons.

Elder Dallin H. Oaks spoke of the choices made by Adam and Eve that led to the Fall. He said (**bold** added for emphasis):

"**It was Eve who first transgressed the limits of Eden in order to initiate the conditions of mortality. Her act**, whatever its nature, **was** formally a transgression but **eternally a glorious necessity** to open the doorway toward eternal life. **Adam showed his wisdom by doing the same**. And thus Eve and 'Adam fell that men might be' [2 Nephi 2:25].

"Some Christians condemn Eve for her act, concluding that she and her daughters are somehow flawed by it. Not the Latter-day Saints! Informed by revelation, **we celebrate Eve's act and honor her wisdom and courage in the great episode, called the Fall**. . . . Brigham Young declared, 'We should never blame Mother Eve, not the least' (*Journal of Discourses,* Vol. 13, p. 145). Joseph Fielding Smith said: 'I never speak of the part Eve took in this fall as a sin, nor do I accuse Adam of a sin. . . . This was a transgression of the law, but not a sin . . . for it was something that Adam and Eve had to do!' [*Doctrines of Salvation,* 1:114–15]" (in Conference Report, October 1993, page 98; or "'The Great Plan of Happiness,'" *Ensign,* November 1993, page 73).

Remember, the Fall was good. In fact, in our gospel discussions, we sometimes say that Adam and Eve "fell forward" rather than just saying that they "fell." It was all part of the Father's plan, and it was now under way. No doubt we rejoiced as premortal spirits upon finding out that the door had now been opened for our coming to earth as mortals.

A vital part of true agency is "owning" the consequences of one's choices. We usually refer to this as accountability. Next, in verses 14–19, we see the Lord teaching Adam and Eve their first lesson on accountability and ownership of the results of their decisions.

14 And **they heard the voice of the Lord God** [*Heavenly Father*],

as they were walking in the garden, in the cool of the day [*"at the time of the evening breeze," see Genesis 3, footnote 3b*]; and **Adam and his wife went to hide themselves** from the presence of the Lord God amongst the trees of the garden.

15 And **I, the Lord God, called unto Adam, and said unto him: Where goest thou** [*the Bible says, "Where art thou" (see Genesis 3:9)—just a small but insightful difference between the incomplete account in Genesis and the revealed account in Moses*]?

16 And **he said: I heard thy voice in the garden, and I was afraid,** because I beheld that I was naked, and I hid myself.

17 And I, the Lord God, said unto Adam: Who told thee thou wast naked? **Hast thou eaten of the tree** whereof I commanded thee that thou shouldst not eat, if so thou shouldst surely die?

Next, we see that Adam is initially reluctant to take direct responsibility for his actions. We are all familiar with this feeling. All of us must eventually learn this lesson, which is inseparably connected with agency.

18 And the man said: **The woman thou gavest me**, and commandest that she should remain with me, she **gave me of the fruit of the tree and I did eat.**

Next, it is Eve's turn. She too is hesitant and attempts to divert attention from her to Satan.

19 And I, **the Lord God, said unto the woman: What is this thing which thou hast done?** And **the woman said: The serpent beguiled me, and I did eat.**

We are taught much about Satan's status in verses 20–21, next.

20 And I, **the Lord God** [*the Father*], **said** unto the serpent: Because thou hast done this **thou shalt be cursed above** [*limited more than*] **all cattle, and above every beast of the field** [*Satan will never get a physical body, nor experience mortality, a blessing that even "cattle" and "every beast of the field" receives*]; **upon thy belly shalt thou go** [*Satan will be the lowest of the low*], and **dust shalt thou eat all the days of thy life** [*perhaps meaning that he will always be behind the Savior, in effect, "eating the Savior's dust"; this could also be a play on words, saying, in effect, that Satan will be "eating dust," associating with mortals and trying to swallow them up in spiritual destruction but never receiving a mortal body himself, one made of the "dust of the ground" (see Moses 3:7)*];

21 And **I will put enmity** [*a natural dislike, intense distrust*] **between thee** [*Satan*] **and the woman, between thy seed** [*Satan's followers, including the one-third who followed him in premortality, as well as those who follow him here on earth*] **and her seed** [*Jesus Christ*]; **and he** [*Christ*] **shall bruise thy head** [*will crush Satan and his kingdom; in other words, he will triumph over Satan and ultimately cast him and his evil followers out completely (see D&C 88:111–14)*], **and thou** [Satan] **shalt bruise his heel** [*will cause suffering, including causing evil men to crucify the Savior and causing pain and sorrow by leading people away from Christ and His gospel*].

Many of the notes supplied in verse 21, above, are taken from the *Old Testament Student Manual.* We will quote it here and add **bold** for teaching purposes.

"**Since Satan has no body** and therefore can have no literal children, **his seed are those who follow him**, both the one-third he led away in the premortal existence and those who follow his enticements in mortality until they come under his power. **The seed of the woman refers to Jesus Christ**, who was the only mortal born of an earthly mother and a Heavenly Father.

"President Joseph Fielding Smith referred to what the Apostle Paul wrote to the Roman Saints: 'Near the close of his epistle to the Roman saints, he said: "And the God of peace shall bruise Satan under your feet shortly. The grace of our Lord Jesus Christ be with you. Amen."' [Romans 16:20.]

"The 'God of peace,' who according to the scriptures is to bruise Satan, is Jesus Christ." (*Answers to Gospel Questions,* 1:3)

"The promise concerning **the bruising of the heel and head** means that while Satan (as the serpent) will bruise the heel of the Savior by leading men to crucify him and seemingly destroy him, in actuality that very act of atonement will give Christ the power to overcome the power that Satan has over men and undo the effects of the Fall. Thus, **the seed of the woman (Christ) shall crush the head of the serpent (Satan and his kingdom) with the very heel that was bruised (the atoning sacrifice)** (*Old Testament Student Manual: Genesis– 2 Samuel,* page 41).

Verse 22, next, is often taken out of the larger context of the scriptures as a whole as well as the plan of salvation and the teachings of our modern prophets, including the Proclamation on the Family. As a result, it becomes negative and quite troubling in the minds of some people. In fact, there is much damaging misunderstanding when it comes to this verse.

Before reading the next two verses, take a moment and answer the following question:

Question

Who got the worst curse, Adam or Eve?

Now go ahead and read verses 22 and 23, and see if you got it right (try not to look at our answer yet). After so doing, read our answer, which is given next.

Answer

Neither Adam nor Eve was cursed! The serpent was cursed (verses 20–21), and the ground was cursed (verse 23).

The point again is that the Fall was good. It was good for Adam and Eve. It was good for us. It was the next step in our being given opportunities to become like our Father in Heaven. Lehi taught us about the need for the Fall and the blessings and opportunities that followed it. He said (**bold** added for emphasis):

2 Nephi 2:22–25

22 And now, behold, **if Adam had not transgressed he would not have fallen**, but he **would have remained in the garden of Eden**. And **all things** which were created **must have** [*would have*] **remained in the same state** in which they were after they were created; and they must have remained **forever**, and had no end.

23 And they would have had **no children**; wherefore they would have remained in a state of **innocence**, having **no joy**, for they knew **no misery**; doing **no good**, for they knew **no sin**.

24 But behold, all things have been done in the wisdom of him who knoweth all things [*in other words, the Fall was an intentional part of the Father's plan*].

25 **Adam fell that men might be; and men are, that they might have joy**.

With the above comments as background, we will read verse 22, taking a bit of poetic license to present it in a negative way, the way in which many read it when they take it out of the larger context of what we know about the plan of salvation. After doing this, we will have President Spencer W. Kimball help us see it in a more positive way.

First, the negative approach. We will overdo it a bit.

22 Unto the woman, I, the Lord

God, said: [*Shame, shame on you for disobeying me. Because of your disobedience*] I will greatly multiply thy sorrow and thy conception [*As a punishment for your disobedience, I will make it hurt bad every time you have a child*]. In sorrow thou shalt bring forth children [*as part of your punishment, you will suffer much sadness and heartache because of your children*], and thy desire shall be to thy husband [*you will have the status of a servant to your husband*], and he shall rule over thee [*because you started it all by your disobedience in the Garden of Eden, I will make you subject to Adam, and he will be your superior*].

In a moment, we will reread verse 22, adding notes that reflect its true context in the plan of salvation. But first, we will quote President Kimball. He said:

"The Lord said to the woman: '. . . in sorrow thou shalt bring forth children.' I wonder if those who translated the Bible might have used the term distress instead of sorrow. It would mean much the same, except I think there is great gladness in most Latter-day Saint homes when there is to be a child there. As He concludes this statement he says, 'and thy desire shall be to thy husband, and he shall rule over thee.' (Gen. 3:16.) I have a question about the word rule. It gives the wrong impression. I would prefer to use the word preside because that's what he does. A righteous husband presides over his wife and family" ("The Blessings and Responsibilities of Womanhood," *Ensign,* March 1976, page 72).

Before we reread verse 22, we would also do well to consult with Eve as to her view of the Fall. After all, she was there and can give us an accurate view of the results as she later thought back on them. We can do so by reading her response to the Fall in Moses 5:11 (we will emphasize things with **bold**):

Moses 5:11

11 And **Eve**, his wife, heard all these things and **was glad**, saying: **Were it not for our transgression we never should have** [*would have*] **had seed** [*children*], and **never should have known good and evil**, and the **joy** of our redemption, and the **eternal life** which God giveth unto all the obedient.

We will now reread verse 22, adding notes that place our understanding of it into the greater context of the overall gospel and plan of salvation, including Eve's teachings and President Kimball's quote, above, along with other helps, including the idea that "sorrow" can mean the trials and tribulations of mortality, or mortality itself. Again, we may overdo it a bit for purposes of emphasizing the positives of this great and vital step in the plan.

22 Unto the woman, I, the Lord God, said: [*Thank you, thank you, thank you!*] **I will greatly multiply thy sorrow** [*because of your choice in the Garden of Eden, I can now give you many years in mortality*] **and thy conception** [*I can send many children into your home*]. **In sorrow** [*in mortality, with the joys and sorrows, pains and distresses that attend it*] **thou shalt bring forth children**, and **thy desire** [*highest loyalty (see Moses 3:24; D&C 42:22)*] **shall be to thy husband**, and **he shall rule over** [*preside and serve, as the Savior does*] **thee.**

Notice, in verse 23, next, that "sorrow" is also used for Adam as he begins the toil and labor that will be his responsibility and opportunity when he also begins mortal life. This is perhaps another indicator that we can consider "sorrow" to be a partial description of mortality, rather than a description of punishment. The same Hebrew word is used in verse 23 as was used for Eve in verse 22, translated as "sorrow" in English.

One of the important lessons we can learn from verse 23 is that the ground was cursed for Adam's "sake"—in other words, for his blessing and benefit. It will be good for his growth and development to have to work for a living.

23 And unto Adam, I, the Lord God, said: **Because thou hast hearkened unto the voice of thy wife** [*which was a very wise thing to do—see quote by Elder Oaks, given after verse 13, above*], **and hast eaten of the fruit of the tree of which I commanded thee, saying—Thou shalt not eat of it** [*unless you choose to become mortal and leave the garden—see quote from Joseph Fielding Smith after Moses 3:17*], **cursed shall be the ground for thy sake; in sorrow** [*in an environment of work, toil, and pain, which will be for your benefit*] **shalt thou eat of it all the days of thy life.**

The Lord continues to describe the conditions of "sorrow" in verses 24–25, next. Anyone who has seen the benefits of hard work can appreciate the benefits of "sorrow."

24 **Thorns also, and thistles shall it** [*the* ground] **bring forth to thee**, and thou shalt eat the herb [*food crops*] of the field.

25 **By the sweat of thy face shalt thou eat bread,** until thou shalt

return unto the ground—for thou shalt surely die [*Satan said this wouldn't happen—he lied; also, this mortal death will open the door for resurrection and for possessing a physical body forever*]—for out of it wast thou taken: for dust thou wast, and unto dust shalt thou return.

> Next, we are given the definition of the name Eve.

26 And Adam called his wife's name Eve, because she was **the mother of all living**; for thus have I, the Lord God, called the first of all women, which are many [*perhaps implying that there are many worlds (see Moses 1:35), all of which have the same plan of salvation as is used on our earth*].

> Next, the Lord provides clothing for Adam and Eve as they leave the Garden of Eden, and he summarizes the fact that they are now on their way into their mortal classroom, already having some understanding of good and evil.

27 Unto Adam, and also unto his wife, did I, the Lord God, make coats of skins, and **clothed them**.

28 And I, the Lord God, said unto mine Only Begotten: Behold, **the man is become as one of us to know good and evil**; and now lest he put forth his hand and partake also of the tree of life, and eat and live forever,

29 Therefore **I, the Lord God, will send him forth from the Garden of Eden**, to till the ground from whence he was taken;

30 For as I, the Lord God, liveth, even so my words cannot return void, for as they go forth out of my mouth they must be fulfilled.

31 **So I drove out the man, and I placed at the east of the Garden of Eden, cherubim and a flaming sword**, which turned every way **to keep the way of the tree of life** [*to prevent Adam and Eve from returning and partaking of the tree of life, thus emphasizing the importance of going through the lessons of mortality, including learning, growing in wisdom and knowledge, making choices, repenting as needed, and so forth, which are a part of the Father's plan for us*].

> In Alma 42, Alma spoke of what would have happened if Adam and Eve had returned and partaken of the tree of life. He said (**bold** added for emphasis):
>
> 2 Now behold, my son, I will explain this thing unto thee. For behold, after the Lord God sent our first parents forth from the garden of Eden, to till the ground, from whence they were taken—yea, he drew out the man, and

he placed at the east end of the garden of Eden, cherubim, and a flaming sword which turned every way, to keep the tree of life—

3 Now, we see that the man had become as God, knowing good and evil; and lest he should put forth his hand, and take also of the tree of life, and eat and live forever, the Lord God placed cherubim and the flaming sword, that he should not partake of the fruit—

4 And thus we see, that there was a time granted unto man to repent, yea, a probationary time, a time to repent and serve God.

5 For behold, **if Adam had put forth his hand immediately, and partaken of the tree of life, he would have lived forever**, according to the word of God, **having no space for repentance**; yea, and also **the word of God would have been void, and the great plan of salvation would have been frustrated**.

6 But behold, it was appointed unto man to die [*it is part of the plan for us to die*]—therefore, as they were cut off from the tree of life they should be cut off from the face of the earth—and man became lost forever, yea, they became fallen man.

7 And now, ye see by this that our first parents [*Adam and Eve*] were cut off both temporally [*physically*] and spiritually from the presence of the Lord; and thus we see they became subjects to follow after their own will [*they were now in a setting in which they could best exercise their agency*].

8 Now behold, **it was not expedient** [*wise, necessary*] **that man should be reclaimed from this temporal death, for that would destroy the great plan of happiness** [*the plan of salvation*].

Verse 32, next, is a reminder to us, as was the case with Moses 1:42, that the book of Moses is, in many cases, advanced doctrine and might overwhelm people with little or no understanding of gospel basics.

32 (And these are the words which I spake unto my servant Moses, and they are true even as I will; and I have spoken them unto you [*Joseph Smith*]. **See thou show them unto no man, until I command you, except to them that believe**. Amen.)

MOSES, CHAPTER 5

(Revealed to Joseph Smith, June–October 1830)

Background

This chapter is the "equivalent" of Genesis 4 in the Bible. One of the dilemmas that arises in this chapter in the Bible is that it appears from that account that the first child of Adam and Eve was Cain; the second, Abel. This leads to a credibility gap in some people's minds when Cain kills Abel and then goes to the land of Nod, where he and his wife have a baby (Genesis 4:16–17). The question comes up as to where Cain's wife came from, since Adam and Eve only had two children at the time. This is used by some to discredit the Bible.

Another concern that arises is that, in the Bible account, it does not seem that God is fair to Cain. It seems that He punishes him severely without giving him a fair chance at being acceptable before God and adequately knowing the dangers of the path he is pursuing with regard to his brother, Abel.

The original account, as given here in Moses, supplies additional details that solve both problems and gives us much more. We will see this during our study of chapter 5.

First, Genesis 4 begins with the birth of Cain, whereas, Moses 5 provides fifteen verses of information before arriving at the birth of Cain. This is another example of the great value of the book of Moses. For instance, in verses 1–2, next, we learn that Adam and Eve had many children before they had Cain and Abel. This solves the first dilemma mentioned in the background, above.

1 And it came to pass that after I, the Lord God, had driven them out, that **Adam began to till the earth, and to have dominion over all the beasts of the field, and to eat his bread by the sweat of his brow**, as I the Lord had commanded him. And **Eve**, also, his wife, **did labor with him** [*a team*].

2 And **Adam knew his wife, and she bare unto him sons and daughters**, and **they began to multiply and to replenish the earth** [*as commanded in Moses 2:28*].

In order to again emphasize the value of the Lord's revealing the original writings of Moses to the Prophet Joseph Smith, we will make a partial list of the many additional things Moses 5 adds to the biblical account in Genesis 4. We will point out nine things added by way of verses 3–15, next. Remember, all of these things happened before Cain and Abel were born.

1. Their sons and daughters married and had children also.

2. Adam and Eve continued to pray and were taught by the Lord, even though they had been cast out of the Garden of Eden.

3. Adam and Eve were given commandments.

4. They offered sacrifices.

5. They were taught about the Atonement of Jesus Christ.

6. They faithfully taught the gospel of Jesus Christ to their children.

7. Satan came among them and spread his false doctrines and deceptions.

8. Apostasy followed disobedience.

9. The power of the Holy Ghost was manifest in the teaching of faith in Jesus Christ and repentance for the remission of sins.

3 And from that time forth, **the sons and daughters of Adam began to divide two and two** in the land [*in other words, they married and settled on places of their own*], and to till the land, and to tend flocks, and **they also begat sons and daughters** [*grandchildren for Adam and Eve*].

Adam will live to be 930 years old (see Moses 6:12), and so we consider that he and Eve would have had a great many children, thus fulfilling the promise of God, given in Moses 4:22, in which He said "I will greatly multiply thy . . . conception." We are not told how long Eve lived, but we assume it was to a ripe old age similar to Adam's. We understand that their years were the same as ours, based on the chronology given in D&C 107:41–53. From this information, we see that Adam was still active and functioning in his priesthood eight generations down the line from him and Eve. Adam was 787 years old at this time, when he ordained Methuselah (D&C 107:50).

By way of additional information, the Jewish historian Josephus, who lived at the time of Christ, indicated that the ancients did live that long and that their ages were measured in our type of years. He said (**bold** added for emphasis):

"Now when Noah had lived three hundred and fifty years after the Flood, and that all that time happily, he died, **having lived the number of nine hundred and fifty** years. But **let no one**, upon comparing the lives of the ancients with our lives, and with the few years which we now live, think that what we have said of them is false [*in other words, don't think that they didn't live that much longer than we do*]; or make the shortness of our lives at present an argument, that neither did they attain to so long a duration of life" (*Josephus, Antiquities of the Jews,* Book 1, chapter 3, verse 9).

President Wilford Woodruff commented on the fact that the ancients did live much longer than we do today. He said:

"The age of man is very short indeed in this day to what it was in ancient days. Men anciently lived to a very great age. When four or five hundred years old they took wives, begat children, and raised up posterity. Today our age is limited to something like three score years and ten [seventy years]" (Wilford Woodruff, in James R. Clark, *Messages of the First Presidency,* Vol. 3, page 319).

We will provide a short list of some of the "ancients" and how long they lived.

- Adam, 930 years (Moses 6:12)
- Seth, 912 years (Moses 6:16)
- Enos, 905 years (Moses 6:18)
- Cainan, 910 years (Moses 6:19)
- Mahalaleel, 895 years (Moses 6:20)
- Jared, 962 years (Moses 6:24)
- Enoch was translated with the City of Enoch at age 430 (Moses 8:1), about 600 years before the flood.
- Methuselah, 969 years (Genesis 5:27)
- Lamech, 777 years (Genesis 5:31)
- Noah, 950 years (Genesis 9:29)

(The Flood occurred approximately 2240 BC)

- Abraham, 175 years (Genesis 25:7)
- Isaac, 180 years (Genesis 35:28)
- Jacob, 147 years (Genesis 47:28)
- Joseph, 110 years (Genesis 50:26)

Next, in verse 4, we are informed that Adam and Eve communicated with God through prayer after being cast out of the Garden of Eden and that the Lord spoke with them from the direction of the Garden.

4 And **Adam and Eve, his wife, called upon the name of the Lord** [*they prayed*], and **they heard the voice of the Lord** from the way toward the Garden of Eden, **speaking unto them**, and they saw him not; for they were shut out from his presence [*this is similar to our general situation now*].

Next, Adam and Eve are commanded to offer sacrifices (Adam will officiate, using his priesthood, and Eve will participate, much the same as when we all participate in the sacrament as priesthood holders administer it to us). Commandments are instructions and invitations from God to us to help us qualify for additional knowledge and blessings, bringing us closer to God. We see this principle clearly taught in the next verses.

5 And **he gave unto them commandments**, that they should **worship the Lord** their God, and should **offer the firstlings** [*the firstborn males—see Deuteronomy 15:19*] **of their flocks, for an offering unto the Lord. And Adam was obedient** unto the commandments of the Lord.

At this point, we will be taught the value of obedience, even when we don't understand the reasons for the commandment or instruction. At first, Adam did not know the purpose of sacrificing the firstborn males of his flocks. All he knew was that he had been commanded by the Lord to do so, and so he did it. Often, such obedience has to persevere for quite some time before the Lord provides the reasons. As you can see from the first line of verse 6, next, such was the case for Adam and Eve.

6 And **after many days** an angel of the Lord appeared unto Adam, saying: Why dost thou offer sacrifices unto the Lord? And Adam said unto him: I know not, save the Lord commanded me.

Watch now as faith and obedience lead to additional knowledge. In fact, there seems to be a pattern here in which faith and obedience lead to additional revelation, which, when obeyed, leads to yet more blessings and revelation, which, when obeyed, lead to additional knowledge and understanding. And so this upward spiral continues in the lives of the faithful. This is a principle and pattern that can continue to operate throughout our lives.

In verse 7, next, the reason for the commandment to sacrifice the firstlings (the firstborn males of the flocks) is given. An angel explains that the sacrificing of the firstborn male, which Adam has been doing as a matter of obedience, is symbolic of the sacrificing of the Son of God.

7 And then the angel spake, saying: **This thing is a similitude of** [*symbolic of*] **the sacrifice of the Only Begotten of the Father,** which is full of grace and truth [*who is full of ability and true doctrine to assist us in returning home to the Father*].

Next, Adam and Eve are taught the importance of worshipping in the name of Jesus Christ and are taught the doctrine of repentance and forgiveness. Again, they are receiving this additional instruction and doctrine because they were obedient to the initial commandments given them.

8 Wherefore, **thou shalt do all that thou doest in the name of the Son,** and **thou shalt repent and call upon God in the name of the Son forevermore.**

Next, one of the greatest blessings of all is given because of obedience. It is the witness of the Holy Ghost.

9 And in that day **the Holy Ghost fell upon Adam, which beareth record of the Father and the Son** [*one of the most important functions of the Holy Ghost*], saying: **I am the Only Begotten of the Father from the beginning** [*the Holy Ghost is bearing special witness that Jesus is the Christ, the Redeemer*], henceforth and forever, that as thou hast fallen **thou mayest be redeemed, and all mankind, even as many as will** [*in other words, all who exercise their agency to follow Christ by keeping His commandments may be redeemed and thus return to live with the Father forever*].

We have been watching as Adam goes rapidly from simple obedience, without knowing why he was commanded to offer sacrifices, to receiving understanding, then to being given the help and witness of the Holy Ghost, which is a tremendous step forward. One of the lessons we learn is that, with the help of the Holy Ghost, one can move rapidly to a higher and much better understanding of the gospel.

Now, in verse 10, next, we will see the power of the Holy Ghost to expand our minds far beyond our normal capabilities, giving us knowledge and perspective that allow us to understand the true purposes of life and to maintain our direction toward exaltation.

One of the most significant teachings in verse 10 deals with the blessings that came as a result of the Fall. We are clearly taught that the Fall was good.

10 And in that day **Adam blessed** [*praised*] **God and was filled** [*with*

the Holy Ghost], and **began to prophesy concerning all the families of the earth**, saying: Blessed be the name of God, for **because of my transgression my eyes are opened, and in this life I shall have joy, and again in the flesh I shall see God.**

We see in verse 11, next, that Eve also has been given great knowledge and powerful testimony because she likewise expresses gladness and joy for the blessings and opportunities that came as a result of the Fall.

11 And **Eve**, his wife, heard all these things and **was glad**, saying: **Were it not for our transgression we never should have had seed** [*we never would have had children*], and **never should have** [*never would have*] **known good and evil**, and the **joy of our redemption**, and the **eternal life** [*exaltation, attaining the highest degree of glory in the celestial kingdom, becoming gods*] **which God giveth unto all the obedient.**

Next, we see that Adam and Eve taught their children all that they had been taught.

12 And **Adam and Eve** blessed [*praised*] the name of God, and they **made all things known unto their sons and their daughters.**

Sadly but not unexpectedly, Satan comes along as recorded in verse 13, next, and leads many of Adam and Eve's posterity astray. Even though we know that opposition is part of the plan, it still hurts to see people fall for the wiles of the devil.

13 And **Satan came among them**, saying: **I am also a son of God** [*perhaps meaning, "I too am righteous—see Moses 7:1, where "sons of God" means "the righteous." If so, he is lying. Another possibility is that he is saying that his ideas and doctrines are just as good as any others, that God's ways are not the only valid ways*]; and **he commanded them** [*he is counterfeiting God*], saying: **Believe it not** [*don't believe what their parents have taught them*]; and they believed it not, and **they loved Satan more than God. And men began from that time forth to be carnal** [*worldly*], **sensual** [*caught up in all forms of sexual immorality*], and **devilish** [*wicked*].

The phrase "they loved Satan more than God" in verse 13 is a pointed statement about any behavior that does not demonstrate loyalty to God. One of the subtleties or traps that the devil uses successfully is that of convincing us that some of our intentional inappropriate behaviors are not all that dangerous. It can be helpful, when involved in such behaviors, to say to one's self, "At this moment, I love Satan more than God." While this may seem a bit strong, it can nevertheless be an effective way to pull us back from such behaviors. Perhaps it is the shock factor that makes this simple technique effective in steering us back onto the straight and narrow path.

Have you noticed that we are being taught quite a bit about the role and function of the Holy Ghost in these verses? We will see more about Him in verse 14, next. By the way, this certainly answers the question, frequently asked, as to whether the Holy Ghost functioned on the earth before the mortal ministry of the Savior.

14 And **the Lord God called upon men by the Holy Ghost** everywhere and commanded them that they should repent;

We are taught in the Doctrine and Covenants that the Holy Ghost can play a major role in bearing witness to people that the gospel of Jesus Christ is true, whether or not they belong to the Church. If nonmembers do not heed the promptings and progress toward baptism, then the Holy Ghost withdraws. We read:

D&C 130:23

23 A man may receive the Holy Ghost, and it may descend upon him and not tarry with him.

A simple and powerful summary of the gospel of Jesus Christ is given in verse 15, next. Such simplicity is difficult to misunderstand!

15 **And as many as believed in the Son, and repented of their sins, should be saved; and as many as believed not and repented not, should be damned** [*stopped in their progression*]; **and the words went forth out of the mouth of God in a firm decree; wherefore they must be fulfilled.**

Now we come to the birth of Cain and Abel. The Book of Moses provides far more information than the Bible about events leading up to Cain's killing of Abel. In fact, it provides a pattern followed by Cain that we would be wise to avoid at all costs.

At the end of verse 16, next, we see that, at an early age, Cain developed an arrogant attitude about God. In verse 17, we are told that Abel had a humble, obedient attitude toward God.

16 And **Adam and Eve, his wife, ceased not to call upon God** [*continued to be faithful to the gospel of Jesus Christ*]. **And Adam knew Eve his wife, and she conceived and**

bare **Cain**, and said: I have gotten a man from the Lord; wherefore he may not reject his words [*as was the case with many of their posterity—see verse 13*]. But behold, Cain hearkened not, saying: **Who is the Lord that I should know him?**

17 And she again conceived and bare his brother **Abel**. And Abel **hearkened unto the voice of the Lord**. And Abel was a keeper of sheep [*a sheep rancher*], but Cain was a tiller of the ground [*a farmer*].

We will pause here long enough to review some steps of the pattern that Cain will follow and that will ultimately make him feel justified in slaying his brother. It is a clever series of steps in a trap set by Satan. The attitudes and rationalizations involved pose danger to all of us unless we avoid them or repent quickly upon realizing that we have begun following this path.

Steps in the Pattern of Deception

1. Having a cocky, arrogant attitude about God and His Church, gospel, and so forth (see verse 16).

2. Loving Satan more than God, enjoying evil more than the things of God (see verse 18).

3. Making your own rules, in opposition to God's, and being angry at God for not accepting your rules for religion as being just as valid as those established by God (verses 19–21).

4. Rejecting opportunities to understand and repent (verses 22–25).

5. Being angry and rejecting God and His servants (verse 26s).

6. Surrounding yourself with friends and peers who enjoy evil just like you, and who support you in your wickedness (verses 27–28).

7. Making secret, dark, covenants with the devil and his evil representatives to destroy the righteous (verses 29–30).

8. Glorying and rejoicing in wickedness (verse 31).

9. Foolishly believing that you have attained true freedom by rejecting the laws of God.

10. Complaining bitterly and blaming others when you finally get caught; refusing to accept full accountability for your actions (verses 38–39).

We will now study the lessons taught in the next several verses.

Ultimately, the steps taken by Cain led him to become a son of perdition. You may wish to read D&C 76:31–35 and compare the details given there to the path followed by Cain.

18 And **Cain loved Satan more than God** [*he loved evil more than righteousness*]. And **Satan commanded him**, saying: Make an offering unto the Lord.

> There is something wrong and completely improper in verse 18. Did you catch it? It is that Satan commands Cain to worship God, to offer sacrifice. The devil would never command us to do something good unless he believed that it could ultimately bring us to him. There is something else wrong with the situation, as reported in verse 19. Can you see it?

19 And **in process of time** [*it apparently took time for Cain to decide to follow Satan's command*] it came to pass that **Cain brought of the fruit of the ground** [*he brought crops, perhaps vegetables and grains*] **an offering unto the Lord.**

> The problem is the type of sacrifice Cain is bringing. Adam's posterity has been commanded to offer the firstlings of the flock (verse 5, above)—in other words, the firstborn males, symbolizing the shedding of the blood of Christ as an atonement for our sins.
>
> Under Satan's direction, Cain has made his own rules. Perhaps one of the things Satan said to Cain was that God discriminates against farmers and blesses ranchers unfairly. Of course, Cain's profession (farming) was just as honorable as Abel's (a rancher—see verse 17, above). It is interesting that verse 17 emphasizes their two chosen careers, perhaps to prepare us for this scene in which Cain offers crops, which represent his livelihood, and in which Abel offers the firstlings of his flocks, representing his chosen livelihood. It may well be that Satan has already put it in Cain's mind that God is prejudiced against farmers, and he may have challenged Cain to offer crops as sacrifice to test God and see if He is fair.
>
> Another important thing to realize here is the fact that Cain held the priesthood, which increased his accountability. Joseph Smith taught (**bold** added for emphasis):
>
> "The power, glory and blessings of the Priesthood could not continue with those who received ordination only [*except*] as their righteousness continued; for **Cain also being authorized to**

offer sacrifice [*in other words, he held the priesthood*], but not offering it in righteousness, was cursed. It signifies, then, that the ordinances must be kept in the very way God has appointed; otherwise their Priesthood will prove a cursing instead of a blessing" (*Teachings of the Prophet Joseph Smith,* page 169).

20 And **Abel,** he also **brought of the firstlings of his flock,** and **of the fat** [*the very best, perhaps implying that Cain did not bring the best of his crops*] **thereof.** And the Lord had respect unto Abel, and to his offering [*the Lord accepted Abel's offering*];

21 **But unto Cain, and to his offering, he had not respect** [*He did not accept it*]. Now **Satan knew this, and it pleased him** [*his plot to trap Cain was working well so far*]. And **Cain was very wroth** [*angry*], and his countenance fell [*he was very unhappy and his face showed it*].

The Prophet Joseph Smith taught us about the reasons that the Lord accepted Abel's sacrifice and rejected Cain's. He said (**bold** added for emphasis):

"**God,** as before remarked, **prepared a sacrifice in the gift of His own Son** who should be sent in due time, to prepare a way, or open a door through which man might enter into the Lord's presence. . . . By faith in this atonement or plan of redemption, **Abel offered** to God a sacrifice that was accepted, which was **the firstlings of the flock. Cain offered of the fruit of the ground,** and was not accepted, because he could not do it in faith, he could have no faith, or could not exercise faith **contrary to the plan of heaven. It must be shedding the blood of the Only Begotten to atone for man**; for this was the plan of redemption; and without the shedding of blood was no remission; and as **the sacrifice was instituted for a type** [*a symbol*]**, by which man was to discern the great Sacrifice which God had prepared; to offer a sacrifice contrary to that, no faith could be exercised, because redemption was not purchased in that way**, nor the power of atonement instituted after that order; **consequently Cain could have no faith**" (*Teachings of the Prophet Joseph Smith,* page 58).

Next, the Lord Jesus Christ talks to Cain, explaining to him what he can do to be accepted also and gently giving him fair warning about what will happen if Cain refuses.

22 And the Lord said unto Cain:

Why art thou wroth? Why is thy countenance fallen?

23 **If thou doest well** [*if Cain follows the commandments, rather than making his own rules*], **thou shalt be accepted. And if thou doest not well, sin lieth at the door, and Satan desireth to have thee**; and **except** [*unless*] **thou shalt hearken unto my commandments, I will deliver thee up** [*a basic rule of the law of justice; in other words, God cannot force us to obey Him and thus obtain mercy; if we choose to disobey, we must be "delivered up" to Satan and his punishments*], and it shall be unto thee according to his desire. And **thou shalt rule over him**;

> It looks like we will have to wait for the final word from the Lord through the living prophet as to the exact meaning of the last phrase in verse 23, above. However, Joseph Smith did say that those with bodies have power over spirits who don't get bodies. He said (**bold** added for emphasis):
>
> "We came to this earth that we might have a body and present it pure before God in the celestial kingdom. The great principle of happiness consists in having a body. **The devil has no body, and herein is his punishment**. He is pleased when he can obtain the tabernacle of man, and when cast out by the Savior he asked to go into the herd of swine, showing that he would prefer a swine's body to having none.
>
> "**All beings who have bodies have power over those who have not**" (*Teachings of the Prophet Joseph Smith,* page 181).

Next, the Lord warns Cain that if he does not change course now, he will become a son of perdition, just like Satan. He will become the physical, mortal leader of Satan's work on earth. "Perdition" means "total loss," "destruction," "complete ruin."

24 For **from this time forth** thou shalt be the father [*author, sponsor*] of his [*Satan's*] lies; **thou shalt be called Perdition** [*if Cain does not repent and cease following Satan, he will become a son of perdition because his rebellion now would be just like Lucifer's rebellion against full and sure knowledge (see verses 22–23*]; for thou wast also before the world [*perhaps a reminder to Cain that he too lived in the premortal existence and was given opportunities there to know right from wrong; in fact, Cain had to have chosen right to the point of qualifying for mortal life, as opposed to the one-third who were cast out with the devil*].

Elder Bruce R. McConkie taught the meaning of "perdition." He said:

"Two persons, Cain and Satan, have received the awesome name-title Perdition. The name signifies that they have no hope whatever of any degree of salvation, that they have wholly given themselves up to iniquity, and that any feeling of righteousness whatever has been destroyed in their breasts" (*Mormon Doctrine*, 566).

The warning to Cain from the Lord continues, in verse 25, next, telling him that if he does not change course now, he will become known throughout the world as the one who committed the first murder and the one who started dark and terrible evil upon the earth.

25 And **it shall be said in time to come—That these abominations were had from Cain; for he rejected the greater counsel** [*the best counsel*] **which was had from God; and this** [*becoming "Perdition"*] **is a cursing which I will put upon thee, except thou repent** [*there is still time for Cain to repent*].

Next, in verse 26, Cain made an agency choice in the face of pure, complete knowledge between good and evil, which has eternal consequences for him.

26 And **Cain was wroth** [*angry*], and **listened not any more to the voice of the Lord, neither to Abel**, his brother, who walked in holiness before the Lord.

Verse 27, next, indicates that Cain had drawn others to follow him in his evil ways before he killed Abel. Verse 28 tells us, in effect, that he chose an evil woman to be his wife. In other words, he surrounded himself with evil friends and family who would support him in his evil ways. You no doubt have seen this type of behavior today among the intentionally wicked.

27 And **Adam and his wife mourned** before the Lord, **because of Cain and his brethren**.

28 And it came to pass that **Cain took one of his brothers' daughters to wife, and they loved Satan more than God.**

Adam and Eve's mourning because of Cain reminds us that many righteous parents find themselves in that situation. Elder Richard G. Scott gave counsel to those who mourn because a loved one has turned away from the Lord to pursue evil. He said:

"Many of you have heavy hearts because a son or daughter, husband or wife, has turned from righteousness to pursue evil. My message is for you.

"Your life is filled with anguish, pain, and, at times, despair. I will tell you how you can be comforted by the Lord.

"First, you must recognize two foundation principles:

1. While there are many things you can do to help a loved one in need, there are some things that must be done by the Lord.

2. Also, no enduring improvement can occur without righteous exercise of agency. Do not attempt to override agency. The Lord himself would not do that. Forced obedience yields no blessings (see D&C 58:26–33).

"I will suggest seven ways you can help. [Elder Scott explained each of the following. You may wish to read the entire article in the May 1988 *Ensign*.]

First—Love without limitations.

Second—Do not condone the transgressions, but extend every hope and support to the transgressor.

Third—Teach truth.

Fourth—Honestly forgive as often as is required.

Fifth—Pray trustingly. "The ... fervent prayer of a righteous man availeth much" (James 5:16).

Sixth—Keep perspective. When you have done all that you can reasonably do, rest the burden in the hands of the Lord.... When the things you realistically can do to help are done, leave the matter in the hands of the Lord and worry no more. Do not feel guilty because you cannot do more. Do not waste your energy on useless worry.... In time, you will feel impressions and know how to give further help. You will find more peace and happiness, will not neglect others that need you, and will be able to give greater help because of that eternal perspective.

"One last suggestion—Never give up on a loved one, never!" ("To Help a Loved One in Need," *Ensign,* May 1988, pp. 60–61).

Verse 29, next, gives an account of one of the most evil and blasphemous scenes of all time. In it, as you can see, Satan invites Cain to covenant with him by his own life (a most sacred type of covenant—see 1 Nephi 4:33) to put his wicked brethren under secret oath by their own lives, and, in the name of Jesus Christ, to keep their covenant from Adam. Satan, in turn, covenants that he will teach Cain how to murder Abel. In this verse, Satan is openly blaspheming and counterfeiting the most sacred covenants we make with God as we enter into ordinances and covenants leading to exaltation.

29 And **Satan said unto Cain**: Swear [*covenant*] unto me by thy throat [*upon your life*], and if thou tell it thou shalt die [*done in secret*]; and **swear thy brethren by their heads** [*make your friends covenant upon their lives*], and **by the living God** [*a mockery of covenants we make in the name of the Father and in the name of Jesus Christ*], **that they tell it not** [*that they keep this dark secret of how to murder a secret*]; for if they tell it, they shall surely die; and this that thy father [Adam] may not know it; and **this day I will deliver thy brother Abel into thine hands** [*Satan will teach Cain how to kill Abel—see verse 31*].

Verse 30, next, is a reminder of how far Satan will go to deceive us into following him. He promises Cain, in effect, that he will be his servant. Mormon warned us against believing that the devil would keep his word. He said (**bold** added for teaching purposes):

Alma 30:60

60 And thus we see the end of him who perverteth the ways of the Lord; and thus we see **that the devil will not support his children** [*followers*] **at the last day, but doth speedily drag them down to hell**.

30 And **Satan sware** [*promised, covenanted*] **unto Cain that he would do according to his commands**. And all these things were done in secret.

It is sad to note how far downward Cain has fallen since the last invitation from the Lord to repent, in verse 25. He turned completely from God and wholly embraced Satan. He now thinks like Satan and acts like Satan, glorying in wickedness, as we see in verse 31, next. All of this is a direct result of intentionally sinning against light.

31 And **Cain said: Truly I am Mahan** [*perhaps meaning "mind," "destroyer," "great one"; see Moses 5:31, footnote d*], **the master of this great secret, that I may murder and get gain** [*obtain others' possessions*]. Wherefore Cain was called **Master Mahan** and **he gloried in his wickedness**.

In verses 32–33, next, we see Cain kill Abel and then glory in what he has done as he considers that he is now "free" and will get all of Abel's possessions. He has intentionally followed Satan and will soon reap the whirlwind.

32 And Cain went into the field, and Cain talked with Abel, his brother. And it came to pass that while they were in the field, **Cain rose up against Abel, his brother, and slew him.**

33 And Cain **gloried in that which he had done**, saying: **I am free**; surely **the flocks of my brother falleth into my hands.**

> Not only do the "flocks of my brother" represent new material wealth for Cain, but it is also likely that they represent, in Cain's distorted way of thinking, a triumph over the animal sacrifices, the firstlings of the flock, sacrificed by Abel, accepted by God in verse 20, above. Thus, it appears that not only was Cain triumphing over Abel, but he was also triumphing over God, in his way of thinking, destroying the sources of his trouble. Surely, one of the important lessons we learn here is that wickedness does not promote rational thought.
>
> Cain's glorying in wickedness does not last long, as we see, beginning in verse 34, next. Satan is significantly absent as a support for Cain in this next scene, as Master Mahan (verse 31) attempts to lie his way out.

34 And **the Lord said unto Cain: Where is Abel, thy brother?** And **he said: I know not.** Am I my brother's keeper?

35 And **the Lord said: What hast thou done? The voice of thy brother's blood cries unto me from the ground.**

> Next, in verses 36–37, we see two curses placed upon Cain.
>
> 1. The earth will not bring forth abundant crops for him.
> 2. He will be a fugitive, running from enemies, real or perceived, and a vagabond, not having a permanent home.

36 And now **thou shalt be cursed** from the earth which hath opened her mouth to receive thy brother's blood from thy hand.

37 **When thou tillest the ground it shall not henceforth yield unto thee her strength. A fugitive and a vagabond shalt thou be in the earth.**

> Next, Cain attempts to divert accountability from himself by blaming others. He specifically blames Satan and also the Lord, and he attempts to invoke sympathy from the Lord. His concern is focused upon himself. He is worried that someone might kill him. You will see that not once in verses 38–39 does Cain mention the victim of his crime. We see much of this today in our

courts of law. Victim's rights seem to be a side issue or no issue at all.

38 And **Cain said unto the Lord: Satan tempted me** because of my brother's flocks. And **I was wroth** [*angry*] also; **for his offering thou didst accept and not mine**; my punishment is greater than I can bear.

39 Behold **thou hast driven me out this day from the face of the Lord**, and from thy face shall I be hid; and **I shall be a fugitive and a vagabond in the earth**; and it shall come to pass, that **he that findeth me will slay me**, because of mine iniquities, for these things are not hid from the Lord.

Next, in verse 40, we are given the reason God placed the "mark" of a dark skin upon Cain (see Moses 7:8). The "curse" and the "mark" are not the same thing.

40 And I the Lord said unto him: Whosoever slayeth thee, vengeance shall be taken on him sevenfold. **And I the Lord set a mark upon Cain, lest any finding him should kill him.**

41 And **Cain was shut out from the presence of the Lord** [*Cain has, in effect, been excommunicated*], and with his wife and many of his brethren dwelt in the land of Nod, on the east of Eden.

As we continue to the end of the chapter, we will see that gross wickedness and secret combinations spread from Cain and his wicked peers doing great individual and collective damage to society (summed up in verse 55).

42 And **Cain knew his wife, and she conceived and bare Enoch** [*not the Enoch who built the City of Enoch*], and **he also begat many sons and daughters**. And he built a city, and he called the name of the city after the name of his son, Enoch.

43 And unto Enoch was born Irad, and other sons and daughters. And Irad begat Mahujael, and other sons and daughters. And Mahujael begat Methusael, and other sons and daughters. And Methusael begat Lamech.

44 And Lamech took unto himself two wives; the name of one being Adah, and the name of the other, Zillah.

45 And Adah bare Jabal; he was the father of such as dwell in tents, and they were keepers of cattle; and his brother's name was Jubal, who was the father of all such as handle the harp and organ.

46 And Zillah, she also bare Tubal Cain, an instructor of every artificer

in brass and iron. And the sister of Tubal Cain was called Naamah.

> Next, we watch as secret combinations infiltrate and begin to destroy their society. Lamech has killed Irad, Cain's grandson, and is afraid for his life. He asks his wives to keep his secret, but they tell everyone, and he is forced to flee and live in hiding. The picture painted here is the exact opposite of a Zion society, where peace and safety prevail because of living the gospel of Jesus Christ.

47 And **Lamech** [*Cain's great-great-great grandson*] **said unto his wives**, Adah and Zillah: Hear my voice, ye wives of Lamech, hearken unto my speech; for **I have slain a man** [*Irad—see verses 49–50*] to my wounding, and a young man to my hurt.

48 If Cain shall be avenged sevenfold, truly Lamech shall be seventy and seven fold;

> In verses 49–53, we watch the spread of secret combinations, Satan worship, and great deceptions and wickedness wherein no one trusts anybody and society is destabilized.

49 For **Lamech having entered into a covenant with Satan**, after the manner of Cain [*just as Cain did*], wherein he became Master Mahan, master of that great secret which was administered unto Cain by Satan; and **Irad**, the son of Enoch, having known their secret, **began to reveal it unto the sons of Adam**;

50 Wherefore **Lamech**, being angry, **slew him**, not like unto Cain, his brother Abel, for the sake of getting gain, but he slew him for the oath's sake [*the secret pact with Satan and fellow members of secret combinations not to reveal murders and plots against others*].

51 For, **from the days of Cain, there was a secret combination**, and **their works were in the dark**, and they knew every man his brother [*other members of the secret combination*].

> You may wish to read more about secret combinations and their deadly effects on society as described in Helaman 6:21–30 and Ether 8:13–25.

52 Wherefore **the Lord cursed Lamech, and his house, and all them that had covenanted with Satan**; for they kept not the commandments of God, and it displeased God, and he ministered not unto them, and **their works were abominations, and began to spread** among all the sons of men. And it was **among the sons of men**.

> It is helpful to offer a bit of

gospel vocabulary work here. The phrase "sons of men," as used in verse 52, above, means the wicked. "Sons of God," as used in Moses 8:13, were the righteous, covenant-keeping followers of God.

Next, in verses 53–54, we are told that Lamech violated his secret oath by telling his wives about his killing of Irad. Thus, he became a target of other members of his secret combination.

53 **And among the daughters of men these things were not spoken** [*apparently meaning that the wicked men who belonged to secret combinations kept it from their wives, as part of the oath they had taken to join the secret groups*], **because** that **Lamech had spoken the secret unto his wives**, and they rebelled against him, and declared these things abroad [*and they told everyone*], and had not compassion;

54 **Wherefore** [*this is why*] **Lamech was despised, and cast out**, and came not among the sons of men, lest he should die [*for fear that they would find him and kill him*].

55 **And thus the works of darkness began to prevail among all the sons of men** [*among all the wicked*].

Verse 55 points out the importance of knowing that the phrase "sons of men" means the wicked and "sons of God" means the righteous (see Moses 7:1). Otherwise, at the end of verse 55, one would tend to believe that secret combinations had taken over everyone and that there were no righteous left. The fact is, there were still "sons of God" on earth at this time, including Adam and Eve (see Moses 6:1–4). In Moses 6:17, many of these righteous had to flee to a "land of promise," where they could worship God in peace.

56 And **God** cursed the earth with a sore curse, and **was angry with the wicked**, with **all the sons of men** whom he had made;

57 For **they would not hearken unto his voice, nor believe on his Only Begotten Son**, even him whom he declared should come in the meridian of time, **who was prepared from before the foundation of the world** [*in other words, Jesus Christ was called to be the Redeemer clear back in premortality*].

58 And thus **the Gospel began to be preached, from the beginning, being declared by holy angels sent forth from the presence of God, and by his own voice, and by the gift of the Holy Ghost.**

We are reminded that Adam and Eve had the gospel of Jesus Christ, including ordinances, in verse 59, next. We will see more of this in Moses 6:65–67.

59 And thus **all things were confirmed unto Adam, by an holy ordinance, and the Gospel preached**, and a decree sent forth, that **it should be in the world, until the end** thereof; and thus it was. Amen.

We will quote Wilford Woodruff to help us understand the phrase "it [*the gospel*] should be in the world, until the end" in verse 59, above. He said (**bold** added for emphasis):

"Now, any man acquainted with the Scriptures can clearly understand that there is but one true Gospel. There never was but one Gospel. Whenever that Gospel has been upon the earth it has been the same in every dispensation. **The ordinances of the Gospel have never been changed from the days of Adam to the present time**, and never will be to the end of time. While there were many sects and parties in existence in the early times, Jesus gave his disciples to understand that there was but one Gospel. He told them what it was. He declared unto them its ordinances. He commissioned them to preach the Gospel to every creature" (in *Journal of Discourses,* Vol. 24, pp. 239–40).

MOSES, CHAPTER 6

(Revealed to Joseph Smith, November–December 1830)

Background

One of the important things we will learn in this chapter is that Adam and Eve were highly educated. They knew how to read and write, and they taught these skills to their children. This is just the opposite of how many in the world view our "first parents." Also, we will be taught that the righteous kept a record of their genealogy and that Adam held the Melchizedek Priesthood.

One of the significant contributions of chapters 6 and 7 of Moses is that they greatly expand our knowledge of Enoch. The book of Genesis contains only five verses about him (Genesis 5:19, 21–24), whereas Moses 6 and 7 contain 115 verses about Enoch and his mission, starting with Moses 6:21. As we study Moses' inspired teachings, we will learn many doctrines and be given a detailed review of much of the plan of salvation.

It is interesting to note that Adam is still alive during the first 243 years of the mission of Enoch (his great-great-great-great grandson). In fact, Enoch mentions that the people of his day know Adam (see Moses 6:45). Adam, who will live to be 930, was 687 years old at the time Enoch was called to preach (at age 65—see Moses 6:25–26).

As we begin our verse-by-verse study of chapter 6, we see that Adam preached the gospel of repentance to his posterity (verse 1) and that Seth is born to accomplish the righteous work that Abel would have done had he not been killed by Cain (verse 2).

1 And **Adam hearkened unto the voice of God** [*was obedient to God's commandments*], and **called upon his sons to repent.**

2 And **Adam knew his wife again** [*the biblical way of saying that Adam and Eve conceived again*], **and she bare a son**, and he called his name **Seth**. And Adam glorified [*praised*] the name of God; for he said: **God hath appointed me another seed, instead** [*in the place of*] **of Abel**, whom Cain slew.

The Doctrine and Covenants tells us that Seth looked just like his father, Adam, and that the only way one could tell them apart was that Adam looked older. We read:

D&C 107:43
43 Because he (Seth) was a perfect man, and his likeness was the express likeness of his father, insomuch that he seemed to be like unto his father in all things, and **could be distinguished from him only by his age**.

Next, we are told that Seth was righteous and that he kept God's commandments, just as Abel had done.

3 And **God revealed himself unto Seth, and he rebelled not, but offered an acceptable sacrifice, like unto his brother Abel**. And to him also was born a son, and he called his name Enos.

4 And **then began these men to call upon the name of the Lord** [*in other words, they were righteous*], and the Lord blessed them;

The "book of remembrance" spoken of in verse 5, next, was a history of Adam and his righteous posterity. It was written under inspiration and is the type of record that later became scripture.

5 And **a book of remembrance** was kept, in the which was recorded, in the language of Adam, for **it was given unto as many as called upon God to write by the spirit of inspiration;**

The "language of Adam" is not in existence today as a complete spoken or written language. However, we do know at least one word because it was revealed to us in D&C 78:20 and 95:17. The word is "Ahman," which is the name of Heavenly Father in the Adamic language. Elder Orson Pratt taught:

"There is one revelation that this people are not generally acquainted with. I think it has never been published, but probably it will be in the Church History. It is given in questions and answers. The first question is, 'What is the name of God in the pure language?' The answer says, 'Ahman.' 'What is the name of the Son of God?' Answer, 'Son Ahman—the greatest of all the parts of God excepting Ahman'" (in *Journal of Discourses,* Vol. 2, p. 342).

Joseph Fielding Smith taught:

"We also learn from the closing verses of this revelation that Jesus Christ is also called Son Ahman. (See D&C 95:17.) Therefore his name is connected with the name of the place where Adam dwelt. For that reason Elder Orson Pratt gives it the interpretation of 'The Valley of God'" (*Church History and Modern Revelation,* Vol. 1, page 310).

Elder Bruce R. McConkie explained this "book of remembrance." He said:

"Adam kept a written account of his faithful descendants in which he recorded their faith and works, their righteousness and devotion, their revelations and visions, and their adherence to the revealed plan of salvation. To signify the importance of honoring our worthy ancestors and of hearkening to the great truths revealed to them, Adam called his record a book of remembrance" (*Mormon Doctrine,* page 100).

Next, we are informed that Adam and Eve knew how to read and write and that they taught their children to do so also. This is a clear reminder that Adam and Eve were intelligent and well-educated.

6 And **by them their children were taught to read and write**, having a language which was pure and undefiled.

Next, Adam prophesies that the priesthood he holds (the Melchizedek Priesthood; he was a high priest—see note accompanying verse 67) will be available to men upon the earth in the last days. In other words, Adam was a great prophet, and he prophesied about our day.

7 Now **this same Priesthood** [*which Adam and his righteous sons, grandsons, and so forth held*], which was in the beginning [*in Adam's day and also in premortality—see Alma 13:3*], **shall be in the end of the world also.**

Joseph Smith explained the topic of verse 7, above. He said (**bold** added for emphasis):

"**The Priesthood was first given to Adam**; he obtained the First Presidency, and held the keys of it from generation to generation. **He obtained it in the Creation, before the world was formed.** . . . The Priesthood is an everlasting principle, and existed with God from eternity, and will to eternity, without beginning of days or end of years. The keys have to be brought from heaven whenever the Gospel is sent. When they are revealed from heaven, it is by Adam's authority" (*Teachings of the Prophet Joseph Smith,* page 157).

The above quote from Joseph Smith reminds us of Adam's high position. It is important that we understand that Adam and Eve were two of the greatest and most valiant spirit children of our Heavenly Father, sent to earth to start things off right. They were highly intelligent, well-educated, married for time and eternity, and wonderful examples as parents who lived gospel-centered lives. Next, in verse 8, we see that they and their righteous posterity kept their genealogy.

In order to understand verse 8, it is helpful to remember, as we mentioned previously (note following Moses 5:55), that "sons of God" is a phrase referring to the righteous (see Moses 7:1), and "sons of men," or "daughters of men," means the wicked. Thus, the phrase "children of God," in verse 8, means the righteous men and women in Adam's day. The wicked generally do not keep their genealogy down through the ages. In fact, some governments have attempted to destroy all sense of family and belonging to extended family by mandating that people can have only one name, which eliminates family names and curtails a sense of belonging to a family unit.

Also in verses 8–9, we are given a brief review and reminder that we are created in the image of God. In other words, we are part of His family. He wants us to know this. We look like Him. He has a body of flesh and bones, just as we do.

8 Now this prophecy Adam spake, as he was moved upon by the Holy Ghost, and **a genealogy was kept of the children of God** [*in other*

words, the righteous posterity of Adam and Eve kept their genealogy, which emphasizes family and belonging to an extended family]. And this was the book of the generations of Adam [*the story of Adam and his posterity*], saying: **In the day that God created man, in the likeness of God made he him**;

9 In the image of his own body, male and female, created he them, and blessed them, and **called their name Adam**, in the day when they were created and **became living souls** [*spirits clothed in physical bodies—see D&C 88:15*] in the land upon the footstool of God [*the earth*].

Did you notice something a bit unusual in verse 9, above, with respect to the name Adam? As used here, it refers to both Adam and Eve. President Spencer W. Kimball gave a brief comment on this. He said:

"'Male and female created he them; and blessed them, and called their name Adam [Mr. and Mrs. Adam, I suppose, or Brother and Sister Adam], in the day when they were created" (Genesis 5:1–2)" ("The Blessings and Responsibilities of Womanhood," *Ensign,* March 1976, page 71).

In verses 10–24, next, we are given a sample of some of the "genealogy" spoken of in verse 8, above. As mentioned earlier (in our note following Moses 5:3), we understand that these people did actually live to be many hundreds of years old and that their "years" were the same as ours. We will use **bold** to highlight these fascinating statistics.

10 And **Adam lived one hundred and thirty years, and begat** a son in his own likeness, after his own image, and called his name **Seth**.

11 And the days of Adam, after he had begotten Seth, were eight hundred years, and he begat many sons and daughters;

12 And **all the days** that **Adam lived** were **nine hundred and thirty years**, and he died.

13 Seth lived one hundred and five years, and begat Enos, and prophesied in all his days, and taught his son Enos in the ways of God; wherefore Enos prophesied also.

14 And Seth lived, after he begat Enos, eight hundred and seven years, and begat many sons and daughters.

15 And the children of men were numerous upon all the face of the land. And in those days Satan had great dominion among men, and raged in their hearts; and from thenceforth came wars and bloodshed; and a man's hand was against

his own brother, in administering death, because of secret works, seeking for power.

16 All the days of **Seth** were **nine hundred and twelve** years, and he died.

> Throughout the scriptures, we see many groups of righteous people who are led away from lands filled with wickedness into a land of promise where they can worship God freely. Verse 17, next, contains the earliest mention of a "land of promise." In this case, Enos, Adam's grandson, and his people were the ones led to the promised land spoken of.

17 And Enos lived ninety years, and begat Cainan. And Enos and the residue of the people of God came out from the land, which was called Shulon, and dwelt in **a land of promise**, which he called after his own son, whom he had named Cainan.

18 And Enos lived, after he begat Cainan, eight hundred and fifteen years, and begat many sons and daughters. And all the days of **Enos** were **nine hundred and five** years, and he died.

19 And Cainan lived seventy years, and begat Mahalaleel; and Cainan lived after he begat Mahalaleel eight hundred and forty years, and begat sons and daughters. And all the days of **Cainan** were **nine hundred and ten** years, and he died.

20 And Mahalaleel lived sixty-five years, and begat Jared; and Mahalaleel lived, after he begat Jared, eight hundred and thirty years, and begat sons and daughters. And all the days of **Mahalaleel** were **eight hundred and ninety-five** years, and he died.

> Next, we see the birth of Enoch. He will be ordained by Adam at age twenty-five (D&C 107:48) and called by the Lord to perform his special mission when he is sixty-five years old. As you will see, he considered himself "but a lad" (verse 31, below) at the time of his call. He will preach the gospel for 365 years before he and the City of Enoch are translated and taken up. Enoch will be 430 years old at the time of his translation (Moses 8:1). At the end of verse 21, you will see that Enoch had a righteous father, who taught him the gospel.

21 And **Jared** lived one hundred and sixty-two years, and **begat Enoch**; and Jared lived, after he begat Enoch, eight hundred years, and begat sons and daughters. And **Jared taught Enoch in all the ways of God.**

22 And **this** [*the brief genealogy in*

the foregoing verses] **is the genealogy of the sons of Adam,** who was **the son of God** [*meaning, among other possibilities, that Adam was righteous (the "sons of God" were the righteous—see note following verse 7, above), that he was the first man (D&C 84:16), and that he was placed on earth by God the Father; in other words, Adam's genealogy does not go back beyond him, on the earth, to a common ancestor he shared with apes or whatever*], with whom God, himself, conversed.

> Verse 23, next, clearly teaches that many righteous people taught the gospel during the time in which Cain and his posterity and associates were sponsoring wickedness, including secret combinations.

23 And **they were preachers of righteousness,** and spake and prophesied, and called upon all men, everywhere, to repent; and **faith was taught unto the children of men.**

24 And it came to pass that all the days of **Jared** were **nine hundred and sixty-two** years, and he died.

25 And Enoch lived sixty-five years, and begat Methuselah.

> Beginning with verse 26, next, Moses writes about Enoch and his mission. From these inspired writings of Moses, revealed to the Prophet Joseph Smith, we learn many "precious things" that were left out of Genesis, in the Bible. Moses' account of Enoch's mission and teachings will continue through Moses 8:2.
>
> First, in verses 26–30, Enoch is called on his mission. He is sixty-five years old at this time (see verse 25, above). At this point, as previously mentioned, Adam is 687 years of age. Enoch was born about 625 years after the Fall of Adam and Eve. The only other references to him in the Bible, in addition to Genesis 5:19–24, are found in Luke 3:37, Hebrews 11:5, and Jude 1:14–15.
>
> As you will sense, Enoch was not expecting this call and was quite reluctant to accept it. This must have been quite touching to Moses as he wrote this account because he went through similar concerns and feelings at the time of his own call to serve as a prophet (see Exodus 3–4, especially Exodus 3:11 and 4:1, 10).
>
> Note how the Lord sets the stage with Enoch as to why it is so important that he accept this call to preach the gospel of Jesus Christ.

26 And it came to pass **that Enoch journeyed in the land,** among the people; and as he journeyed, **the**

Spirit of God descended out of heaven, and abode upon him.**

27 And **he heard a voice** from heaven, **saying: Enoch, my son, prophesy unto this people, and say unto them—Repent,** for thus saith the Lord: I am angry with this people, and my fierce anger is kindled against them; for **their hearts have waxed** [*grown*] **hard,** and **their ears are dull of hearing** [*they are spiritually deaf*], and **their eyes cannot see afar off** [*they lack wisdom; they cannot see the future consequences of their present actions and philosophies*];

28 And for these **many generations**, ever since the day that I created them, **have** they **gone astray**, and have **denied me**, and have **sought their own counsels** [*have left God and gone their own ways*] **in the dark** [*spiritual darkness*]; and in their own **abominations** [*extreme wickedness*] have they devised **murder**, and have **not kept the commandments**, which I gave unto their father [*ancestor*], Adam.

29 Wherefore, **they have foresworn themselves** [*made covenants with God and then broken them*], and, **by their oaths** [*including those made as they joined secret combinations—see Moses 5:51, 6:15*], **they have brought upon themselves death** [*spiritual and physical, in many cases*]; and a hell [*the spirit prison*] I have prepared for them, **if they repent not** [*they can still repent; it is not too late*];

30 And **this is a decree** [*an absolute*], which I have sent forth in the beginning of the world, from my own mouth, **from the foundation thereof** [*clear back in the premortal life; in other words, this is part of the plan of salvation*], and **by the mouths of my servants, thy fathers** [*ancestors*], **have I decreed it** [*the gospel of repentance and salvation, which Enoch is being called to preach*], even as **it shall be sent forth in the world, unto the ends thereof** [*the gospel will ultimately be preached throughout the world*].

Next, we see Enoch's humility and concerns about his inadequacies.

31 And **when Enoch had heard these words, he bowed himself to the earth**, before the Lord, and spake before the Lord, saying: **Why is it that I have found favor in thy sight, and am but a lad** [*of sixty-five years of age; a "lad" compared to Adam and others still alive who were much older and more experienced in preaching*], and **all the people hate me; for I am slow of speech**; wherefore [*why*] am I thy servant [*why have You called me*]?

In addition to being relatively young and inexperienced, Enoch expressed two major concerns about his ability to be effective in carrying out this call from the Lord. They are:

1. "All the people hate me," which implies that, in such a wicked society, his life would be in danger if he started openly preaching the gospel.

2. "I am slow of speech," which implies that he had great difficulty speaking and was quite ineffective in communicating.

The Lord will address both of these concerns next, in verse 32, if Enoch is obedient and goes forth in faith to do the Lord's will.

32 And the Lord said unto Enoch: **Go forth** and do as I have commanded thee, and **no man shall pierce thee** [*he will be given physical protection*]. **Open thy mouth, and it shall be filled, and I will give thee utterance** [*his inability or disability in communicating will be healed*], **for all flesh is in my hands** [*I can do these things for you*]**, and I will do as seemeth me good.**

Next, in this "MTC" conducted by the Lord for Enoch, he is instructed as to what to say. Furthermore, the Savior prophesies concerning the power over nature that He will give to Enoch.

33 **Say unto this people: Choose ye this day, to serve the Lord God who made you.**

34 Behold **my Spirit is upon you,** wherefore **all thy words will I justify** [*support*]; and the **mountains shall flee before you** [*the mountains will move at his command—see Moses 7:13*], and the **rivers shall turn from their course** [*Moses 7:13*]; and **thou shalt abide in me, and I in you** [*we will be a team*]; **therefore walk with me.**

Next, Enoch obeys a simple command that leads to his seeing a tremendous vision. This vision will give him the perspective that God has and will enable him to carry out his mission despite impossible odds.

35 And the Lord spake unto Enoch, and said unto him: **Anoint thine eyes with clay, and wash them, and thou shalt see.** And he did so.

The instruction of the Savior to put clay on his closed eyes and then wash it off and "see" reminds us of the blind man spoken of in John 9:6–7 who was healed of his blindness on the Sabbath day by the Master. We will take a moment to read this account from the Bible:

John 9:6–7

6 When he [*the Savior*] had thus spoken, he spat on the ground, and made clay of the spittle, and **he anointed the eyes of the blind man with the clay,**

7 And said unto him, Go, wash in the pool of Siloam, (which is by interpretation, Sent.) [*"Sent," capitalized, is another name for Christ, the one "sent" by the Father to heal us from our "blindness"*] **He went his way therefore, and washed, and came seeing.**

Next, we are given a brief glimpse of what Enoch saw in this vision. From this time forth, his reputation begins to spread throughout the land.

36 And **he beheld the spirits that God had created; and he beheld also things which were not visible to the natural eye**; and from thenceforth came the saying abroad in the land: **A seer hath the Lord raised up unto his people.**

We will pause to take a closer look at the word "seer." It is an important gospel vocabulary word. Seers are vital to our salvation. We sustain the members of the First Presidency and the Quorum of the Twelve Apostles as "prophets, **seers**, and revelators." Elder John A. Widtsoe, of the Twelve, taught:

"A seer is one who sees with spiritual eyes. He perceives the meaning of that which seems obscure to others; therefore he is an interpreter and clarifier of eternal truth. He foresees the future from the past and the present (*Evidences and Reconciliations,* 258).

The Book of Mormon teaches us more about what seers do for us.

Mosiah 8:17

17 But a seer can know of things which are past, and also of things which are to come, and by them shall all things be revealed, or, rather, shall secret things be made manifest, and hidden things shall come to light, and things which are not known shall be made known by them, and also things shall be made known by them which otherwise could not be known.

Joseph Smith gave further instructions about the role of seers. He taught us what past seers **saw**, emphasizing that they saw into the future and prophesied about it. He said (**bold** added for teaching purposes):

"Wherefore, we again say, search the revelations of God; study the prophecies, and **rejoice that God grants unto the world**

Seers and Prophets. **They are they who saw** the mysteries of godliness; **they saw** the flood before it came; **they saw** angels ascending and descending upon a ladder that reached from earth to heaven; **they saw** the stone cut out of the mountain, which filled the whole earth; **they saw** the Son of God come from the regions of bliss and dwell with men on earth; **they saw** the deliverer come out of Zion, and turn away ungodliness from Jacob; **they saw** the glory of the Lord when he showed the transfiguration of the earth on the mount; **they saw** every mountain laid low and every valley exalted when the Lord was taking vengeance upon the wicked; **they saw** truth spring out of the earth, and righteousness look down from heaven in the last days, before the Lord came the second time to gather his elect; **they saw** the end of wickedness on earth, and the Sabbath of creation crowned with peace; **they saw** the end of the glorious thousand years, when Satan was loosed for a little season; **they saw** the day of judgment when all men received according to their works, and **they saw** the heaven and the earth flee away to make room for the city of God, when the righteous receive an inheritance in eternity" (*Teachings of the Prophet Joseph Smith*, pp. 12–13).

We will continue now with Moses' account of Enoch's mission. As you will see, people have become curious as to who this "wild man" is (verse 38).

37 And it came to pass that **Enoch went forth** in the land, **among the people**, standing upon the hills and the high places, and cried with a loud voice, **testifying against their works**; and **all men were offended because of him** [*the wicked don't like to be told of their sins*].

38 And **they came forth to hear him**, upon the high places, saying unto the tent-keepers: Tarry ye here and keep the tents, while we go yonder to behold [*to see*] the seer, for he prophesieth, and **there is a strange thing in the land; a wild man hath come among us**.

Next, in verse 39, we see the Lord's promise to Enoch of physical protection (verse 32) in action.

39 And it came to pass when they heard him, **no man laid hands on him**; for fear came on all them that heard him; **for he walked with God** [*as invited to do so by the Lord—see end of verse 34*].

According to verse 40, next, there has been such commotion and curiosity about Enoch among these wicked people that they have selected one of their number to approach him directly and ask him who he really is. Perhaps this implies that they were so afraid of Enoch (verse 39, above) that they didn't dare get that close to him themselves.

40 And **there came a man unto him**, whose name was Mahijah, **and said** unto him: **Tell us plainly who thou art, and from whence thou comest?**

41 And he said unto them: **I came out from the land of Cainan** [*the "promised land" to which Enos and his righteous followers had been led; see verse 17*], the land of my fathers, **a land of righteousness** unto this day. And my father [*Jared; see verse 21*] taught me in all the ways of God [*a reminder of the powerful influence of righteous fathers*].

Next, in verses 42–46, Enoch continues to answer their question as to who he is and where he comes from. We feel the skillful flow and power of his words, and we see the promise of the Lord to him being fulfilled (verse 32), overcoming Enoch's concern about being "slow of speech" (verse 31).

42 And it came to pass, **as I journeyed** from the land of Cainan, by the sea east, **I beheld a vision;** and lo, **the heavens I saw**, and **the Lord spake with me**, and gave me commandment; wherefore, for this cause, to keep the commandment, I speak forth these words.

One of the lessons we learn from verse 43, next, is the importance of having God be a part of our personal identity in our own minds.

43 And Enoch continued his speech, saying: The Lord which spake with me, the same is the God of heaven, and **he is my God** [*part of Enoch's identity*], and your God, and ye are my brethren, and why counsel ye yourselves, and deny the God of heaven [*why do you support each other in denying God*]?

One more comment about having our commitment to God be an integral part of our self-image. President Henry D. Moyle, counselor in the First Presidency, once told us as a group of missionaries serving in Austria that foremost in our minds should be the fact that we are members of the Lord's true church. He told us of his being on a train when a fellow passenger suddenly asked him, "What are you?" Without thinking, President Moyle immediately replied, "A Mormon." He could have told the man that he was a businessman, a civic leader, a philanthropist, a leader in The Church of Jesus Christ of Latter-day Saints, headquartered in Salt Lake City, Utah, or any one of several titles and positions he held. He told us that his response startled him at the time, but that, as he later thought about it, he was pleased with it because it was genuine. He was first and foremost "a Mormon."

As Enoch continues, he eloquently bears witness of God as the Creator, teaches about the Fall of Adam and Eve, reminds them all of the fact that they have been placed on earth by the God of heaven, points their minds to their living ancestors back to Adam, whom they know, and talks of their scriptures (the book of remembrance), which have been kept as commanded by the Lord.

44 **The heavens he made; the earth is his footstool** [*a scriptural phrase symbolizing that the earth and its contents are subject to God*]; and the foundation thereof is his. Behold, **he laid it** [*He created the earth*], **an host of men hath he brought** in upon the face thereof.

45 And **death hath come upon our fathers** [*our ancestors; in other words, all are subject to death because of the Fall*]; nevertheless **we know them**, and cannot deny, and even the first of all **we know**, even **Adam**.

Verse 45 is another reminder that the genealogy of man does not go back beyond Adam, who is the "first of all."

46 For **a book of remembrance we have written among us, according to the pattern given by the finger of God**; and it is given **in our own language** [*perhaps implying that it is readily accessible and easy for anyone to read, and that these people could and should read their scriptures, which explain the purposes of their being on earth*].

Enoch has become a masterful teacher under the guidance and power of the Lord. As we study his sermon, which continues in verses 47–68, next, we will not only learn much more about Adam and what he was taught about the gospel, but we will also be taught much about the Fall and the Atonement of Jesus Christ.

Remember that many of the wicked people to whom Enoch preaches the gospel will repent and become a Zion people, ultimately being translated and taken up with the City of Enoch. We are watching the very beginnings of this great conversion of souls as we study these next verses. Pay close attention to the basics of the plan of salvation that can lead to such complete conversion.

47 And **as Enoch spake** forth the words of God, **the people trembled**, and could not stand in his presence.

> A correct understanding of the Fall of Adam and Eve is essential to complete conversion. Next, Enoch teaches that the Fall was good. Mortality and the physical death that accompanies it are necessary if we want resurrected bodies. The trials and tribulations of mortality are part of the plan of salvation. Satan's opposition and temptation are necessary for the exercising of our agency.

48 And he said unto them: **Because that Adam fell, we are** [*Adam's Fall resulted in our being mortals upon the earth*]; and **by his fall came death**; and **we are made partakers of misery and woe.**

49 Behold **Satan hath come among the children of men, and tempteth them to worship him**; and **men have become carnal** [*worldly, materialistic, lacking in spirituality*], **sensual** [*involved in sexual immorality*], and **devilish** [*evil, wicked*], and are shut out from the presence of God.

> The solution to the situations explained in verses 48–49 is given in simple, clear terms, beginning in verse 50. Adam will be used as an example.

50 But God hath made known unto our fathers that **all men must repent**.

51 And **he called upon our father** [*ancestor*] **Adam** by his own voice, saying: I am God; I made the world, and men before they were in the flesh [*a reference to our premortal life as spirit children of God; in other words, the Father has a plan for us*].

> Next, Enoch explains that Adam was taught what we refer to as the "first principles and ordinances of the gospel" (fourth article of faith), namely, faith, repentance, baptism, and the gift of the Holy Ghost.

52 And he also said unto him: If thou wilt **turn unto me**, and **hearken unto** [*obey*] **my voice**, and **believe**, and **repent** of all thy transgressions, and **be baptized**, even in water [*by immersion*], in the name of mine Only Begotten Son, who is full of grace and truth [*full of power to save us*], which is Jesus Christ, the only name which shall be given under heaven [*there is only one gospel with the power to save us*], whereby salvation shall come unto the children of men, ye shall receive **the gift of the Holy Ghost**, asking all things in his name [*the name of Jesus Christ*], and whatsoever ye shall ask, it shall be given you.

Next, in verse 53, Enoch explains that Adam had a question about why baptism is necessary, including why it was to be done by immersion. The Lord's answer will be given over several verses and summarized with beautiful symbolism in verses 59–60.

But before answering the question, the Lord puts Adam's mind at ease about his having partaken of the forbidden fruit in the Garden of Eden.

53 And our father Adam spake unto the Lord, and said: **Why is it that men must repent and be baptized in water?** And the Lord said unto Adam: Behold **I have forgiven thee thy transgression in the Garden of Eden.**

With that concern off his mind, the way is open for Adam to concentrate on the answer to his question about baptism. First, in verse 54, next, the Savior will address the issue of original sin, apparently a prevalent false doctrine spread by Satan in Adam's day. Those who believed in original sin (that children are born unclean because of Adam and Eve's transgression and fall) would believe that babies are unclean and must be baptized. The Savior will teach Adam that babies are not unclean and that they do not carry the sins of the parents, but that as they grow up and become accountable, they will need baptism. As stated in verse 54, this correct doctrine will spread throughout the land.

54 **Hence came the saying abroad among the people, that the Son of God hath atoned for original guilt** [*see second article of faith*], wherein **the sins of the parents cannot be answered upon the heads of the children**, for **they are whole** [*clean, pure*] from the foundation of the world.

What really happens to children and why they will eventually need to be baptized is clearly taught next, as the Lord continues to answer Adam's question about the need for baptism.

55 And the Lord spake unto Adam, saying: **Inasmuch as** [*since it is a fact that*] **thy children are conceived in sin** [*born into a world that contains much sin and wickedness*], even so **when they begin to grow up, sin conceiveth in their hearts** [*they begin to get sinful ideas and thoughts*], and **they taste the bitter, that they may know to prize the good** [*part of the plan for "opposition in all things"—see 2 Nephi 2:11*].

Elder McConkie taught the following about the phrase "conceived in sin," in verse 56, above:

"Conceived in sin" means "born

into a world of sin" (*A New Witness for the Articles of Faith*, page 101).

Next, the doctrine of agency is taught as it relates to baptism. Children who are old enough to distinguish between right and wrong become accountable (at age eight—see D&C 68:25–28). Thus, they become "agents unto themselves" (verse 56) and need baptism.

56 And **it is given unto them to know good from evil** [*they soon begin gaining the ability to differentiate between good and evil*]; **wherefore** [*this is the reason*] **they are agents unto themselves** [*thus, they can begin to exercise their moral agency*], and I have given unto you another law and commandment [*to teach repentance to your children, as described, beginning in verse 57, next*].

57 **Wherefore** [*therefore*] **teach** it unto **your children, that all men, everywhere, must repent, or they can in nowise inherit the kingdom of God** [*the celestial kingdom*], for no unclean thing can dwell there, or dwell in his [*the Father's*] presence; for, in the language of Adam, **Man of Holiness** is his name, and **the name of his Only Begotten is the Son of Man** [*of Holiness*], even Jesus Christ, a righteous Judge, who shall come in the meridian of time [*referring to the time of Christ's mortal mission on earth*].

The last half of verse 57 gives us an important clarification as to why Jesus is often referred to as the "Son of Man" in the scriptures. Over the years, students have often asked me why Jesus is referred to in this way, rather than as the "Son of God." They felt that calling Him the "Son of Man" did not represent who He was and that the phrase made it sound like He was the son of a mortal man rather than of the Father. An example of their concern is found in Matthew, where we read of the Savior's healing of the man with palsy (**bold** added for emphasis):

Matthew 9:6
6 But that ye may know that **the Son of man** hath power on earth to forgive sins, (then saith he to the sick of the palsy,) Arise, take up thy bed, and go unto thine house.

It was always a pleasure to point out to them that the answer is found in the last part of verse 57, above. The complete phrase is, in effect, that Jesus is the "Son of Man of Holiness." In other words, He is the Son of the Father.

Next, Adam was commanded to make sure that he and Eve

surrounded their children with the gospel.

58 Therefore **I give unto you a commandment, to teach these things freely unto your children**, saying:

Next, Adam is told to teach his children about the Fall and the Atonement. Pay close attention in verse 59 to the words "water," "blood," and "spirit." Note that they are given in a different order in the second half of verse 59 than in the first half. Note also that the second time they are given, the word "spirit" is capitalized. Significant symbolism is involved here. We will give verse 59, using **bold** to highlight these three words and their order. Then we will repeat verse 59, adding several notes.

59 That by reason of transgression cometh the fall, which fall bringeth death, and inasmuch as ye were born into the world by **water**, and **blood**, and the **spirit**, which I have made, and so became of dust a living soul, even so ye must be born again into the kingdom of heaven, of **water**, and of the **Spirit**, and be cleansed by **blood**, even the blood of mine Only Begotten; that ye might be sanctified from all sin, and enjoy the words of eternal life in this world, and eternal life in the world to come, even immortal glory;

As mentioned above, this verse points out that there is much intentional symbolism between the process of physical birth and the process of spiritual rebirth, or being "born again," through the Atonement of Jesus Christ, with the help and guidance of the Holy Ghost. Water, blood, and spirit are involved in both. We will now add several notes to verse 59 as we go through it again.

Verse 59 repeated

59 That **by reason of** [*because of Adam and Eve's*] **transgression cometh the fall**, which fall **bringeth death** [*eventual physical death and spiritual death, meaning, being cut off from the direct presence of God*], and **inasmuch as** [*since*] **ye were born** [*physical birth*] **into the world by water** [*amniotic fluid*], and **blood** [*which accompanies physical birth*], and the **spirit** [*your premortal spirit, which is now in your physical body*], **which I have made** [*the Father is the father of our premortal spirits—see Hebrews 12:9*], **and so became of dust** [*the physical elements of the earth that form our mortal bodies*] **a living soul** [*the body and spirit combined together form a "soul"—see D&C 88:15*], **even so ye must be born again** [*spiritually*] **into the kingdom of heaven** [*celestial glory*], **of water** [*baptism*], **and of the Spirit** [*the*

gift of the Holy Ghost], and be cleansed by **blood** [*the Atonement of Christ*], even the blood of mine Only Begotten; **that ye might be sanctified** [*made pure, clean, fit to be in the presence of God*] **from all sin, and enjoy the words of eternal life** [*the gospel of Christ*] **in this world, and eternal life** [*exaltation*] **in the world to come, even immortal glory;**

Verse 60, next, is a brief review of what was taught in more detail in verse 59, above.

60 For by the **water** [*baptism*] ye keep the commandment; by the **Spirit** [*the Holy Ghost*] ye are justified, and by the **blood** [*of Christ—in other words, the Atonement*] ye are sanctified;

We will summarize what Adam was commanded to teach his children in verses 59–60:

1. The transgression of Adam and Eve brought the Fall (which was good—see 2 Nephi 2:22–25).

2. The Fall brought us the opportunity for mortal birth (and the experiences and trials of mortality) and physical death (thus opening the door for resurrection).

3. The Fall also brought spiritual death (being cut off from the direct presence of God) and the need for spiritual rebirth, or being "born again" back into the presence of God.

4. By being baptized, we keep the commandment to be baptized (verse 60). But there is more to it than just being immersed in water by one holding proper authority.

5. After baptism, we are given the gift of the Holy Ghost. By following the teachings and promptings of the Holy Ghost, we are "justified"—in other words, lined up in harmony with God's laws and thus placed in a position to access the Atonement of Christ.

The word "justified" as used here is similar to the word as used in computer language and word processing today. When we tell a computer to "justify" a margin, it lines things up in perfect harmony throughout the document. So it also is with the word "justified" here in verse 60. By our listening to and obeying the promptings of the Holy Ghost, we are gradually "lined up" in harmony with God, enabling the cleansing blood of Christ to cleanse us and "sanctify" us.

6. As we follow the guidance of the Holy Ghost, we access

the cleansing blood of Christ in our lives and are made clean from sin and fit to be in the presence of God—in other words, we are "sanctified" (verse 60). Thus, we become worthy to dwell with God in celestial glory forever.

Next, in verse 61, we are taught the importance of having the Holy Ghost with us. We will point out several of the functions and attributes of the Holy Ghost with **bold**.

61 Therefore it [*the privilege of having the gift of the Holy Ghost*] is given to abide in you; **the record of heaven** [*the Holy Ghost, the source of our testimonies—see footnote 61a in your Pearl of Great Price*]; **the Comforter** [*the Holy Ghost*]; the **peaceable things of immortal glory**; the **truth of all things**; that which **quickeneth** [*gives life to*] **all things**, which **maketh alive all things**; that which **knoweth all things**, and **hath all power** according to **wisdom, mercy, truth, justice,** and **judgment.**

No wonder faithful Saints who have the gift of the Holy Ghost are said to have a special glow about them! They do!

Elder Parley P. Pratt taught about the functions of the Holy Ghost. He said:

"The gift of the Holy Spirit adapts itself to all these organs or attributes. It quickens all the intellectual faculties, increases, enlarges, expands and purifies all the natural passions and affections; and adapts them, by the gift of wisdom, to their lawful use. It inspires, develops, cultivates and matures all the fine-toned sympathies, joys, tastes, kindred feelings and affections of our nature. It inspires virtue, kindness, goodness, tenderness, gentleness and charity. It develops beauty of person, form and features. It tends to health, vigor, animation and social feeling. It develops and invigorates all the faculties of the physical and intellectual man. It strengthens, invigorates, and gives tone to the nerves. In short, it is, as it were, marrow to the bone, joy to the heart, light to the eyes, music to the ears, and life to the whole being" (*Key to the Science of Theology/A Voice of Warning*, page 101).

Verse 62, next, clearly teaches that the Atonement of Jesus Christ is the central focus of the plan of salvation.

62 And now, behold, I say unto you: **This is the plan of salvation** unto all men, **through the blood of mine Only Begotten**, who shall come in the meridian of time.

Sometimes people wonder if we overdo it a bit on symbolism as we teach the gospel. Verse 63, next, indicates that there is probably far more symbolism of God's involvement in our lives than we realize. It is all around us and is constantly bearing witness to us that God exists, that we are His children, and that He has had this world created for us.

63 And behold, **all things have their likeness** [*symbolism*], and **all things are created and made to bear record of me**, both things which are **temporal** [*including physical creations*], and things which are **spiritual; things which are in the heavens above**, and things which are **on the earth**, and things which are **in the earth**, and things which are **under the earth**, both above and beneath: **all things bear record of me**.

As you can see, from the above verses, Adam and Eve were taught the gospel of Jesus Christ. They had a great knowledge of the plan of salvation, which they taught their children. Next, in verse 64, we see that Adam was baptized. Obviously, so was Eve.

(Remember, in context, that Enoch is teaching these things about Adam to the wicked people who are listening to him).

Adam Is Baptized

64 And it came to pass, **when the Lord had spoken with Adam**, our father [*ancestor; Enoch's great-great-great-great grandfather*], that **Adam** cried [*prayed*] unto the Lord, and he **was caught away by the Spirit of the Lord**, and was carried down into the water, and was **laid under the water**, and was **brought forth out of the water** [*in other words, Adam was baptized by immersion*].

65 And **thus he was baptized**, and the Spirit of God descended upon him, and thus he was born of the Spirit, and became quickened in the inner man.

Students sometimes ask who the "Spirit of the Lord" was in verse 64, above, and how a spirit could baptize a physical man. It is an interesting question, but we do not have the answer. It is one of the things for which we will have to wait. Perhaps we can ask Adam or Eve when we get to the other side. Or perhaps we will have to wait until the Savior reveals "all things" right after His Second Coming (D&C 101:32–34).

Next, we are taught that Adam received the gift of the Holy Ghost.

Adam Receives the Gift of the Holy Ghost

66 And he heard a voice out of heaven, saying: Thou art **baptized with fire, and with the Holy Ghost**. This is the record [*the Holy Ghost is the one who testifies and bears witness*] of the Father, and the Son, from henceforth and forever;

> Obviously, both Adam and Eve received the saving ordinances of the gospel. Elder McConkie taught (**bold** added for emphasis):
>
> "**Adam and Eve**—our first parents, our common ancestors, the mother and father of all living—**had the fulness of the everlasting gospel**. They received the plan of salvation from God himself.... They saw God, knew his laws, entertained angels, received revelations, beheld visions, and were in tune with the Infinite. They exercised faith in the Lord Jesus Christ; repented of their sins; **were baptized** in similitude of the death, burial, and resurrection of the Promised Messiah; and **received the gift of the Holy Ghost**. They **were endowed** with power from on high, **were sealed** in the new and everlasting covenant of marriage, and **received the fulness of the ordinances of the house of the Lord**" (*Mortal Messiah,* Vol. 1, pp. 228–29).

Adam Is Given the Melchizedek Priesthood

67 And **thou art after the order of** [*you hold the same priesthood as*] **him** [*Jesus Christ*] **who was without beginning of days or end of years**, from all eternity to all eternity.

The "order," in verse 67, above, means high priest in the Melchizedek Priesthood. Wilford Woodruff taught that Adam held the keys of presidency in this priesthood. He quoted Joseph Smith, saying:

"The Prophet Joseph taught us that father Adam was the first man on the earth to whom God gave the keys of the everlasting priesthood. He held the keys of the presidency, and was the first man who did hold them" (*Discourses of Wilford Woodruff,* page 66).

Concerning the Melchizedek Priesthood and the keys of presidency given to Adam, the Doctrine and Covenants teaches:

D&C 107:41
This order was instituted in the days of Adam.

Verse 68, next, summarizes the results of Adam's living the gospel, which was first preached on this earth to him and his wife, Eve. Through it, we can all be united again with God.

68 Behold, **thou art one in me**, a son of God; and thus [*through faith, repentance, baptism, and the gift of the Holy Ghost*] may all become my sons [*becoming "sons and daughters unto God" (D&C 76:24) is a scriptural phrase meaning to attain exaltation in the highest degree in the celestial kingdom*]. Amen.

MOSES, CHAPTER 7
(Revealed to Joseph Smith, December 1830)

Background

As we begin chapter 7, Enoch continues his speech to the people, begun in chapter 6 when they had a spokesman approach him and ask, "Tell us plainly who thou art, and from whence thou comest?" (Moses 6:40).

Having told them that he came from the righteous land of Cainan, a land of promise to which Enoch's great-great-grandfather Enos had led a group of righteous followers who were fleeing wickedness (Moses 6:17), Enoch then taught them that he was a prophet of God, and he told them about the gospel of Jesus Christ that had been preached to Adam and Eve. He taught them about the Fall and the Atonement, the necessity of faith, repentance, baptism, the gift of the Holy Ghost, and the Melchizedek Priesthood (Moses 6:44–68).

As we study chapter 7, we will learn much more about Enoch's mission as it continues. He will see a vision in which he will be shown "all things, even unto the end of the world" (verse 67). In studying this chapter, we will be given the advantage of seeing the big picture as it was shown to Enoch. It will strengthen our testimonies and give us the perspective of God on many issues. Among the many things we will learn about Enoch's mission are:

1. He will see the Savior and talk to Him face-to-face (Verse 4).

2. He will see a vision in which the descendants of Cain destroy the people of Shum. He will see that Cain's descendants do not prosper (verses 5–8).

3. He will see many lands and peoples in vision and be told to go to them and preach the gospel (verses 9–11).

4. He will move mountains and change the course of rivers, in direct fulfillment of the Lord's promises to him in

Moses 6:34 (verse 13).

5. He will be made a powerful preacher and teacher, in direct fulfillment of Moses 6:32 (verse 13).

6. Terrible wars and much bloodshed occurred during the time Enoch was preaching and gathering the righteous, but the faithful Saints who followed Enoch prospered and established a Zion people (verses 16–19).

7. He will see a vision in which he sees all of the inhabitants of the earth and the eventual taking of the City of Enoch up into heaven (verses 20–22).

8. As this vision continues, Enoch will see wickedness spread throughout the world before the Flood. He will see Satan and his angels laughing at the wickedness upon the earth and rejoicing in their evil success. He sees as the people of the world are warned of the destruction that awaits them (the Flood) if they do not repent. He also sees many converted and caught up to join the righteous in the City of Enoch before the Flood cleanses the earth of wickedness (verses 23–27).

9. He will be perplexed when he sees God weeping because of the wickedness upon the earth, and we will listen carefully for the answer to Enoch's question, "How is it that thou canst weep?" (verses 28–40).

10. We will be taught again about the relationship between knowledge and agency and be shown the reasons for the Flood (verses 32–34).

11. We will be told that our earth is the most wicked world (verse 36).

12. We will watch as Enoch, himself, weeps because of the wickedness he sees in the vision (verses 41–44).

13. Enoch will see the Savior's mortal ministry, including His crucifixion (verses 45–55).

14. Enoch will feel the pain of the earth because of the wickedness upon her, and we will feel to ask, with him, several times during the vision, "When shall the earth rest?" (verses 48–58). The answer will be given in verse 64. The earth will finally rest from wickedness during the Millennium.

15. Enoch will see the restoration of the gospel in the last days as it shines forth into the spiritual darkness and wickedness that beset the whole earth (verses 60–62).

16. Enoch will see the building of the New Jerusalem and will see his city, the City of Enoch, meet the Saints in the New Jerusalem as the Millennium begins (verses 62–65).

17. He will see some signs of the times in the last days, including natural disasters and the despair and gloom that is falling upon the wicked in our day (verse 66).

With the above outline of this chapter in mind, we will begin our verse-by-verse study. In verse 1, next, Enoch will continue his sermon, telling his listeners of the great blessings of being obedient to God's commandments and the awful consequences of ignoring the gospel message.

1 And it came to pass that **Enoch continued his speech**, saying: Behold, our father [*ancestor*] **Adam taught these things**, and **many have believed and become the sons of God** [*have become righteous followers of God, qualifying for salvation*], and **many have believed not, and have perished in their sins**, and are looking forth with fear, in torment, for the fiery indignation of the wrath of God to be poured out upon them.

As Enoch's mission continues, he is commanded to climb Mount Simeon. We do not know where that was. As he obeys, the heavens open and he is transfigured (in order to withstand the presence of the Lord) and talks to the Savior face to face.

2 And from that time forth Enoch began to prophesy, saying unto the people, that: As I was journeying, and stood upon the place Mahujah, and cried [*prayed*] unto the Lord, there came a voice out of heaven, saying—**Turn ye, and get ye upon the mount Simeon.**

3 And it came to pass that I turned and went up on the mount; and as I stood upon the mount, **I beheld the heavens open**, and **I was clothed upon with glory** [*transfigured—see Moses 1:2, 11*];

4 And **I saw the Lord** [*Jesus Christ—see Moses 7:4, footnote a*]; and he stood before my face, and **he talked with me**, even as a man talketh one with another, **face to face; and he said unto me: Look, and I will show unto thee the world for the space of many generations.**

Next, in verses 5–8, Enoch sees in vision that the descendents of Cain destroy the people of Shum and take over their land. He sees also that the descendents of Cain do not prosper.

5 And it came to pass that **I beheld in the valley of Shum**, and lo, a great people which dwelt in tents, which were **the people of Shum**.

6 And again the Lord said unto me: Look; and **I looked towards the north, and I beheld the people of Canaan** [*Cain's descendents—see verses 8, 12, and 22; compare with Abraham 1:21, 24*], which dwelt in tents.

7 And the Lord said unto me: Prophesy; and **I prophesied, saying: Behold the people of Canaan**, which are numerous, **shall go forth in battle array against the people of Shum, and shall slay them that they shall utterly be destroyed**; and the people of Canaan shall divide themselves in the land, and **the land shall be barren and unfruitful**, and none other people shall dwell there but the people of Canaan;

8 For behold, **the Lord shall curse the land with much heat**, and the **barrenness** thereof shall go forth forever; and there was **a blackness** [*see also verse 22*] **came upon all the children of Canaan**, that they were despised among all people.

Next, Enoch sees many lands and peoples and is told to go to them and preach the gospel.

9 And it came to pass that **the Lord said unto me: Look; and I looked, and I beheld the land of Sharon**, and the land of **Enoch**, and the land of **Omner**, and the land of **Heni**, and the land of **Shem**, and the land of **Haner**, and the land of **Hanannihah**, and **all the inhabitants** thereof;

10 And the Lord said unto me: **Go to this people, and say unto them—Repent**, lest I come out and smite them with a curse, and they die.

In verse 11, next, Enoch is given wording that is reflected in the baptismal prayer we use today. We will quote it here before we continue to verse 11.

D&C 20:73

73 Having been commissioned of Jesus Christ, I baptize you **in the name of the Father**, and of the **Son**, and of the **Holy Ghost**. Amen.

11 And he gave unto me a commandment that I should **baptize in the name of the Father**, and of the **Son**, which is full of grace and truth, and of the **Holy Ghost**, which beareth record of the Father and the Son.

At this point in the Lord's plan, the gospel was preached to all but the residents of the land of Canaan (verse 11, next). This may be a concern for some. It may be helpful to remember that during the Savior's mortal ministry, the gospel was to be taken only to the Israelites in the Holy Land. During the days of Moses and the children of Israel, the priesthood was held only by members of the tribe of Levi. The Lord has His reasons for what He does and we are wise to have complete faith in Him, knowing that the day will come when the righteous will have all of their questions answered.

We know that in the Lord's timetable, the gospel will be taught to all, whether on earth or in the spirit world mission field. Before the day of final judgment, everyone will be given the opportunity to hear and understand the pure gospel of Jesus Christ and then accept it or reject it according to their God-given agency. God is completely fair.

12 And it came to pass that **Enoch continued to call upon all the people, save it were** [*except*] **the people of Canaan, to repent;**

At the time of Enoch's call, he was promised by the Lord that he would be given power to move mountains and rivers (Moses 6:34). An example of this promise being fulfilled is recorded in verse 13, next. It will be fascinating to get more details someday. This advantage in battle must have been somewhat disturbing to the enemies of the people of God.

13 And so great was the faith of **Enoch** that he **led the people of God**, and **their enemies came to battle against them**; and **he spake** the word of the Lord, and **the earth trembled, and the mountains fled** [*moved*], **even according to his command**; and the **rivers of water were turned out of their course**; and the roar of the lions was heard out of the wilderness; and **all nations feared greatly, so powerful was the word of Enoch**, and **so great was the power of the language which God had given him** [*another fulfillment of the promise of the Lord—see Moses 6:32*].

We do not know anything about the land mentioned in verse 14, next, other than what is given here. It sounds, perhaps, as if their enemies were more afraid of Enoch and his Zion people than they were to venture out onto an unstable, new landmass in order to increase the distance between them.

14 **There also came up a land out of the depth of the sea, and so great was the fear of the enemies**

of the people of God, that they fled and stood afar off and went upon the land which came up out of the depth of the sea.

> We presume that the "giants" mentioned in verse 15, next, were large men, perhaps like Goliath or even like many basketball players we see today. They would be formidable enemies in hand-to-hand combat. The Bible mentions giants, one of whom was King Og, of Bashan (spoken of in Deuteronomy), who was one of the last of a race of "giants." He used a bed that was thirteen and a half feet long by six feet wide (see Deuteronomy 3:11). The giants of Enoch's day were likewise afraid of Enoch and his people.

15 And **the giants of the land, also, stood afar off**; and there went forth a curse upon all people that fought against God;

> Since we live in a day of "wars and rumors of wars" (Matthew 24:6), when the world is filled with wickedness and danger, verses 16–17, next, are especially helpful to us. They remind us that the thing that counts is having the Lord with us.

16 And from that time forth **there were wars and bloodshed among them**; but **the Lord came and dwelt with his people, and they dwelt in righteousness**.

17 The fear of the Lord was upon all nations, so great was the glory of the Lord, which was upon his people. And **the Lord blessed the land, and they were blessed upon the mountains, and upon the high places, and did flourish**.

> You may wish to mark verse 18, next, in your own scriptures. It is one of the most-quoted definitions of a "Zion" people. It teaches us that we must be peacemakers, righteous, and generous if we desire to live in celestial glory.

18 And **the Lord called his people Zion**, because **they were of one heart and one mind**, and **dwelt in righteousness**; and there was **no poor among them**.

> The only way to establish Zion among us is to live according to celestial law (D&C 105:5). Such living requires that we become "pure in heart," as stated in D&C 97:21.
>
> Next, we are told that Enoch and his people built a city. It was called, among other names, the City of Enoch.

19 And Enoch continued his preaching in righteousness unto the people of God. And it came to pass in his days, that **he built a city that was called the City**

of Holiness, even Zion.

President Spencer W. Kimball described the residents of this city. He said:

"Zion is a name given by the Lord to his covenant people, who are characterized by purity of heart and faithfulness in caring for the poor, the needy, and the distressed. (See D&C 97:21.) "... This highest order of priesthood society is founded on the doctrines of love, service, work, self-reliance, and stewardship, all of which are circumscribed by the covenant of consecration" ("Welfare Services: The Gospel in Action," *Ensign,* November 1977, page 78).

President Marion G. Romney, of the First Presidency, described a Zion society as follows:

"Always the aim has been unity, oneness, and equality among the members of the church of Christ. As an example, I call your attention to the record of Enoch, how he and his people reached a state of unity when the rest of the world was at war. [Moses 7:15–17.] 'And the Lord called his people Zion.' Why? 'Because they were of one heart and one mind, and dwelt in righteousness; and there was no poor among them'" ("Unity," *Ensign,* May 1983, page 17).

Next, in verses 20–21, we are given to understand that Enoch expected his City of Zion to remain permanently on the earth. The Lord explained to him that such would not be the case. Rather, because of increasing wickedness on earth, Enoch's city would eventually be translated and taken up into heaven (Moses 7:69). This translation took place 604 years before the Flood. In fact, Noah was born four years after Enoch and his city were taken up, and he was six hundred years old when he entered the ark (Genesis 7:6).

20 And it came to pass that **Enoch talked with the Lord; and he said unto the Lord: Surely Zion shall dwell in safety forever.** But the Lord said unto Enoch: Zion have I blessed, but **the residue** [*remainder*] **of the people have I cursed.**

If the word "cursed," as used at the end of verse 20, above, is misunderstood, it can make God look unfair and biased. Of course, He is not. When God "curses" people, it is generally another way of saying that He turns them over to the law of justice, which requires that they be punished for their sins and wickedness.

God operates according to the laws of mercy and justice. When people use their agency to obey

MOSES 7

the laws of the gospel, the law of mercy takes over in their behalf. They repent, are forgiven of their sins, reap the bountiful harvest of gospel living, and eventually return to live with the Father in celestial glory forever.

However, if they use their agency to choose evil and wickedness, they "curse" themselves in the sense that they subject themselves to the law of justice, which requires that those who do not access the Atonement of Christ become subject to the punishment of God.

Next, in verse 21, the Lord shows Enoch all the people on earth as well as the City of Enoch being translated and taken up to Heaven.

21 And it came to pass that the Lord showed unto Enoch all the inhabitants of the earth; and he beheld, and lo, **Zion** [*the City of Enoch*], **in process of time, was taken up into heaven.** And the Lord said unto Enoch: Behold mine abode forever.

Next, Enoch is shown that the posterity of Cain did not mix with the rest of the population during the time period depicted in this part of the vision.

22 And **Enoch also beheld** [*saw*] **the residue of** [*the rest of*] **the people** which were the sons [*descendants*] of Adam; and **they were a mixture of all the seed of Adam save** [*except*] **it was the seed of Cain,** for **the seed of Cain were black, and had not place among them.**

One of the great blessings of our day is that we live in the long-awaited time when the gospel is going forth into all the world. The priesthood is available to all worthy males. This is according to the revelation that President Spencer W. Kimball received in 1978 (see Official Declaration—2 at the end of your Doctrine and Covenants). Thus, the ordinances of exaltation are available to all Church members who choose to qualify for them. This is part of the fulfillment of the signs of the times—that the gospel will be preached to every nation, kindred, tongue, and people before the Second Coming (see D&C 42:58).

Next, Enoch is shown what will take place on the earth between the time his City is taken up and the time of the Flood.

23 And after that Zion was taken up into heaven, **Enoch beheld, and lo, all the nations of the earth were before him** [*in the vision*];

24 And there came **generation upon generation;** and **Enoch was high and lifted up, even in the**

bosom of the Father, and of the Son of Man [*Enoch was with the Father and the Son as he saw this part of the vision*]; and behold, **the power of Satan was upon all the face of the earth** [*which would lead to the cleansing of the earth by flood*].

25 And **he saw angels descending out of heaven**; and he heard a loud voice saying: **Wo, wo be unto the inhabitants of the earth** [*the inhabitants of the earth are being warned of the destruction that will come if they don't repent*].

26 And **he beheld Satan**; and he had **a great chain in his hand** [*symbolic of the captivity of sin and spiritual darkness*], and it veiled the whole face of the earth with [*spiritual*] darkness; and **he looked up and laughed, and his angels rejoiced**.

> Verse 26, above, reminds us of the attitude of Satan and his angels as they laugh and rejoice at the destruction of the wicked in America at the time of the crucifixion of the Savior (3 Nephi 9:2).
>
> Next, we see that the gospel was preached and there were many converts to the Church during this time, after the City of Enoch had been taken up and before the Flood. These righteous saints were translated

and taken up to live in the City of Enoch.

27 And **Enoch beheld angels descending out of heaven, bearing testimony of the Father and Son**; and **the Holy Ghost fell on many** [*bringing true conversion and righteousness into their lives*], and **they were caught up** [*translated*] by the powers of heaven **into Zion** [*the City of Enoch*].

> Next in the vision, Enoch will be startled to see God and heaven weeping. He will ask some questions as a result.

28 And it came to pass that **the God of heaven** looked upon the residue of the people [*the wicked who remained on the earth*], and he **wept**; and Enoch bore record of it, saying: **How is it that the heavens weep, and shed forth their tears as the rain upon the mountains?**

29 And Enoch said unto the Lord: **How is it that thou canst weep, seeing thou art holy, and from all eternity to all eternity?**

> As Enoch continues with his question, we are taught that there are countless earths that have already been created (compare with Moses 1:33, 35).

30 And were it possible that man could number the particles of the earth, yea, **millions of earths like this, it would not be a beginning**

to the number of thy creations; and thy curtains are stretched out still [*God is still creating more earths*]; and yet thou art there, and thy bosom is there; and also thou art just; thou art merciful and kind forever;

31 And thou hast taken Zion to thine own bosom, from all thy creations, from all eternity to all eternity; and **naught** [*nothing*] **but peace, justice, and truth is the habitation of thy throne; and mercy shall go before thy face and have no end; how is it thou canst weep?**

> Apparently, from what we see in the above verses, Enoch had thought that there was nothing but peace in being a god. He is surprised to see God weeping. There is an important insight for us in his response. It is that godhood is by far the happiest and most satisfying lifestyle in the universe (see last part of D&C 132:16, 20), yet there is sadness and concern when children use their God-given agency to choose evil instead of good. Agency is a key principle and law in the universe. Knowledge and commandments enable people to use agency and be accountable for the outcome. This can bring happiness or sadness to parents. Gods are parents. The Lord will explain this to Enoch in verses 32–33, next.

32 **The Lord said unto Enoch: Behold** [*look at*] **these thy brethren** [*in other words, look at all these wicked people in the vision*]; **they are the workmanship of mine own hands** [*they are My children*], **and I gave unto them their knowledge**, in the day I created them; and in the Garden of Eden, gave I unto man his **agency;**

33 And **unto thy brethren have I said, and also given commandment, that they should love one another, and that they should choose me** [*be loyal to Me above all else*], **their Father; but behold** [*look*], **they are without affection, and they hate their own blood;**

> Next, the Lord explains to Enoch that because of gross wickedness upon the earth, which he is being shown in the vision, He will flood the earth.

34 And **the fire of mine indignation** [*anger*] **is kindled against them**; and **in my hot displeasure will I send in the floods upon them**, for my fierce anger is kindled against them.

> In verse 35, next, we are given several names for God. These name-titles reflect attributes of God.

35 Behold, I am God; **Man of Holiness** is my name; **Man of Counsel** is my name; and **Endless**

and **Eternal** is my name, also.

Verse 36, next, is somewhat famous in the Church. It is the verse that tells us that we live on the most wicked earth God has created. We will do a bit more with the verse after reading it.

36 Wherefore, I can stretch forth mine hands and hold all the creations which I have made [*the Lord is fully aware of all His creations*]; and mine eye can pierce them [*see what is happening on them*] also, and **among all the workmanship of mine hands there has not been so great wickedness as among thy brethren.**

After reading verse 36, above, students often ask, "What did we do to deserve being sent to this earth?" They feel that they must have done something wrong in premortality to be sent here. I have responded that my feeling is that it is a great honor to be sent to this earth, the world to which the Savior was sent to gain His mortal body and serve His mortal mission, the earth upon which was performed the infinite Atonement of Jesus Christ, which blesses the inhabitants of all the Father's worlds—past, present, and future (D&C 76:24). To me, they should be asking what they did right to deserve such an honor!

Next, in verse 37, the Lord summarizes the reason why the heavens weep over the wicked.

37 But behold, their sins shall be upon the heads of their fathers [*their wicked, rebellious ancestors*]; Satan shall be their father [*the author of their misery*], and **misery shall be their doom**; and the whole heavens shall weep over them, even all the workmanship of mine hands; wherefore **should not the heavens weep, seeing these shall suffer?**

38 But behold, **these which thine eyes are upon shall perish in the floods**; and behold, I will shut them up [*will lock them up*]; **a prison** [*the spirit prison—see 1 Peter 3:19–20*] **have I prepared for them.**

Note in verse 39, next, that two words are capitalized. They are "That" and "Chosen." Both refer to Jesus Christ. That is why they are capitalized.

Another thing, before we read verse 39. In this verse, Jesus is speaking directly for the Father in what is often referred to as "divine investiture" (see note following Moses 1:3). Perhaps you have noticed in the foregoing verses that He switches often between speaking for Himself and speaking as if He were the Father. This is common practice, and the context is the way we must determine whether it is Jesus speaking for Himself or quoting the Father. A helpful key is found in the writings of Joseph Fielding Smith. He said:

"All revelation since the fall has come through Jesus Christ, who is the Jehovah of the Old Testament. In all of the scriptures where God is mentioned and where he appeared, it was Jehovah who talked with Abraham, Noah, Enoch, Moses and all the prophets. He is the God of Israel, the Holy One of Israel; the one who led that nation out of Egyptian bondage, and who gave and fulfilled the Law of Moses. The Father has never dealt with man directly and personally since the fall, and he has never appeared except to introduce and bear record of the Son. Thus the Inspired Version [the Joseph Smith Translation of the Bible] records that "no man hath seen God at any time, except he hath borne record of the Son."

"In giving revelations our Savior speaks at times for himself; at other times for the Father, and in the Father's name, as though he were the Father ["divine investiture"], and yet it is Jesus Christ, our Redeemer who gives the message. So, we see in Doctrine and Covenants 29:1 that he introduces himself as 'Jesus Christ, your Redeemer,' but in the closing part of the revelation [example: verses 42 and 46] he speaks for the Father, and in the Father's name as though he were the Father, and yet it is still Jesus who is speaking, for the Father has put his name on him for that purpose" (*Doctrines of Salvation,* Vol. 1, page 27).

As we read verse 39, now, we learn that there is hope for the spirits in prison, but these wicked will be in prison, tormented because of their wickedness, until Christ finishes His mortal mission. We know from D&C 138 that He set up missionary work in the spirit prison between the time of His crucifixion and resurrection.

39 And **That** [*Jesus Christ*] **which I have chosen hath pled before my face** [*in other words, Jesus is our "advocate before the Father"—D&C 45:3–5*]. Wherefore, **he suffereth for their sins** [*Christ atoned for the sins of all—see 2 Nephi 9:21*]; **inasmuch as** [*if*] **they will repent** in the day that my Chosen [*Jesus*] shall return unto me [*when the Savior has finished His mortal mission, and the preaching of the gospel is taken to the spirits in prison*], and **until that day** [*until they hear and accept the gospel in the spirit prison*] **they shall be in torment;**

40 Wherefore [*this is why*], **for this shall the heavens weep**, yea, and all the workmanship of mine hands.

Next, Enoch weeps also. He is growing much in understanding and perspective during the vision, and now he has the same feelings as the Lord has about wickedness among the people.

41 And it came to pass that the Lord spake unto Enoch, and told Enoch all the doings of the children of men; wherefore **Enoch** knew, and looked upon their wickedness, and their misery, and **wept** and stretched forth his arms, and his heart swelled wide as eternity; and his bowels yearned [*every fiber of his being yearned for people to be righteous*]; and all eternity shook.

42 And **Enoch also saw Noah, and his family**; that the posterity of all the sons of Noah should be saved with a temporal [*physical*] salvation [*in other words, Enoch saw in the vision that Noah and his family would be saved from the flood, and would repopulate the earth*];

43 Wherefore **Enoch saw that Noah built an ark**; and that **the Lord smiled upon it, and held it in his own hand** [*protected it from the ravages of the Flood*]; **but upon the residue of the wicked** [*the rest of the people on earth, all of whom were wicked*] **the floods came and swallowed them up.**

At this point of the vision, we see Enoch discouraged and refusing to be comforted. Indeed, at this point, it can be depressing for all of us. But the Lord has a solution that will cause joy and happiness to enter our souls. He tells Enoch to cheer up at the end of verse 44, next. Watch for the reason in the next several verses.

44 And **as Enoch saw this, he had bitterness of soul, and wept over his brethren**, and said unto the heavens: **I will refuse to be comforted**; but the Lord said unto Enoch: **Lift up your heart, and be glad**; and **look**.

Elder Neal A. Maxwell spoke of Enoch's despair in verse 44, above. He said:

"If Enoch had not looked and been spiritually informed, he would have seen the human condition in isolation from the grand reality. If God were not there, Enoch's 'Why?' would have become an unanswered scream of despair!

"At first, Enoch refused 'to be comforted' (Moses 7:44). Finally, he saw God's plan, the later coming of the Messiah in the meridian of time, and the eventual triumph of God's purposes" (in Conference Report, October 1987, page 36; or "'Yet Thou Art

There,'" *Ensign,* November 1987, pp. 30–31).

Have you paid attention to the marvelous teaching techniques employed by the Master Teacher in this vision being given to Enoch? Have you felt the drama and tension building in the past few verses, preparing Enoch for the reason he can rejoice? When the mind is properly prepared, the lessons sink deep and become ingrained in the student. It is a privilege for us to also be taught by the Master as we study these "pearls of great price."

As Enoch "looks," the stage is set for the reason he can "lift up [his] heart, and be glad" (verse 44, above). He sees the future, from the time the Flood recedes and Noah and his family leave the ark. He sees God's plan unfold, with the Savior's mortal mission and Atonement as its center focus. This is the reason he can rejoice.

45 And it came to pass that **Enoch looked**; and **from Noah, he beheld all the families of the earth**; and he cried unto the Lord, saying: **When shall the day of the Lord come** [*when will the Savior come to earth*]? **When shall the blood of the Righteous** [*Christ*] **be shed** [*when will the Atonement be accomplished*], **that all they that mourn** [*for their sins; in other words, truly repent for their sins*] **may be sanctified** [*cleansed by the blood of Christ*] **and have eternal life** [*exaltation*]?

Next, the Lord answers Enoch's question as to when the Savior will come to earth for His mortal mission. It will be three thousand years in the future, from the time of Enoch.

46 And the Lord said: **It shall be in the meridian** [*the high point—see definition of "meridian" in various dictionaries*] **of time**, in the days of wickedness and vengeance [*when great wickedness is upon the earth*].

47 And behold, **Enoch saw the day of the coming of the Son of Man, even in the flesh** [*in a mortal body*]; **and his soul rejoiced** [*as the Lord said he could, at the end of verse 44, above*], saying: **The Righteous** [*Christ*] **is lifted up** [*crucified*], and **the Lamb** [*Christ*] **is slain** [*the Son of God will be sacrificed for the sins of the world*] **from the foundation of the world** [*planned and presented in the Father's plan for us, in the premortal councils*]; and **through faith** [*in Jesus Christ*] I am in the bosom of the Father [*I can return to live with the Father forever*], **and** behold, **Zion** [*Enoch's city and people*] **is with me.**

Next, in verses 48–49, Enoch hears the earth mourn because of the great wickedness upon her. He hears her ask when she will find relief and peace from the terrible wickedness on her. By the way, we know that the earth was baptized via the Flood and will be cleansed by fire at the Second Coming, symbolic of the Holy Ghost. It will then have a thousand years of peace during the Millennium, will die and be resurrected (D&C 88:26), and will become the celestial kingdom (D&C 130:9) for the righteous who have lived on it, including Christ.

48 And it came to pass that **Enoch looked upon the earth**; and he **heard a voice from the bowels thereof, saying: Wo, wo is me, the mother of men** [*the provider of nutrition, ecosystem, and so forth, which sustains mortal life*]; **I am pained**, I am **weary**, because of the wickedness of my children. **When shall I rest, and be cleansed from the filthiness** which is gone forth out of me? **When will my Creator sanctify me, that I may rest, and righteousness for a season abide upon my face?**

49 And **when Enoch heard the earth mourn, he wept**, and cried unto the Lord, saying: **O Lord, wilt thou not have compassion upon the earth?** Wilt thou not bless the children [*posterity*] of Noah?

Joseph Fielding Smith explained that the earth is a living thing. He said:

"The Lord here [in Doctrine and Covenants 88] informs us that the earth on which we dwell is a living thing, and that the time must come when it will be sanctified from all unrighteousness. In the Pearl of Great Price, when Enoch is conversing with the Lord, he hears the earth crying for deliverance from the iniquity upon her face. . . . It is not the fault of the earth that wickedness prevails upon her face, for she has been true to the law which she received and that law is the celestial law. Therefore the Lord says that the earth shall be sanctified from all unrighteousness" (*Church History and Modern Revelation,* Vol. 1, pp. 366–67).

Next, Enoch pleads with the Lord to never flood the earth again. As you can feel, Enoch has become active in this vision. It is similar to the growth and increasing involvement of the servant in the allegory of the olive tree, given in Jacob 5, as the Master schools and teaches Enoch.

50 And it came to pass that **Enoch continued** his cry unto the Lord, **saying: I ask thee, O Lord, in**

the name of thine Only Begotten, even Jesus Christ, that thou wilt have mercy upon Noah and his seed [*the descendants of Noah, which means all people after the Flood*]**, that the earth might never more be covered by the floods.**

51 And **the Lord** could not withhold [*hold back*]; and he **covenanted with Enoch**, and sware [*covenanted*] unto him with an oath [*the most solemn promise possible*], **that he would stay the floods** [*that there would not be another universal flood*]; **that he would call upon** [*preach the gospel to*] **the children** [*posterity*] **of Noah**;

52 And he sent forth an unalterable decree, that a remnant of his [*Noah's*] seed should always be found among all nations, while the earth should stand [*in other words, there would never be a complete destruction of the inhabitants of the earth*];

> Next, in verse 53, Enoch is told that the Messiah will be a descendant of Noah. He is then given a brief summary of some of the name-titles of the Savior that describe His mission. Then he is taught that it takes work to access the blessings of the Atonement and that there is absolute security in building our lives on the "Rock" (Jesus Christ).

53 And the Lord said: Blessed is he [*Noah*] through whose seed **Messiah shall come; for he saith—I am Messiah** [*meaning "the anointed," "the King and Deliverer"—see Bible Dictionary, under "Messiah"*]**, the King of Zion** [*the King of the pure in heart—see D&C 97:21*]**, the Rock of Heaven, which is broad as eternity** [*whose Atonement is infinite*]**; whoso** [*whoever*] **cometh in at the gate** [*repentance and baptism—see 2 Nephi 31:17–18*] **and climbeth up by me** [*continues to progress in the gospel of Jesus Christ*] **shall never fall**; wherefore, blessed are they of whom I have spoken, for **they shall come forth with songs of everlasting joy** [*they will receive exaltation*].

> Enoch is still concerned about the earth and her feelings. In verse 54, next, he asks if the earth will obtain relief from wickedness when the Savior comes on earth to fulfill His mortal mission.

54 And it came to pass that Enoch cried unto the Lord, saying: **When the Son of Man cometh in the flesh, shall the earth rest?** I pray thee, show me these things.

> In answer to Enoch's question, the Savior continues the vision, showing him that there will still be great wickedness upon the earth during His mission. In fact,

He will be crucified. The earth will not yet be free of wickedness.

55 And **the Lord said unto Enoch: Look, and he looked and beheld the Son of Man lifted up on the cross** [*being crucified*], after the manner of men [*as was the common practice*];

56 And he heard a loud voice; and the heavens were veiled; and all the creations of God mourned; and **the earth groaned**; and the rocks were rent [*torn apart*]; and the saints arose [*were resurrected; this is the first part of the celestial resurrection, and it occurred at the time of Christ's resurrection*], and were crowned at the right hand of the Son of Man, with crowns of glory;

The Doctrine and Covenants tells us who the "saints" in verse 56, above, are. As you will see, they are all those, from Adam and Eve down to the resurrection of Christ, who are worthy of celestial glory. This would include Enoch and the people in his city, as well as John the Baptist, who was beheaded by Herod (Matthew 14:10) near the end of the second year of the Savior's mortal mission.

D&C 133:54–55

54 Yea, and Enoch also, and they who were with him; the prophets who were before him [*including Adam*]; and Noah also, and they who were before him; and Moses also, and they who were before him;

55 And from Moses to Elijah, and from Elijah to John, who **were with Christ in his resurrection**, and the holy apostles, with Abraham, Isaac, and Jacob, shall be in the presence of the Lamb.

In verse 57, next, Enoch sees that many who die and enter spirit prison accept the gospel there and are saved (see D&C 138:58–59). Those who don't accept it remain in spiritual darkness until the final judgment.

57 And as **many of the spirits as were in prison came forth, and stood on the right hand of God** [*symbolic of salvation; "right hand" symbolizes making and keeping covenants with God*]; and **the remainder were reserved in chains of darkness until the judgment of the great day** [*final Judgment Day*].

Enoch is still concerned about the earth's feelings, and he exercises the privilege of asking the Lord more questions.

58 And again **Enoch wept and cried unto the Lord, saying: When shall the earth rest?**

There seems to be a sense, in

verse 59, next, that Enoch is a bit worried that he is asking too many questions. Thus, after seeing in vision the Savior's ascension into heaven following His resurrection, he explains to the Lord why he keeps asking questions.

59 And **Enoch beheld the Son of Man ascend up unto the Father**; and he called unto the Lord, saying: **Wilt thou not come again upon the earth?** Forasmuch as thou art God, and I know thee, and **thou hast sworn unto me** [*made covenants with me*]**, and commanded me that I should ask** in the name of thine Only Begotten; thou hast made me, and given unto me a right to thy throne [*the Lord brought Enoch into His presence, where he could ask questions*], and not of myself, but through thine own grace; **wherefore** [*this is the reason*]**, I ask thee if thou wilt not come again on the earth.**

> The Savior answers Enoch's question, telling him that He will come again in the last days. He came to Joseph Smith in the First Vision and has come many times since. These "comings" of the Savior will culminate in the Second Coming.

60 And **the Lord said** unto Enoch: **As I live** [*the strongest type of promise or covenant in biblical culture*]**, even so will I come in the last days** [*to restore the gospel, which will lead up to the Second Coming*]**,** in the days of wickedness and vengeance [*when the earth is full of wickedness*]**,** to fulfil the oath [*promise, covenant*] which I have made unto you concerning the children of Noah [*to preach the gospel to all the world—see end of verse 51, above*];

> The Lord tells Enoch in verse 61, next, that the day will come when the earth will be freed from wickedness, but then He informs him of the final scenes before the Second Coming.
>
> The earth's "rest" will begin with the thousand years of millennial peace. There will be a "little season" after the Millennium (D&C 88:111–14) during which Satan will be let loose and wickedness will again rage on the earth. This final battle between good and evil will be called the Battle of Gog and Magog. After the devil and his evil followers are banished forever, the earth will be celestialized and finally "rest" as a celestial planet (see D&C 130:9–11).

61 And **the day shall come that the earth shall rest** [*beginning with the Millennium*]**, but before that day the heavens shall be darkened,** and **a veil of darkness** [*spiritual darkness*] **shall cover the earth**; and the heavens shall shake,

and also the earth [*perhaps including natural disasters, earthquakes, and so forth*]; **and great tribulations shall be among the children of men**, but my people will I preserve [*a comforting promise for the Saints in the last days*];

Next, Enoch is told about the restoration of the gospel through Joseph Smith and the coming forth of the Book of Mormon.

62 And **righteousness will I send down out of heaven** [*the restoration of the gospel through heavenly visions and manifestations*]; and **truth will I send forth out of the earth** [*the Book of Mormon*], **to bear testimony of mine Only Begotten** [*Jesus Christ*]; **his resurrection** from the dead; yea, and **also the resurrection of all men; and righteousness and truth will I cause to sweep the earth as with a flood** [*the gospel will be preached to every nation and people*], **to gather out mine elect** [*those who will accept the gospel and keep the commandments*] **from the four quarters of the earth** [*from the entire earth*], unto a place which I shall prepare, an Holy City [*the New Jerusalem*], that my people may gird up their loins [*prepare*], and be looking forth for the time of my coming; for there shall be my tabernacle [*Christ will visit the people in the New Jerusalem*], and it shall be called Zion, a New Jerusalem.

Next, Jesus tells Enoch that he and the people of his City of Enoch will meet the residents of the New Jerusalem (to be built in Independence, Jackson County, Missouri) and that it will be a joyous meeting.

63 And **the Lord said unto Enoch: Then shalt thou and all thy city** [*all the people in the City of Enoch*] **meet them** [*the inhabitants of the New Jerusalem*] there, and we will receive them into our bosom, and they shall see us; and we will fall upon their necks [*embrace, hug them*], and they shall fall upon our necks, and we will kiss each other;

Next, in verse 64, Enoch is finally told when the earth will rest.

64 And there shall be mine abode, and it shall be Zion, which shall come forth out of all the creations [*righteous, covenant-keeping converts from all nations will join Zion*] which I have made; **and for the space of a thousand years the earth shall rest** [*the earth will "rest" and have peace and freedom from wickedness during the Millennium*].

In verse 65, next, Enoch is shown in vision the Millennium. Then, in verse 66, he is shown the wickedness on earth before the Second Coming and that the sea will cause great devastations (compare with D&C 88:90, which speaks of "the waves of the sea heaving themselves beyond their bounds.") He is also taught that there will be much despair and giving up hope, coupled with fear, in the last days.

65 And it came to pass that **Enoch saw the day of the coming of the Son of Man** [*the Second Coming*], in the last days, **to dwell on the earth in righteousness for the space of a thousand years;**

Joseph Fielding Smith explained who would remain on earth during the Millennium, after the destruction of the wicked at the Second Coming. He said:

"When the reign of Jesus Christ comes during the millennium, only those who have lived the telestial law will be removed. It is recorded in the Bible and other standard works of the Church that the earth will be cleansed of all its corruption and wickedness. Those who have lived virtuous lives, who have been honest in their dealings with their fellow man and have endeavored to do good to the best of their understanding, shall remain. . . .

"The gospel will be taught far more intensely and with greater power during the millennium until all the inhabitants of the earth shall embrace it. Satan shall be bound so that he cannot tempt any man. Should any man refuse to repent and accept the gospel under those conditions then he would be accursed [Isaiah 65:20]. Through the revelations given to the prophets we learn that during the reign of Jesus Christ for a thousand years, eventually all people will embrace the truth" (*Answers to Gospel Questions,* Vol. 1, page 108, 110–11).

66 But **before that day** he saw **great tribulations among the wicked**; and he also saw **the sea**, that it **was troubled**, and **men's hearts failing them** [*much discouragement, depression, gloom, and doom*], looking forth with fear for the judgments [*punishments*] of the Almighty God, which should come upon the wicked.

Next, Enoch, who has wept much during this vision, receives a "fulness of joy" as he sees the final results of the Atonement of Christ in the lives of the faithful.

67 And **the Lord showed Enoch all things, even unto the end of the world;** and **he** saw the day of the righteous [*the faithful Saints*], the hour of their redemption, and **received a fulness of joy;**

In verses 68–69, next, Moses (who is writing this account—see Moses 1:40–41) concludes his account of Enoch and his people.

68 And **all the days of Zion** [*the City of Enoch*], in the days of Enoch, **were three hundred and sixty-five years** [*the City of Enoch existed on earth for 365 years*].

69 And **Enoch and all his people walked with God, and he dwelt in the midst of Zion**; and it came to pass that Zion was not, for God received it up into his own bosom [*the City of Enoch was translated and taken up to heaven—see D&C 107:49*]; and from thence [*from that time*] went forth the saying, Zion Is Fled.

President Brigham Young gave us a bit more information about the translation of Enoch and the City of Enoch. He taught that Enoch and his people were translated "with the region they inhabited, their houses, gardens, fields, cattle and all their possessions" (*Discourses of Brigham Young,* page 105).

MOSES, CHAPTER 8

(Revealed to Joseph Smith, February 1831)

Background

This is the final chapter in the book of Moses, as revealed to the Prophet Joseph Smith. It basically covers Genesis 5:23–6:13. Verses 1–15 give us a brief genealogy from the time the City of Enoch was taken up (604 years before the Flood) to the time that Noah began his service as a prophet and teacher of the gospel.

1 And all the days of Enoch were four hundred and thirty years [*and then he was translated*].

We learn from verse 2, next, that there were prophecies about Noah in the earliest times. In fact, God had covenanted with Enoch that Noah would be from his posterity. Therefore, Enoch's son Methuselah did not go up with his father in the City of Enoch when it was translated. Methuselah will be Noah's grandfather, and Enoch will be his great-grandfather.

2 And it came to pass that **Methuselah, the son of Enoch, was not taken** [*up with the City of Enoch*], that the covenants of **the Lord** might be fulfilled, which he made to Enoch; for he truly **covenanted with Enoch that Noah should be of the fruit of his loins** [*in other words, his descendant*].

It appears from the end of verse 3, next, that Methuselah became prideful about the fact that Noah was to be born through his posterity.

3 And it came to pass that **Methuselah** prophesied that from his loins should spring all the kingdoms of the earth (through Noah), and he **took glory unto himself.**

> The information in verse 4, next, was left out of the Bible.

4 And there came forth **a great famine** into the land, and **the Lord cursed the earth** with a sore [*severe*] curse, and **many** of the inhabitants thereof **died.**

5 And it came to pass that Methuselah lived one hundred and eighty-seven years, and begat Lamech [*Noah's father*];

6 And Methuselah lived, after he begat Lamech, seven hundred and eighty-two years, and begat sons and daughters;

> As you can see in verse 7, next, Methuselah lived 969 years, which is the longest of anyone on record. He died in the year that the Flood came. You may wish to review the note following Moses 5:3 in this study guide concerning how long people lived before the Flood.

7 And **all the days of Methuselah were nine hundred and sixty-nine years**, and he died.

> Next, Noah comes on the scene. He will preach the gospel for at least 120 years (verse 17), and his mission to preach the gospel to the wicked inhabitants of the earth, before the Flood, will be over when he enters the ark at age six hundred.

8 And **Lamech lived one hundred and eighty-two years, and begat a son,**

9 And he called his name **Noah**, saying: This son shall comfort us concerning our work and toil of our hands, because of the ground which the Lord hath cursed [*probably a reference to the famine, mentioned in verse 4*].

10 And Lamech lived, after he begat Noah, five hundred and ninety-five years, and begat sons and daughters;

11 And **all the days of Lamech were seven hundred and seventy-seven years**, and he died.

> The three sons of Noah, mentioned in verse 12, next, were righteous (verses 13 and 27) and all held the Melchizedek Priesthood, according to the *Pearl of Great Price Student Manual,* which says (**bold** added for emphasis):
>
> "A list of the 'sons of God,' which began in Moses 5:8–25, continues in Moses 8 with the addition of Lamech (v. 5), Noah (v. 9), and Noah's three sons (v. 12). **These brethren were all**

holders of the higher priesthood (see D&C 107:40–52)" (*Pearl of Great Price Student Manual,* page 26).

12 And Noah was four hundred and fifty years old, and begat **Japheth**; and forty-two years afterward he begat **Shem** of her who was the mother of Japheth, and when he was five hundred years old he begat **Ham**.

13 And **Noah and his sons hearkened unto the Lord, and gave heed** [*and obeyed His commandments*]**, and they were called the sons of God** [*a term meaning that they were righteous followers of God*].

A brief reminder here will be helpful concerning the meaning of the scriptural phrases "sons of God" and "sons of men," or "daughters of God" and "daughters of men." Sons or daughters of God means the righteous, and sons or daughters of men means the wicked. We will see these terms and variations of them in the next verses.

14 And when these men began to multiply on the face of the earth, and daughters were born unto them, the **sons of men** (men who were not loyal to God) saw that those daughters were fair, and they took them wives, even as they chose [*apparently these women were willing to marry outside the Church*].

15 And the Lord said unto Noah: **The daughters of thy sons have sold themselves** [*have intentionally distanced themselves from God*]; for behold mine anger is kindled against the **sons of men**, for they will not hearken to my voice.

Joseph Fielding Smith commented on the scriptural terminology mentioned above. He said (**bold** added for emphasis):

"Because the daughters of Noah married the **sons of men** contrary to the teachings of the Lord, his anger was kindled, and this offense was one cause that brought to pass the universal flood.

. . . The daughters who had been born, evidently under the covenant, and were the **daughters of the sons of God**, that is to say of those who held the priesthood, were transgressing the commandment of the Lord and were marrying out of the Church. Thus they were cutting themselves off from the blessings of the priesthood contrary to the teachings of Noah and the will of God. . . .

"Today there are foolish daughters of those who hold this same priesthood who are violating this commandment and marrying the sons of men; there are also some of the sons of those who hold the priesthood who are marrying the daughters of men. All of this is contrary to the will of God just as much as it was in the days of Noah" (*Answers to Gospel Questions,* Vol. 1, pp. 136–37).

From verse 16, next, we understand that Noah taught the gospel of Jesus Christ just as it was taught to Adam and Eve.

16 And it came to pass that **Noah prophesied, and taught the things of God, even as it was in the beginning.**

We learn from verse 17, next, that there are limits as to how long the Spirit of the Lord will work with the wicked to get them to repent. After so long, the Spirit withdraws. While this is sad, it reminds us of the fact that agency is a supreme principle and that God will not violate it. We are indeed "free to choose liberty and eternal life, through the great Mediator of all men, or to choose captivity and death, according to the captivity and power of the devil" (2 Nephi 2:27).

The warning in verse 17, next, includes a 120-year grace period before the sending of the Flood.

17 And the Lord said unto Noah: **My Spirit shall not always strive with man** [*the rebellious and wicked*], for he shall know that all flesh shall die; **yet his days shall be an hundred and twenty years; and if men do not repent, I will send in the floods upon them.**

18 And in those days there were giants [*apparently extra large races of people*] on the earth, and they sought Noah to take away his life; but the Lord was with Noah, and the power of the Lord was upon him.

Next, we see that Noah was a high priest in the Melchizedek Priesthood. He was ordained to the priesthood at age ten by his grandfather, Methuselah, according to D&C 107:52. Whether this was the ordination referred to in verse 19 or is a later ordination, we do not know. Whatever the case, Noah is now sent on his mission to preach the gospel.

19 And **the Lord** [*Jesus Christ*] **ordained Noah after his own order** [*gave him the same priesthood He holds; Christ is a high priest*], and **commanded him that he should go forth and declare his gospel unto the children of men**, even as it was given unto Enoch.

It must have been difficult for Noah to know and appreciate the gospel and its wonderful power to redeem and give sweet purpose and meaning to life and then see it rejected by the people (verses 20–21, next). Remember, though, that his mission was not without some success. Moses 7:27 informs us that many accepted the gospel and were taken up to join the City of Enoch.

20 And it came to pass that Noah called upon the **children of men** [*the wicked—see note following verse 13, above, concerning this terminology*] that they should repent; **but they hearkened not unto his words;**

Not only did the people reject his message, but they also taunted him, saying, in effect, that they were righteous and successful and didn't need the gospel he preached. This sounds very much like the arrogant statements of Nephi's brothers as they bore testimony to him that the wicked people of Jerusalem were righteous (1 Nephi 17:22).

21 And also, after that they had heard him, **they came up before him,** saying: Behold, **we are the sons of God** [*we are righteous*]; have we not taken unto ourselves the daughters of men? And **are we not eating and drinking, and marrying and giving in marriage?** And **our wives bear unto us children, and the same are mighty men,** which are like unto men of old, men of great renown. And **they hearkened not unto the words of Noah.**

One of the great dangers of deliberately choosing to rebel against God is that it takes more and more evil and wicked gratification to satisfy wicked desires, until the wicked are completely caught up in devising more and more depraved activities to satisfy their carnal and devilish lusts. In verse 22, next, we see that these people had arrived at this point, where their minds were engaged in evil constantly.

22 And God saw that **the wickedness of men had become great** in the earth; and **every man was lifted up in the imagination of the thoughts of his heart, being only evil continually.**

Despite this great opposition, Noah continued preaching the gospel of Jesus Christ to the people (verse 23). You can see, in verse 24, that he taught the same basic message that our missionaries preach today.

23 And it came to pass that **Noah continued his preaching unto the people,** saying: Hearken, and give heed unto my words;

24 **Believe** and **repent** of your sins and **be baptized** in the name of Jesus Christ, the Son of God, even as our fathers, and ye shall **receive**

the Holy Ghost, that ye may have all things made manifest; and if ye do not this, the floods will come in upon you; nevertheless they hearkened not.

Verses 25–26, next, represent a significant change from the text in the Bible. We will quote Genesis 6:6–7 here so that you can easily compare it with verses 25–26. We will use **bold** to point things out.

<u>Genesis 6:6–7</u>
6 And **it repented the Lord** that he had made man on the earth, and it grieved him at his heart.

7 And the Lord said, I will destroy man whom I have created from the face of the earth; both man, and beast, and the creeping thing, and the fowls of the air; for **it repenteth me that I have made them**.

25 And **it repented Noah**, and his heart was pained that the Lord had made man on the earth, and it grieved him at the heart.

26 And the Lord said: I will destroy man whom I have created, from the face of the earth, both man and beast, and the creeping things, and the fowls of the air; **for it repenteth Noah that I have created them**, and that I have made them; and he hath called upon me; for they have sought his life.

The rendering of these verses in the Bible makes it sound like God felt that He had made a mistake in putting people on earth. God is perfect and doesn't make mistakes. It would be tragic to believe that He does, and it would make it difficult to have complete faith in Him. Thankfully, Moses 8:25–26 straightens this out.

27 And thus **Noah found grace in the eyes of the Lord**; for **Noah** was a just man, and perfect in his generation; and he **walked with God, as did also his three sons, Shem, Ham, and Japheth.**

The word "perfect" is used in verse 27, above, in reference to Noah. Since Christ was the only perfect person to live on earth, we will quote Elder Mark E. Petersen to help us understand the phrase "perfect in his generation." We will use **bold** for emphasis.

"Noah, who built the ark, was one of God's greatest servants, chosen before he was born as were others of the prophets. He was no eccentric, as many have supposed. Neither was he a mythical figure created only in legend. Noah was real. . . .

"Let no one downgrade the life and mission of this great prophet. **Noah was so near perfect** in his day that he literally walked and talked with God. . . .

"Few men in any age were as great as Noah. In many respects he was like Adam, the first man. Both had served as ministering angels in the presence of God even after their mortal experience" (*Noah and the Flood,* pp. 1–2).

The repetition in verses 28–30, next, serves to emphasize the reasons for the destruction of the wicked by the Flood.

28 The **earth was corrupt** before God, and it was **filled with violence.**

29 And God looked upon the earth, and, behold, **it was corrupt,** for all flesh had corrupted its way upon the earth.

30 And God said unto Noah: The end of all flesh is come before me, for **the earth is filled with violence,** and behold I will destroy all flesh from off the earth.

Elder Parley P. Pratt taught that rampant sexual immorality was one of the chief reasons for the destruction of the wicked with the Flood. He said:

"The people before the flood, and also the Sodomites [the residents of Sodom, who openly taught homosexuality] and Canaanites [after the flood], had carried these corruptions and degeneracies so far that God, in mercy, destroyed them and thus put an end to the procreation of races so degenerate and abominable; while Noah, Abraham, Melchizedek, and others who were taught in the true laws of procreation [the Lord's law, including the law of chastity] 'were perfect in their generation,' and trained their children in the same laws" (*Key to the Science of Theology,* page 106).

THE BOOK OF ABRAHAM

TRANSLATED FROM THE PAPYRUS BY JOSEPH SMITH

General Background

Abraham was born about 2000 BC. He lived to be 175 years of age and is one of the best-known prophets of all time. The writings of Abraham, given here in the Pearl of Great Price, are a translation from a papyrus scroll (one of several such scrolls that came into the hands of the Church in Kirtland, Ohio, in 1835, along with four Egyptian mummies). See heading to the Book of Abraham in the Pearl of Great Price. Joseph Smith translated these writings of Abraham by the gift and power of God, thus adding much to our knowledge of Abraham and his teachings.

It is quite likely that Abraham knew Noah, since Noah lived for another 349 years after the Flood. Noah entered the ark at age 600 and left the ark about a year later. He lived to be 950 years old (see Genesis 7:6; 9:29). From the limited biblical chronology we have available, it appears that Abraham was born several years before Noah died. Abraham's father, Terah, would have been alive for the last 200 or so years of Noah's life, and his grandfather, Peleg, who lived 239 years, would have lived and died while Noah was still alive.

To those who have family members, parents, grandparents, and other relatives who are not faithful in the Church and who live with a certain sense of loneliness as a result, despite all the happiness provided by living the gospel, Abraham provides good company. As you will see, his father and other extended family members apostatized from the true gospel. In fact, they were so bitter against Abraham for worshipping God that they helped nominate him to be a human sacrifice in their area. See Facsimile No. 1, at the beginning of the Book of Abraham. Although Abraham's father repented for a while, he reverted to his old ways.

Despite family opposition, Abraham created his own eternal family unit. He made and kept covenants with the Lord and thus successfully attained joy and eternal exaltation. He has already become a God (D&C 132:29, 37).

ABRAHAM, CHAPTER 1

Background

In this chapter, we will be given many details about Abraham's life, which are not available elsewhere in scripture. As we begin, we see that Abraham lived in "the land of the Chaldeans" (verse 1). Genesis 11:28 tells us that "Ur of the Chaldees" is the "land of [*Abraham's*] nativity"; in other words, Abraham was born in Ur. On a map in our day, Ur would be in Iraq, in the area of the modern town of Mugheir. It is about 150 miles inland from the Persian Gulf, to the northwest. The "Chaldeans" were residents of southern Babylon. Chaldea was another name for southern Babylon.

Although Egypt was 875 miles west of Ur, it was influential in the lives of the citizens of Ur in Abraham's day. As we will see, beginning with verse 6, the religion of Egypt was a dominant influence in Ur. In fact, as depicted in Facsimile No. 1, one of Pharaoh's priests attempted to sacrifice Abraham on the altar. We will learn more about this from Abraham, beginning with verse 12.

One of the things we learn about Abraham, in verse 1, is that he was gentle and modest. He gives the understatement of the ages in the last half of this verse. We know from this chapter that he was almost offered as a human sacrifice, at the request of his relatives (verse 7), and that there was great anger against him when the priest of Pharaoh was struck dead by the Lord as he attempted to kill Abraham and when the temple of Pharaoh in Ur was destroyed. Thus, there was a public outcry against Abraham, the perceived cause of the destruction of the people's priest and shrine. With this as a setting, we read verse 1 (**bold** added for emphasis):

1 In the land of the Chaldeans, at the residence of my fathers [*in other words, in Abraham's home town*], **I, Abraham, saw that it was needful for me to obtain another place of residence;**

He will make another understatement at the end of Abraham 2:12. His quiet modesty of words is indeed exemplary.

As mentioned above, Abraham's father and extended family were apostates. In other words, they had once belonged to the true religion given from God through Noah and his righteous sons but had left it (see verse 5). They had turned to idol worship and the evil indulgences and practices that accompanied it. Verse 2, next, tells us that Abraham did not go with them in this departure from truth. Rather, he recognized the value of the gospel of Christ and stayed true to it. He gives his reasons for so doing in verses 2–4.

2 And, finding **there was greater happiness** and **peace** and **rest** for me, I sought for the blessings of the fathers, and the right [*of holding the Melchizedek Priesthood—see end of this verse*] whereunto I should be ordained to administer the same; having been myself a follower of righteousness, **desiring also to be one who possessed great knowledge**, and **to be a greater follower of righteousness**, and **to possess a greater knowledge** [*have on-going revelation and instruction*], and **to be a father of many nations** [*desiring to have a large posterity*], **a prince of peace**, and **desiring to receive instructions**, and **to keep the commandments of God, I became a** rightful heir, a **High Priest**, holding the right [*the Melchizedek Priesthood*] belonging to the fathers [*his righteous ancestors, including Shem, Noah, and so on back to Adam*].

We see in verse 3, next, that Abraham was a high priest in the Melchizedek Priesthood.

3 **It** [*the office of high priest in the Melchizedek Priesthood mentioned in verse 2, above*] **was conferred upon me from the fathers**; it came down from the fathers, from the beginning of time [*from the time of Adam—see note in this study guide for Moses 6:67, which tells us that Adam was a high priest in the Melchizedek Priesthood*], yea, **even from the beginning, or before the foundation of the earth** [*worthy men held this priesthood in premortality—compare with Alma 13:3*], down to the present time, even the right of the firstborn, or the first man, who is Adam, or first father, through the fathers unto me.

According to the Doctrine and Covenants, Abraham received his priesthood from Melchizedek. We read:

D&C 84:14

14 Which **Abraham received the priesthood from Melchizedek**, who received it through the lineage of his fathers, even till Noah;

Joseph Smith gave further detail about Abraham's meeting with Melchizedek and his subsequent ordination. He said:

"Abraham says to Melchizedek, I believe all that thou hast taught me concerning the priesthood and the coming of the Son of Man; so Melchizedek ordained Abraham and sent him away. Abraham rejoiced, saying, Now I have a priesthood" (*History of the Church,* Vol. 5, page 555).

4 I sought for mine appointment unto the Priesthood [*Abraham lived worthily and sought to be ordained a high priest in the Melchizedek Priesthood*] according to the appointment of God [*according to the pattern approved and established by the Lord*] unto the fathers concerning the seed [*perhaps meaning the pattern of father to son, established in the days of Adam*].

It may be that verse 4, above, is the introductory sentence of Abraham's explanation as to why he received the priesthood from Melchizedek (D&C 84:14), rather than from his father, Terah. It appears that he "sought" it from his "fathers" (direct ancestors), but they had apostatized and thus could not give it to him. This no doubt caused him much sorrow and heartache. He explains their apostasy, beginning in verse 5.

5 **My fathers having turned from their righteousness** [*they were once faithful to God*], **and from the holy commandments** which the Lord their God had given unto them, **unto the worshiping of the gods of the heathen** [*they had turned to idol worship*], **utterly refused to hearken to my voice;**

The four "gods," or idols, mentioned in verse 6, next, were Egyptian idols. You can see this by looking at Facsimile No. 1, and looking at Figures 5–8, which are depicted as jars underneath the table-altar upon which Abraham has been placed in preparation for his sacrifice. As stated in verse 5, above, Abraham's father and other ancestors had joined the Egyptian religion in Ur, in which idols were worshipped and human sacrifice was practiced. If you look in the layers under the four jars (representing the four gods mentioned above), you will see a crocodile lurking. It represents Pharaoh, as a god (see figure 9). The vital organs of the victim being sacrificed were placed in these jars and then poured out to a live crocodile as a part of worshipping Pharaoh as a god.

Human sacrifice is one of the worst of all blasphemies promoted by Satan. It is an abominable mockery of the sacrifice of the Son of God.

6 For **their hearts were set to do evil**, and were **wholly** [*completely*] **turned** to the god of **Elkenah**, and the god of **Libnah**, and the god of **Mahmackrah**, and the god of **Korash**, and **the god of Pharaoh**, king of Egypt;

7 Therefore **they turned their hearts to the sacrifice of the heathen in offering up their children unto these dumb idols** [*idols that*

are inanimate, deaf and dumb, having no capacity to hear or speak], and **hearkened not unto my voice, but endeavored to take away my life by the hand of the priest of Elkenah** [*in other words, they attempted to murder Abraham, under the guise of religious worship, using the priest of Pharaoh as their executioner*]. **The priest of Elkenah was also the priest of Pharaoh.**

> Next, Abraham explains that the Egyptian custom of sacrificing humans to their false gods had become firmly established in Chaldea, Abraham's homeland. He will mention specific instances of such sacrifices.

8 **Now, at this time it was the custom of the priest of Pharaoh**, the king of Egypt, **to offer up upon the altar** which was built in the land of Chaldea, for the offering unto these strange [*foreign*] gods, **men, women, and children.**

9 And it came to pass that **the priest made an offering unto the god of Pharaoh**, and **also unto the god of Shagreel**, even after the manner of the Egyptians. Now the god of Shagreel was the sun.

10 Even **the thank-offering of a child** did the priest of Pharaoh offer upon the altar which stood by the hill called Potiphar's Hill, at the head of the plain of Olishem.

> In verse 11, next, we see another example, in addition to Abraham, of the practice among these wicked people of using human sacrifice to get rid of those who opposed them.

11 Now, **this priest had offered upon this altar three virgins at one time**, who were the daughters of Onitah, one of the royal descent directly from the loins of Ham. **These virgins were offered up because of their virtue; they would not bow down to worship gods of wood or of stone** [*idols*], **therefore they were killed upon this altar**, and it was done after the manner of the Egyptians.

> Next, Abraham modestly gives us a few details of his almost being sacrificed. He tells us that he has included a drawing (Facsimile No. 1) that will help us understand what happened.

12 And it came to pass that **the priests laid violence upon me, that they might slay me also, as they did those virgins upon this altar**; and **that you may have a knowledge of this altar, I will refer you to the representation** [*drawing*] at the commencement of this record.

> Next, he tells us that the altar upon which victims were sacrificed looked like a bed.

13 **It** [*the* altar] **was made after the**

form of a bedstead [*it was made like a bed*], such as was had among the Chaldeans, and **it stood before the gods of Elkenah, Libnah, Mahmackrah, Korash, and also a god like unto that of Pharaoh, king of Egypt.**

14 That you may have an understanding of these gods, I have given you the fashion [*a drawing*] of them in the figures [*figures 5–9*] at the beginning, which manner of figures is called by the Chaldeans Rahleenos, which signifies **hieroglyphics.**

There is an important lesson for us in Facsimile No. 1. There is much symbolism in what Abraham did literally. It is that he was willing to put his "all" on the altar of sacrifice in order to remain true to God. In the facsimile, he is remaining loyal to the Lord at all costs. By doing so, he showed his great faith. Having such faith, he was enabled to pray fervently to be redeemed from the evil that was about to descend upon him. Figure 1 represents the "Angel of the Lord" who came and rescued Abraham. This "Angel" can represent Christ, who literally redeems us from the evils and sins of the world when we follow Him no matter what the cost.

If you look at the facsimile again, you will see the knife held in the hand of the priest of Pharaoh, ready to sacrifice Abraham. In verse 15, Abraham tells us what happened next.

15 And **as they lifted up their hands upon me, that they might offer me up** and take away my life, behold, **I lifted up my voice** [*prayed*] **unto the Lord my God, and the Lord hearkened and heard, and he filled me with the vision of the Almighty** [*he saw the Savior—see verse 16*]**, and the angel of his presence stood by me, and immediately unloosed my bands** [*untied him*];

16 And **his voice was unto me: Abraham, Abraham, behold, my name is Jehovah** [*the name of Christ in the Old Testament*]**, and I have heard thee, and have come down to deliver thee,** and **to take thee away** from thy father's house, and from all thy kinsfolk, into a strange land which thou knowest not of;

One of the important messages we see in verse 16, above, and verse 17, next, is that in order to follow Christ, we must leave the worldly influences around us.

17 And this **because they have turned their hearts away from me**, to worship the god of Elkenah, and the god of Libnah, and the god of Mahmackrah, and the god of Korash, and the god of Pharaoh,

king of Egypt; therefore I have come down to visit [*punish*] them, and to destroy him [*the priest*] who hath lifted up his hand against thee, Abraham, my son, to take away thy life.

> As you can see, in verse 18, next, when we leave the world and follow Christ, we are not alone.
>
> Verses 18–19 contain part of the Abrahamic covenant, the covenant that the Lord made with Abraham and through which the faithful in all ages since Abraham are blessed. This includes the faithful Saints in our day. We will speak in more detail about this when we get to Abraham 2:9–11. These are blessings and promises to us if we make covenants (which provide direction and security) and remain faithful.

18 Behold, **I will lead thee by my hand**, and **I will take thee, to put upon thee my name**, even **the Priesthood** of thy father, and **my power shall be over thee**.

19 As it was with Noah so shall it be with thee; but **through thy ministry my name shall be known in the earth forever**, for I am thy God.

> Next, Abraham gives a few more details as to what happened to the shrine of Egyptian gods in Ur, at which Abraham was nearly sacrificed.

20 Behold, Potiphar's Hill was in the land of Ur, of Chaldea. And **the Lord broke down the altar of Elkenah, and of the gods** [*the idols*] **of the land, and utterly destroyed them, and smote the priest that he died**; and **there was great mourning in Chaldea, and also in the court of Pharaoh** [*in other words, news of this destruction reached Egypt, almost nine hundred miles away*]; which Pharaoh signifies king by royal blood.

> Sadly, as you saw in verse 20, above, instead of repenting and turning to the true God, who obviously had great power over their "dumb" idols (verse 7) and false priests, these wicked people mourned the loss of their evil religious symbols and shrine. This is a reminder that wickedness does not promote rational thought.
>
> Next, in verses 21–27, Abraham gives us some detail explaining that the descendants of Cain were not allowed to hold the priesthood. One of the great blessings of our day is that all worthy men may now receive the priesthood, as revealed by the Lord to President Spencer W. Kimball in 1978 (see Doctrine and Covenants—Declaration 2, at the end of your Doctrine and Covenants). Thus,

the full gospel can now go to all the world in fulfillment of many prophecies to that effect, including Daniel 2:35, 44–45.

These next verses may not help us explain to those who do not believe in the Pearl of Great Price the fact that not all men have been allowed to hold the priesthood throughout most of the history of the world. However, they are helpful to us because they inform us that this practice did not originate in the early days of the restored gospel in this dispensation.

Abraham will explain that the king of Egypt in his day could not hold the priesthood. From what he says, we understand that Noah's son Ham, a righteous man (see Moses 8:13, 27), and his wife, Egyptus, came through the Flood with Noah and his wife, as well as with Ham's brothers, Japheth and Shem, and their wives—a total of eight people on the ark (see 1 Peter 3:20). Egyptus was a descendant of Cain. Thus, the restriction pertaining to the priesthood was preserved after the Flood through the posterity of Ham and Egyptus.

Ham's daughter, who was also named Egyptus, settled Egypt. Therefore, the Egyptians in Abraham's day could not hold the true priesthood.

21 Now **this king of Egypt** [*the Pharaoh mentioned at the end of verse 20, above*] **was a descendant from the loins of Ham, and was a partaker of the blood of the Canaanites** [*descendants of Cain*] **by birth.**

The word "Canaanites" is used both in verse 21, above, and in verse 22, next. According to Genesis 10:6, Ham and Egyptus named their fourth son Canaan. This is where the name Canaanites comes from. You can read more about this in your Bible Dictionary under "Canaan" and under "Canaanite."

22 **From this descent** [*from Ham and Egyptus*] **sprang all the Egyptians, and thus the blood of the Canaanites was preserved in the land.**

23 **The land of Egypt being first discovered by a woman, who was the daughter of Ham, and the daughter of Egyptus**, which in the Chaldean signifies Egypt, which signifies that which is forbidden;

24 When this woman discovered the land it was under water [*the waters of the Flood hadn't yet receded from it*], who afterward settled her sons in it; and **thus, from Ham, sprang that race which preserved the curse** [*of not holding the priesthood*] **in the land.**

From verses 25–27, we learn that the oldest son of Egyptus—in other words, a grandson of Ham and Egyptus and a great-grandson of Noah and his wife—became the first pharaoh. He was a righteous man and received a blessing from his great-grandfather, Noah.

25 Now **the first government of Egypt was established by Pharaoh, the eldest son of Egyptus, the daughter of Ham**, and it was after the manner of [*patterned after*] the government of Ham, which was patriarchal [*passed down from father to son*].

26 **Pharaoh,** being **a righteous man,** established his kingdom and **judged his people wisely and justly all his days**, seeking earnestly to imitate that order [*the patriarchal order*] established by the fathers [*righteous men, back to Adam*] in the first generations, in the days of the first patriarchal reign, even in the reign of Adam, and also of **Noah**, his father [*great-grandfather*], who **blessed him with the blessings of the earth, and with the blessings of wisdom**, but **cursed him as pertaining to the Priesthood** [*in other words, he was not allowed to hold the priesthood*].

27 Now, **Pharaoh being of that lineage by which he could not have the right of Priesthood**, notwithstanding [*even though*] the Pharaohs would fain claim [*pretend to claim*] it from Noah, through Ham [*even though many later Pharaohs falsely claimed to have the true priesthood from Noah through Ham*], therefore **my father** [Terah] **was led away by their idolatry** [*their idol worship*];

28 But I shall endeavor, hereafter, to delineate [*to give and make notes about; to describe*] the chronology running back from myself to the beginning of the creation, for the records have come into my hands, which I hold unto this present time [*Abraham had scriptures and historical records in his possession; see also verse 31*].

Abraham now picks up the story of what happened after the shrine and the priest of Pharaoh were destroyed. Remember that this destruction took place at the time Abraham was freed from the sacrificial altar by the Lord.

29 Now, **after the priest of Elkenah** [*the one who had tried to sacrifice Abraham*] **was smitten that he died**, there came a fulfilment of those things which were said unto me concerning the land of Chaldea, that there should be **a famine in the land.**

One of the positive results of the famine, initially, was that Abraham's father repented and returned to God. Unfortunately, when things began going well for him again, he returned to his old ways (Abraham 2:5). This is one of the dangers of prosperity. Thus, Abraham is well acquainted with the joy and heartache that come and go when loved ones return to God when they are humbled but then leave again when prosperity and safety are once again theirs.

As we continue, Abraham tells us that because of the famine, his father repented of his evil plots against him.

30 Accordingly **a famine prevailed throughout all the land of Chaldea**, and **my father** was sorely [*severely*] tormented because of the famine, and he **repented** of the evil which he had determined against me, to take away my life.

Abraham will tell us more about the effects of the famine on him and his family in chapter 2. In the meantime, as Abraham closes chapter 1, we see that one of the main topics for him so far in these writings has been the importance of the priesthood and the blessings that flow to us from it. He emphasizes this again now.

31 But the records of the fathers, even the patriarchs, **concerning the right of Priesthood**, the Lord my God preserved in mine own hands; therefore a knowledge of the beginning of the creation, and also of the planets, and of the stars, as they were made known unto the fathers, have I kept even unto this day, and I shall endeavor to write some of these things upon this record, for the benefit of my posterity [*all of us*] that shall come after me.

ABRAHAM, CHAPTER 2

Background

This chapter contains one of the most important matters in all of scripture for each of us. It concerns the blessings of Abraham, the Abrahamic covenant. Each of us who has had a patriarchal blessing has had our mind pointed to the "blessings of Abraham, Isaac, and Jacob." These are the blessings that make exaltation possible to us. This chapter contains a summary of these blessings in verses 9–11. We will discuss them when we get there.

But first, in verses 1–8, father Abraham tells us what happened to him and his family after they left Ur. We will do a quick bit of genealogy on Abraham's family at the time he leaves Ur, which will be helpful in the next verses. We will use Genesis 11:26–29 as our source.

> **Terah** (his father)
>
> **Abraham**
>
> **Nahor** (his brother)
>
> **Haran** (his brother)
>
> **Sarah** (his niece)
>
> **Lot** (his nephew)
>
> **Milcah** (his niece)

As you will see, Haran, Abraham's brother, will die because of the famine. Abraham will marry his niece, Sarai (Sarah), and Nahor will marry his niece, Milcah. To marry close relatives was not unusual in Abraham's day. Lot will travel with his uncles, Abraham and Nahor, and with his grandfather, Terah.

1 Now the Lord God caused the **famine** to wax sore [*grow severe*] in the land of Ur, insomuch that **Haran, my brother, died**; but Terah, my father, yet lived in the land of Ur, of the Chaldees.

> Next, Abraham tells us that he married his niece, Sarai (her name will be changed to Sarah in conjunction with the Lord's covenant with Abraham and Sarai that they will have a child—Isaac (see Genesis 17:15). It is interesting that a name change was often associated with covenant making in ancient times.

2 And it came to pass that **I, Abraham, took Sarai to wife**, and **Nahor, my brother, took Milcah to wife**, who was the daughter of Haran.

3 Now **the Lord had said unto me: Abraham, get thee out of thy country**, and from thy kindred, and from thy father's house, unto a land that I will show thee.

> Next, Abraham tells us who went with him as he obeyed the Lord's commandment to leave.

4 **Therefore I left the land of Ur**, of the Chaldees, **to go into the land of Canaan**; and **I took Lot**, my brother's son, **and his wife, and Sarai my wife**; and **also my father followed after me**, unto the land which we denominated [*named*] Haran.

> From the wording in verse 4, above, it sounds as if Abraham's father, Terah, followed Abraham later. Of course, it could be that when Abraham determined to leave, as commanded by the Lord, Terah followed him. Whatever the case, they settled for a time in a place they named Haran, which was located far north and a bit east of what we know today as the Holy Land.
>
> Sadly, when things started going

well in Haran, which they apparently did—when Abraham leaves Haran, they have "substance" and converts with them (verses 14–15)—his father apostatizes again and remains in Haran. He will die there at age 205 (Genesis 11:32).

5 And **the famine abated** [*ceased*]; and **my father tarried** [*remained*] **in Haran** and dwelt there, as there were **many flocks in Haran** [*prosperity*]; and **my father turned again unto his idolatry**, therefore he continued in Haran.

Next, in verses 6–12, the Savior appears to Abraham and commands him to leave Haran with his family and followers. The Lord makes a covenant with him that is of vital interest to each of us. The details of the covenant are given in verses 9–11.

6 But **I, Abraham, and Lot**, my brother's son, **prayed unto the Lord**, and **the Lord appeared unto me, and said** unto me: **Arise**, and take Lot with thee; for **I have purposed to take thee away out of Haran, and to make of thee a minister to bear my name** in a strange land [*basically, the area of the Holy Land today*] **which I will give unto thy seed** [*posterity*] **after thee** for an everlasting possession, when they hearken to my voice.

A very important matter, which is often misunderstood, is mentioned in verse 6, above. Did you notice to whom the "strange land" is to be given? The answer is to Abraham's "seed." And which of the major factions fighting over the Holy Land today are Abraham's seed? Answer: both Jews and Arabs. Abraham is a highly revered ancestor for both peoples.

In an address given at Brigham Young University on February 4, 1979, President Howard W. Hunter reminded us that both the Jews and the Arabs are children of Abraham and thus, the promises given to Abraham apply to both (David B. Galbraith, "President Howard W. Hunter, 1907–1995: A Man of Peace," *Brigham Young Magazine,* May 1995, page 5).

Next, the Savior identifies Himself to Abraham. As He does so, we see Him confirming Abraham's wisdom in rejecting idol worship. Idols can do none of the things Jehovah can. None of them is a god. He is!

7 For **I am the Lord thy God**; I dwell in heaven; the earth is my footstool; I stretch my hand over the sea, and it obeys my voice; I cause the wind and the fire to be my chariot; I say to the mountains—Depart hence—and behold,

they are taken away by a whirlwind, in an instant, suddenly.

8 **My name is Jehovah**, and I know the end from the beginning; therefore **my hand shall be over thee** [*the Lord's blessings will be upon Abraham and his righteous posterity*].

> You may wish to bracket or put a box around verses 9–11 in your own scriptures, or otherwise mark them. They constitute a concise summary of the "blessings of Abraham, Isaac, and Jacob, as promised to faithful, covenant-keeping members of the Church. They are often referred to in patriarchal blessings. These verses contain the basics of the Abrahamic covenant.
>
> We will first go through verses 9–11, using **bold** to point out the basic elements of the covenant. Then, we will repeat the verses, adding notes and commentary.

9 And **I will make of thee a great nation**, and **I will bless thee above measure**, and **make thy name great among all nations**, and **thou shalt be a blessing unto thy seed after thee**, that **in their hands they shall bear this ministry and Priesthood unto all nations**;

10 And **I will bless them through thy name**; for **as many as receive this Gospel shall be called after thy name**, and **shall be accounted thy seed**, and **shall rise up and bless thee, as their father**;

11 And **I will bless them that bless thee, and curse them that curse thee**; and **in thee (that is, in thy Priesthood) and in thy seed (that is, thy Priesthood)**, for I give unto thee a promise that this right shall continue in thee, and **in thy seed after thee (that is to say, the literal seed, or the seed of the body) shall all the families of the earth be blessed**, even **with the blessings of the Gospel**, which are the blessings of **salvation**, even of **life eternal**.

> As mentioned above, we will now repeat verses 9–11, adding notes and commentary as we go. Remember that at the time Abraham was given these promises, he and Sarai had no children. He is sixty-two years old at this point, and she is fifty-two years old (see verse 14).
>
> Note how many different ways of saying "exaltation" (the highest degree of glory in the celestial kingdom) are used in these verses. Some of the blessings promised are literal for Abraham here on earth; others are symbolic of exaltation for him as well as for the faithful in the eternities.

Verses 9–11, repeated

9 And **I will make of thee a great nation** [*literal for Abraham on earth; symbolic of exaltation*], and **I will bless thee above measure** [*exaltation; the blessings of exaltation are beyond measuring*], and **make thy name great among all nations** [*literal for Abraham; symbolic of exaltation for the faithful, wherein they become gods and their names become great among all the worlds they create*], and thou shalt be a blessing unto **thy seed after thee**, that in their hands they **shall bear this ministry and Priesthood unto all nations** [*through Abraham and his righteous posterity (the righteous of Israel), the gospel of Jesus Christ with the blessings of the priesthood will be taken throughout the world*];

10 And I will bless them through thy name; for **as many as receive this Gospel shall be called after thy name** [*all who accept the gospel and live it become "Abraham's seed"; whether they are literal descendants or are adopted in, it makes no difference; they too receive the promises made to Abraham*], **and shall be accounted thy seed** [*in other words, heirs to the promises and obligations of Abraham*], and shall rise up and bless [*praise*] thee, as their father [*ancestor*];

11 And **I will bless them that bless thee, and curse them that curse thee** [*in other words, the Lord will be on our side*]; and in thee (that is, **in thy Priesthood**) and in thy seed (that is, thy Priesthood), for I give unto thee a promise that this right shall continue in thee, and in thy seed after thee (that is to say, the literal seed, or the seed of the body) **shall all the families of the earth be blessed**, even **with the blessings of the Gospel**, which are the blessings of **salvation**, even of **life eternal** [*exaltation as gods, in the highest degree of glory of the celestial kingdom*].

As you can see, the main emphasis in the blessings and promises given to Abraham is exaltation. Thus, those who inherit the blessings of Abraham (through baptism and other covenants) and live worthy of them will be exalted.

The phrase "life eternal" in verse 11, above, is the same as "eternal life." As used in the scriptures, both phrases always mean "exaltation." Exaltation means becoming gods and living in the family unit forever. "Immortality," on the other hand, means being resurrected and living forever. All who have ever been born will be resurrected and live forever, whether in outer darkness or in telestial, terrestrial, or celestial glory. But only those who attain the highest glory in the celestial kingdom (D&C 131:1–4) receive "eternal life." An example of the use of "immortality" and "eternal life" as two separate scriptural concepts is found in Moses, as follows:

Moses 1:39
39 For behold, this is my work and my glory—to bring to pass the **immortality** [*resurrection*] and **eternal life** [*exaltation*] of man.

We will go through these verses one more time, this time pointing out our obligations as members of covenant Israel.

Verses 9–11, repeated again
9 And I will make of thee **a great nation** [*marry, and have children, where possible*], and I will bless thee above measure, and make thy name great among all nations, and **thou shalt be a blessing unto thy seed after thee** [*be a blessing and influence for good to our families*], that in their hands they shall **bear this ministry and Priesthood unto all nations** [*serve formal missions where possible, preach the gospel, and be missionaries under all circumstances, thus making the ordinances of the priesthood available to others*];

10 And I will bless them through thy name; for **as many as receive this Gospel shall be called after thy name** [*do all we can to ensure that our posterity are blessed by the gospel*], and shall be accounted thy seed, and shall rise up and bless thee, as their father [*do our best to pass the gospel of Jesus Christ on to our children, grandchildren, and so forth*];

11 And I will bless them that bless thee, and curse them that curse thee; and in thee (that is, in thy **Priesthood**) and in thy seed (that is, thy Priesthood), for I give unto thee a promise that this right shall continue in thee [*make sure we honor the priesthood and the priesthood ordinances we have received*], and in thy seed after thee (that is to say, the literal seed, or the seed of the body) **shall all the families of the earth be blessed** [*be a blessing for others, constantly*], even with the blessings of the Gospel, which are the blessings of salvation, even of life eternal.

In verses 12–13, next, we see the gentle greatness and humility of Abraham as he once again uses an understatement (see also Abraham 1:1) to express his feelings. He has been saved from death on the altar. He has seen the Savior and, though still childless, has been told that his posterity will grow into nations and that his name will be honored and revered throughout the world. Not only that, his posterity will take the gospel and priesthood to all nations.

12 Now, after the Lord had withdrawn from speaking to me, and withdrawn his face from me, I said in my heart: **Thy servant has sought thee earnestly; now I have found thee;**

13 Thou didst send thine angel to deliver me from the gods of Elkenah, and **I will do well to hearken unto thy voice**, therefore let thy servant rise up and depart in peace.

14 So **I, Abraham, departed** as the Lord had said unto me, and Lot with me; and **I, Abraham, was sixty and two years old when I departed out of Haran.**

As Abraham and his company depart, they will head southwest toward what we know today as the Holy Land. As stated in verse 14, above, he is now sixty-two years of age. That makes Sarai fifty-two years old. They have thirty-eight more years of trial of their faith ahead of them before the Lord's promise will be fulfilled that they will have a child. Abraham will be a hundred and Sarah will be ninety when Isaac is born.

15 And **I took Sarai** [*her name will be changed to Sarah in Genesis 17:15, which means "princess" in Hebrew, and "queen" in the Akkadian language*], whom I took to wife when I was in Ur, in Chaldea, **and Lot,** my brother's son, **and all our substance that we had gathered** [*it appears that by now Abraham has gathered considerable wealth*], **and the souls** [*converts*] **that we had won in Haran**, and came forth in the way to [*direction of*] the land of Canaan, and dwelt in tents as we came on our way;

16 Therefore, eternity was our covering and our rock and our salvation, as we journeyed from Haran by the way of Jershon, to come to the land of Canaan.

Abraham informs us that he continued to worship God faithfully during his travels. In verse 17, next, we see the charity in Abraham's heart as he continues to pray for the blessings of the Lord upon his father and relatives, who have been significant enemies to him.

17 Now **I, Abraham, built an altar** in the land of Jershon, and **made an offering unto the Lord**, and **prayed that the famine might be turned away from my father's house**, that they might not perish.

18 And then we passed from Jershon through the land unto the place of Sechem; it was situated in the plains of Moreh, and we had already come into the borders of

the land of the Canaanites [*a land full of idol worship and attendant wickedness*], and **I offered sacrifice** there in the plains of Moreh, **and called on the Lord devoutly**, because we had already come into the land of **this idolatrous nation**.

In verse 19, next, the Savior appears to Abraham and tells him that the land he is now traveling through will be given to his posterity.

One thing you might take note of is that upon entering Canaan, which he refers to as "the land of this idolatrous nation," Abraham builds several altars. Perhaps an important message for us might be that when we are faced with increased opposition to our personal righteousness, it is wise to increase our time spent with the things of God.

19 And **the Lord appeared** unto me in answer to my prayers, **and said** unto me: **Unto thy seed will I give this land**.

20 And I, Abraham, arose from the place of the altar which I had built unto the Lord, and removed from thence unto a mountain on the east of Bethel, and pitched my tent there, Bethel on the west, and Hai on the east; and **there I built another altar unto the Lord**, and called again upon the name of the Lord.

As Abraham informs us, the great famine that caused so much devastation in Ur is evident also in the land of the Canaanites. At this point in his journeying, Abraham determines to travel on to Egypt. This will pose a particular problem for Abraham and Sarai because she is a beautiful woman.

By culture and tradition, the Egyptian pharaohs at this time in Egypt would never commit adultery. But they didn't hesitate to murder a man if they desired his wife. After the death of her husband, a wife would then be available. Thus, a pharaoh could then marry her and he would not be committing adultery. We will quote from the *Old Testament Student Manual*:

"The idea that Abraham, the great man of righteousness, seems to have told a deliberate lie in order to protect his own life has troubled many students of the Old Testament. That his life was in danger because of Sarah's beauty seems quite clear. It seems peculiar, but **whereas the Egyptian pharaohs had a strong aversion to committing adultery with another man's wife, they had no qualms about murdering the man to free his spouse for remarriage**.

"'To kill the husband in order

to possess himself of his wife seems to have been a common royal custom in those days. A papyrus tells of a Pharaoh who, acting on the advice of one of his princes, sent armed men to fetch a beautiful woman and make away with her husband. Another Pharaoh is promised by his priest on his tombstone that even after death he will kill Palestinian sheiks and include their wives in his harem (Kasher, *Encyclopedia of Biblical Interpretation,* 2:128).

"**Some scholars have noted that Abraham could validly state that Sarah was his sister. First of all, the Hebrew words brother and sister were often used for other blood relatives**. (See Genesis 14:14, in which Lot, Abraham's nephew, is called 'his brother.') Because Abraham and Haran, Sarah's father, were brothers, Sarah was Abraham's niece and thus could be called sister.

"Another ancient custom permitted a woman to be adopted as a man's sister upon their marriage to give her greater legal and social status (see *Encyclopedia Judaica,* s.v. 'Sarah,' 14:866). Also, it is not unlikely that when Haran died Terah legally adopted Haran's children as his own, thus making Sarah Abraham's sister" (*Old Testament Student Manual: Genesis–2 Samuel, Religion 301,* page 66).

With the above explanations in mind, there is one more issue that is far more important than any other. It is the simple fact that the Lord told Abraham to ask Sarah to claim that she was his sister. Unfortunately, the Bible leaves this fact out (Genesis 12:10–13). We will see the Lord's counsel for solving the problem in verses 21–24, next.

21 And I, Abraham, journeyed, going on still towards the south; and there was a continuation of a famine in the land; and **I, Abraham, concluded to go down into Egypt**, to sojourn there, **for the famine became very grievous.**

22 And it came to pass **when I was come near to enter into Egypt, the Lord said unto me: Behold, Sarai, thy wife, is a very fair woman to look upon;**

23 Therefore it shall come to pass, **when the Egyptians shall see her, they will say—She is his wife; and they will kill you, but they will save her alive**; therefore see that ye do on this wise [*here is what you should do*]:

24 **Let her say unto the Egyptians, she is thy sister**, and thy soul shall live [*your body will remain alive*].

Next, in verse 25, Abraham brings up the subject with his wife.

25 And it came to pass that **I, Abraham, told Sarai, my wife, all that the Lord had said unto me**—Therefore **say unto them** [*the Egyptians*], I pray thee [*please*], **thou art my sister, that it may be well with me for thy sake** [*so that I can remain alive and also watch out for you*], **and my soul shall live because of thee** [*you can save my life*].

Elder Mark E. Petersen of the Quorum of the Twelve explained this situation as follows:

"To protect himself, Abraham had told Pharaoh that Sarah was his sister, which of course she was. Had he divulged that she was his wife, he might have been slain. But as his sister, Pharaoh was willing to buy her at a good price" (*Abraham, Friend of God*, page 69)

Elder Bruce R. McConkie taught:

"The Lord never sends apostles and prophets and righteous men to minister to his people without placing women of like spiritual stature at their sides. Adam stands as the great high priest, under Christ, to rule as a natural patriarch over all men of all ages, but he cannot rule alone; Eve, his wife, rules at his side, having like caliber and attainments to his own. Abraham is tested as few men have been when the Lord commands him to offer Isaac upon the altar (Gen. 22:1–19); and Sarah struggles with like problems when the Lord directs that she withhold from the Egyptians her status as Abraham's wife. . . . And so it goes, in all dispensations and at all times when there are holy men there are also holy women. Neither stands alone before the Lord. The exaltation of the one is dependent upon that of the other" (*Doctrinal New Testament Commentary,* Vol. 3, page 302).

Many Christians are quite critical of Abraham, claiming that it was out of character and disappointing that such an otherwise great man would lie to the Egyptians about his wife. An *Ensign* article regarding this matter, written by S. Kent Brown, is helpful. Here is a quote from it:

"For Abraham and Sarah, Egypt constituted a place of refuge from the famine raging at the time of their arrival in Canaan (see Gen. 12:10). Interestingly, while Abraham and Sarah enjoyed respite from Canaan's drought, their visit to Egypt provided Sarah with one of her most difficult trials.

"Most are familiar with the story

of Sarah posing as Abraham's sister (see Gen. 12:11–15). Even though Abraham later insisted that Sarah was his sister through his father, but not his mother (see Gen. 20:12), many students have felt confused with this explanation. It was not until the discovery of ancient Hurrian legal texts at the site of Nuzi, a city east of Ashur, the capital of ancient Assyria, that we obtained a clearer background for this incident.

"The Hurrians were people who flourished about the time of Abraham, and later. Their kingdom included the land of Haran in which Abraham and Sarah lived for a number of years before moving to Canaan (see Gen. 11:31; Gen. 12:5). Interestingly, only in stories dealing with Sarah and Rebecca do we find the claim made that the wife was also a sister to her husband (see Gen. 12:10–20; Gen. 20:2–6; Gen. 26:1–11). Rebecca, like Sarah, spent her youth growing up in Haran, no doubt in contact with Hurrians.

"The contact is important when we learn that under Hurrian law women were frequently adopted as sisters by their husbands either before or during the marriage ceremony. Such a dual status, both wife and sister, had important consequences for a woman. It guaranteed to her special legal and social protections and opportunities which were simply not available to women in any other culture of the Near East. Because Sarah had lived within the Hurrian culture for a number of years, it is not unlikely that she enjoyed this status in her marriage, a status common among Hurrians. Therefore, Abraham's claim that Sarah was his sister upon their entry into the land of Egypt is not far-fetched in the least. Further, it is possible that Terah, Abraham's father, had adopted Sarah before her marriage to Abraham and that this is the meaning of the passage in Genesis 20:12. This particular practice, on the part of a prospective father-in-law, is documented from the Nuzi tablets. (See E. A. Speiser, 'The Wife-Sister Motif in the Patriarchal Narratives,' in *Biblical and Other Studies* [Cambridge, Mass.: Harvard Univ. Press, 1963], pp. 15–28.)

"In Genesis, Abraham is said to have insisted that Sarah was his sister because he feared for his life. The incident is clarified in the Book of Abraham where we learn it was revealed to Abraham that Sarah would maintain that she was his sister (see Abr. 2:21–25).

"This placed the burden on

Sarah. Would she risk her own rights as wife in order to preserve the life of her husband as the Lord had asked? Indeed, Sarah's visit to Egypt became a period of intense trial for her. Even though the Lord protected her from the pharaoh's intent to make her his wife—and protected her virtue—the pharaoh was nevertheless allowed to take her into his household (Gen. 12:15–20). We see, then, that Egypt represented at the same time a haven from the famine and a place of testing for Sarah" ("Biblical Egypt: Land of Refuge, Land of Bondage," *Ensign,* September 1980, pp. 45, 47).

Genesis 12:14–20 informs us that when Abraham and Sarah arrived in Egypt, Sarah was protected by the Lord, and Abraham was treated very well, perhaps in an attempt by Pharaoh to impress Sarah and gain her favor. Abraham was invited by Pharaoh to teach in his court (see Facsimile No. 3). We learn from Josephus, the Jewish historian, that Abraham was invited to teach mathematics and astronomy while there. This would, of course, be in addition to the gospel. It appears likely that they stayed twelve to thirteen years in Egypt, and Genesis 13:2 tells us that they were wealthy when they left.

ABRAHAM, CHAPTER 3

Background

We are taught many things in this chapter. Perhaps one of the most important is the fact that this life is a test (verse 25). Some people get a bit confused on this issue. They begin discussing God's foreknowledge and our agency and end up concluding that our future on Judgment Day is already determined because of His knowledge of the future. Regardless of discussions and debates on the subject, the revealed answer to the whole question is that this life is a test. We are indeed determining our future by whether we keep the commandments in this life (provided we are familiar with the gospel here).

One of the best-known doctrines in this chapter is the doctrine concerning the "noble and great" spirits, many of whom were reserved to come forth in this last dispensation. Also, a brief discussion of our "first estate" and "second estate" is presented here by Abraham. Among other things, Abraham will also teach us about intelligences and spirits and will give us a brief glimpse into the premortal councils during which Jesus was chosen to be the Redeemer, and Satan was rejected.

Before teaching us these doctrines, however, Abraham will provide a background and setting for us, using the stars and planets as examples, emphasizing that they are well organized and that some of them govern the others. Using these examples, he will lead us to the fact that some spirits in premortality progressed more rapidly than others, becoming great and noble. He will also teach us that just as there are grand, governing planets, such as Kolob, so also is there a grand, governing being, namely, God.

Abraham tells us that through the Urim and Thummim (verse 1), he was taught much about the stars and planets. These lessons in astronomy took place before he journeyed to Egypt (see verse 15). Abraham uses Facsimile No. 2 to illustrate much of what he was taught about the relationships among the planets and much more. This reminds us that there was great revealed knowledge in ancient times about the stars and planets. Much of this was lost during periods of apostasy.

As we begin our study of chapter 3, we run into the term "Urim and Thummim." The Bible Dictionary informs us that "Urim and Thummim" is a Hebrew term that means "Lights and Perfections." It also tells us that there is more than one Urim and Thummim. Joseph Smith had the one used by the brother of Jared. Abraham had one and learned much, including the things he summarizes for us in this chapter. It is interesting that he received it while he lived in Ur (verse 1), which would mean that it was given to him relatively early in his life.

1 And **I, Abraham, had the Urim and Thummim**, which the Lord my God had given unto me, in Ur of the Chaldees;

2 And **I saw the stars**, that they were very great, and that **one of them** [*Kolob*] **was nearest unto the throne of God**; and there were many great ones which were near unto it;

> Once in a while, members get Kolob confused with the actual planet on which Heavenly Father resides. They are not the same. As you saw in verse 2, above, Kolob is the planet nearest to the planet on which the Father lives.
>
> As Abraham continues, he points out that some planets govern others. He is leading up to the point that some spirits progress more than others through their agency choices and thus become the "great and noble" whom God appoints to be rulers (verse 23).

3 And the Lord said unto me: **These are the governing ones**; and the name of **the great one is Kolob**, because it is near unto me, for I am the Lord thy God: I have set this one to govern all those which belong to the same order as that upon which thou standest.

> We learn from verse 4, next, that the planet on which God resides has the same time system as Kolob. The Lord further informs us that one thousand years on our earth is one day on Kolob. You can see this same fact taught in the explanation of Fig. 1 provided for Facsimile No. 2. We are taught the same thing in 2 Peter 3:8.

4 And the Lord said unto me, by the Urim and Thummim, that **Kolob was after the manner of the Lord, according to its times and seasons in the revolutions thereof**; that one revolution was **a day unto the Lord**, after his manner of reckoning, it being **one thousand years** according to the time appointed unto that [*our earth*] whereon thou standest. **This is the reckoning of the Lord's time, according to the reckoning of Kolob.**

> Next, Abraham teaches us about our moon, explaining that a day on the moon is longer than our earth days. It is worth noting that much of this knowledge about astronomy, which Abraham taught in ancient times, was lost during the dark ages.

5 And the Lord said unto me: **The planet which is the lesser light** [*the moon*], lesser than that which is to rule the day [*the sun*], even the night, is above or greater than that upon which thou standest in point of reckoning, for it **moveth in order** [*in its orbit*] **more slow**; this is in order because it standeth above the earth upon which thou standest, therefore **the reckoning of its time is not so many as to its number of days, and of months, and of years** [*compared to the earth; one day on the moon, from when the sun rises on one horizon to when it sets on the opposite horizon, is about twenty-nine days on earth*].

> Abraham is now going to lead us to a major point he makes in verse 19, namely, that there are various levels of intelligence and that God is the most intelligent of all.
>
> As he teaches us, he will repeat a rather interesting phrase several times. It is "these two facts exist." He uses it (or something similar) in verses 6, 8, 16, 17, 18 (twice), and 19 (twice). We will use **bold** to point these out as we go along. His point will be that where you have two related things, there will always be

something higher than they are. And as you pursue this "order," moving higher and higher, you will eventually come to God. In other words, God is the force behind the organization and order in the universe.

To put it simply, the order in the universe bears witness that there is a God.

Another way to put it might be that, if we follow the simple teachings and commandments placed before us by the Lord, we will progress upward, seeing and understanding more and greater things. As we receive those things into our lives, we progress yet further and see more and yet greater things. If we continue this upward spiral, it leads to becoming like God (compare to D&C 88:49).

This process is illustrated in the example of the universe. First we see the earth, then we see the moon above it, and then we the sun above them both. Then we see larger stars beyond the sun, then the galaxy, then clusters of galaxies beyond it, and so forth, which ultimately leads to God. D&C 88:12–13 confirms this.

Let's sit down in Abraham's classroom now and listen carefully as this great prophet astronomer teaches us that all things in the universe have their order and proper relationship to each other. So, likewise, is there an "order of the gospel" as we move higher and higher, eventually keeping our second estate (verse 26) and becoming like God. Abraham will be quoting the Savior as he teaches us.

6 And the Lord said unto me: Now, Abraham, **these two facts exist** [*the sun rules the day, and the moon rules the night—see end of this verse*], behold thine eyes see it; it is given unto thee to know the times of reckoning, and the set time, yea, the set time of the earth upon which thou standest, and **the set time of the greater light** [*the sun*] **which is set to rule the day**, and **the set time of the lesser light** [*the moon*] **which is set to rule the night.**

7 Now the set time of the lesser light is a longer time as to its reckoning than the reckoning of the time of the earth upon which thou standest [*the moon has longer "days" than the earth*].

8 And **where these two facts exist**, there shall be **another fact above them**, that is, there shall be another planet whose reckoning of time shall be longer still [*there will be planets which have longer days than either the earth or the moon*];

The Savior continues reasoning with Abraham, explaining that there are planets above other planets that have longer and longer days, until you arrive at Kolob, which has the longest days of all in this order of planets, namely, one thousand earth years to one of its days. The same time system is used on the planet upon which God lives.

9 And thus **there shall be the reckoning of the time of one planet above another, until thou come nigh unto Kolob**, which Kolob is after the reckoning of the Lord's time [*Kolob uses the same time system used by the celestial planet upon which God resides*]; which Kolob is set nigh [*near*] unto the throne of God, to govern all those planets which belong to the same order as that upon which thou standest.

Perhaps one of the main implied messages in verse 10, next, is that just as Abraham is being taught about the orbits and time systems of the planets and stars leading up to Kolob and God's planet, so also will the Lord teach him the order of things, commandments, ordinances, and so forth leading up to his returning to the presence of God.

10 And **it is given unto thee to know the set time of all the stars that are set to give light, until thou come near unto the throne of God**.

Abraham points out that he was instructed by the Savior Himself, face to face.

11 Thus **I, Abraham, talked with the Lord, face to face**, as one man talketh with another; and he told me of the works [*creations*] which his hands had made;

12 And **he said unto me: My son, my son** [*a term of closeness and endearment*] (and his hand was stretched out), behold I will show you all these. And he put his hand upon mine eyes, and **I saw those things which his hands had made**, which were many [*an understatement*]; and they multiplied before mine eyes, and **I could not see the end thereof**.

13 And he said unto me: This is Shinehah, which is the **sun**. And he said unto me: Kokob, which is star. And he said unto me: Olea, which is the **moon**. And he said unto me: Kokaubeam, which signifies **stars**, or all the great lights, which were in the firmament of heaven [*the night sky*].

As the Savior teaches Abraham, he repeats His covenant and promise to Abraham that his posterity will be infinite in number.

14 And it was in the night time when the Lord spake these words unto me: **I will multiply thee,**

and thy seed after thee, like unto these; and if thou canst count the number of sands, so shall be the number of thy seeds.

We know from verse 15, next, that Abraham was taught all these things before he and Sarah went to Egypt. Thus, we understand that he taught the Egyptians much about astronomy.

15 And the Lord said unto me: **Abraham, I show these things unto thee before ye go into Egypt**, that ye may declare all these words.

In verses 16–19, we see the transition from stars and planets to people and God. The main point of this part of the lesson is made in these verses.

16 **If <u>two things exist</u>, and there be one above the other, there shall be greater things above them**; therefore Kolob is the greatest of all the Kokaubeam [*stars*] that thou hast seen, because it is nearest unto me [*the closer to God we come, the greater we become*].

17 Now, **if <u>there be two things</u>, one above the other**, and **the moon** be **above the earth**, then it may be that **a planet or a star may exist above it**; and there is nothing that the Lord thy God shall take in his heart to do but what he will do it [*"with God all things are possible"—Matthew 19:26*].

We learn from verses 18–19, next, that, just as there are different magnitudes among stars and planets, so also there are differing degrees of intelligence and progression among spirits. Spirits progressed at different rates during premortality because of agency choices. Joseph Fielding Smith taught this. He said:

"We know they were all innocent in the beginning; but the right of free agency which was given to them enabled some to outstrip others, and thus, through the eons of immortal existence, to become more intelligent, more faithful, for they were free to act for themselves, to think for themselves, to receive the truth or rebel against it" (*Doctrines of Salvation,* Vol. 1, page 59).

18 Howbeit that [*the fact of the matter is—see definition of "howbeit" in the 1828 Noah Webster Dictionary*] he made the greater star; as, **also, if <u>there be two spirits</u>, and one shall be more intelligent than the other**, yet <u>**these two spirits**</u>, notwithstanding [*even though*] one is more intelligent than the other, **have no beginning**; they existed before, they shall have **no end**, they shall exist after, for they are gnolaum, or eternal.

19 And the Lord said unto me:

These two facts do exist, that there are **two spirits**, **one being more intelligent than the other; there shall be another more intelligent than they; I am the Lord thy God, I am more intelligent than they all** [*in other words, God is the central focus and supreme creative power of the universe*].

At this point in the lesson, the Lord stops to remind Abraham that He is the one who sent the angel to free him from the sacrificial altar when he was about to be sacrificed. This appears to be a practical example given by the Savior at this point in the lesson to Abraham that He does, indeed, have power over all things.

20 The Lord thy God sent his angel to deliver thee from the hands of the priest of Elkenah.

We will pause a moment here to clarify some gospel vocabulary. Abraham is using three words interchangeably in these verses to mean premortal spirits. They are "intelligence," "spirit," and "soul." We will quote from the *Pearl of Great Price Student Manual* on this subject (**bold** added for emphasis):

"Abraham learned that there are varying degrees of intelligence among Heavenly Father's spirit children. (**Abraham called the spirit children of our Heavenly Father 'spirits'** in Abraham 3:18–19, **'intelligences'** in verse 22, and **'souls'** in verse 23.) He learned that God dwelled in the midst of all the spirits or intelligences and that God 'is more intelligent than they all' (v. 19)" (*Pearl of Great Price Student Manual,* page 37).

In other words, here in these verses we are taught about spirit children of the Father during our premortal existence. In many gospel discussions in our day, we differentiate between these three words as follows:

1. Intelligence: what we were before we were born to our Heavenly Parents as spirit children. This intelligence is eternal. It had no beginning. Joseph Smith taught this. He said (**bold** added for emphasis):

"I am dwelling on the immortality of the spirit of man. Is it logical to say that the intelligence of spirits is immortal, and yet that it has a beginning? **The intelligence of spirits had no beginning**, neither will it have an end. That is good logic" (*History of the Church,* Vol. 6, page 311).

Joseph Fielding Smith taught (**bold** added for emphasis):

"Some of our writers have endeavored to explain what an intelligence is, but to do so is futile, for we have never been given any insight into this matter beyond what the Lord has fragmentarily revealed. We know, however, that **there is something called intelligence, which always existed. It is the real eternal part of man**, which was not created or made. **This intelligence combined with the spirit constitutes a spiritual** identity or **individual**.

"**The spirit of man, then, is a combination of the intelligence and the spirit,** which is an entity begotten of God" (*Progress of Man,* page 11).

2.   **Spirit:** We were born to our Heavenly Parents as spirit sons and daughters. At that point, our intelligence was clothed in a spirit body. We became spirit beings. It is these spirits about which Abraham is teaching us. The spirit matter (D&C 131:7–8) from which our spirit bodies are created is eternal, but we began our life as spirits when we were born to our Heavenly Parents.

3.   **Soul:** Technically speaking, in our modern gospel vocabulary, "soul" means the spirit and body combined (see D&C 88:15).

The Lord continues the lesson that God is more intelligent than all. If we did not understand and believe this, we would not be able to worship and obey Him with full faith. This is a vital lesson and reinforcement for Abraham, who came from a culture in which idol worshippers believed in gods who warred among themselves, sometimes winning and sometimes losing. Against this background of false gods and idol worship, the Savior bears witness to Abraham that He does have all power and all intelligence. As we continue, we will see the words "intelligences" and "souls" both used to mean premortal spirits.

21 **I dwell in the midst of them all**; I now, therefore, have come down unto thee to declare [*teach, explain, show*] unto thee the works which my hands have made, wherein **my wisdom excelleth them all**, for **I rule in the heavens above, and in the earth beneath, in all wisdom and prudence, over all the intelligences** [*spirits—see verse 23*] thine eyes have seen from the beginning; I came down in the beginning in the midst of all the **intelligences** thou hast seen.

22 Now the Lord had shown unto me, Abraham, the **intelligences** [*spirits—see verse 23*] that were organized before the world was; and among all these there were many of the **noble and great ones;**

We know from modern revelation that many of these "noble and great ones" have been reserved to come to earth in the last days. They are a major reason that the Church will not go into apostasy again, as has been the case with each preceding dispensation. In the October 1989 general conference of the Church, Elder Marvin J. Ashton quoted President Ezra Taft Benson on this subject as follows (**bold** added for emphasis):

"I share with you a statement of President Benson made to a gathering of youth in Southern California after he became President of the Church: '**For nearly six thousand years, God has held you in reserve to make your appearance in the final days before the Second Coming**. Every previous gospel dispensation has drifted into apostasy, but ours will not. . . . **God has saved for the final inning some of his strongest children, who will help bear off the kingdom triumphantly**. And that is where you come in, for you are the generation that must be prepared to meet your God. . . . Make no mistake about it—you are a marked generation. There has never been more expected of the faithful in such a short period of time as there is of us. . . . Each day we personally make many decisions that show where our support will go. The final outcome is certain—the forces of righteousness will finally win. What remains to be seen is where each of us personally, now and in the future, will stand in this fight—and how tall we will stand. Will we be true to our last-days, foreordained mission?'" (Marvin J. Ashton, "'Stalwart and Brave We Stand,'" *Ensign,* November 1989, pp. 36–37).

23 And God saw these **souls** [*spirits*] that they were good, and he stood in the midst of them, and he said: **These I will make my rulers**; for **he stood among those that were spirits**, and he saw that they were good; and he said unto me: **Abraham, thou art one of them; thou wast chosen before thou wast born** [*Abraham was foreordained to be a prophet while yet a spirit in premortality*].

We understand from verse 24, next, in combination with verses 22–23, above, that many of the "noble and great" assisted with the creation of the earth. Joseph Fielding Smith taught:

"It is true that Adam helped to form this earth. He labored with our Savior Jesus Christ. I have a strong view or conviction that there were others also who assisted them. Perhaps Noah and Enoch; and why not Joseph Smith, and those who were appointed to be rulers before the earth was formed?" (*Doctrines of Salvation,* Vol. 1, pp. 74–75).

Note the use of the word "we" in verse 24, next, implying that many of the noble and great assisted the Savior in creating the world.

24 And **there stood one among them** [*the noble and great ones*] **that was like unto God** [*in other words, this was Jesus Christ*], and **he** [*Jesus*] **said unto those who were with him: We** will go down, for there is space there, and **we** will take of these materials, and **we** will make an earth whereon these may dwell;

> Students sometimes ask why the first part of verse 24, above, doesn't just come right out and say "Jehovah" or "Jesus," instead of saying "one . . . like unto God." We see similar wording in other places in scripture. One example is found in 1 Nephi 1:8, wherein Nephi writes that his father "thought he saw God," rather than simply saying, "he saw God." Daniel 3:25 says that the king saw a fourth person in the fiery furnace with Shadrach, Meshach, and Abednego who was "like the Son of God," rather than saying he saw a fourth person, and it was Jesus. Yet another example is Revelation 1:13, where

the Savior is standing in the midst of the seven candlesticks. The reference to Him, though, is indirect. It is "one like unto the Son of man." You will see another example in verse 27, near the end of this chapter.

What you are seeing here is the Old Testament custom of being careful not to use the name of God inappropriately. Rather than risk taking the name of God in vain, writers often referred to Him indirectly. Abraham is part of this culture of extreme care when using the name of God. Thus, we see the careful, indirect form of referring to Deity here in the Pearl of Great Price. Our world would be much different if such care existed today as part of our culture.

As mentioned in the introduction to this chapter, verse 25, next, contains an important doctrine. It is a revealed truth that lays to rest many false conclusions reached while discussing the foreknowledge of God and the agency of man. It states, simply and concisely, that we have been sent here to earth to be tested.

25 **And we** [*the Gods*] **will prove** [*test*] **them** [*the premortal spirits being sent to earth*] **herewith** [*by creating an earth and sending them to it*]**, to see if they will do all things whatsoever the Lord their**

God shall command them;

Many times over my years of teaching, students have come to class quite concerned that their agency here on earth is, in the eternal realities, of little or no consequence. For example, a student came to class on a Monday still somewhat shaken from a discussion in his Sunday School class the previous day. The topic of God's knowledge of the future had come up, and the conclusion of the class was that because God knows all things, past, present, and future, He could tell us all, right now, what our lot will be on the final Day of Judgment. All we are doing here is proving to ourselves that God is right about us.

This was obviously disturbing to the young man because it made it sound as if what he does in this life really doesn't count. I told him that I don't understand all there is to know about God's foreknowledge and our use of agency. However, I know where the final answer is found that addresses this dilemma. It is in Abraham 3:25. We read it together in class, and he was relieved.

This is one of those cases in which the Lord has given us the final answer to the question without giving us all the information leading up to the answer. Perhaps we couldn't understand it all. But the answer is vital. It is that we are indeed determining our future by the agency choices we make here on earth, provided we have a knowledge and understanding of the gospel of Jesus Christ.

Next, we are taught about the "first estate" and the "second estate." The term "first estate" is used in Jude 1:6, in the New Testament. We will define these gospel terms:

First Estate

Our premortal life as spirits. The phrase "keep their first estate" means to earn the right to be born on earth and receive a physical body. Thus, those who didn't keep their first estate are Satan and the one-third who were cast out with him.

Second Estate

Our life on earth. Those who do not have a fair chance to hear and understand the gospel here on earth will get the opportunity in the postmortal spirit world. Those who "keep their second estate" are those who keep God's commandments and thus qualify to return to the presence of the Father and become like Him.

Remember that the scene Abraham is showing us here is taking place during our premortal life, where preparations are being made to create our earth and send the spirits to earth who have qualified for that next step in their progression.

26 And **they who keep their first estate shall be added upon** [*the premortal spirits who are worthy will be allowed to continue their progression by going to earth to gain a physical body, gain knowledge and experience, and be tested*]; and **they who keep not their first estate** [*the spirits who joined Lucifer and rebelled against God*] shall not have glory in the same kingdom with those who keep their first estate [*including the fact that they will not attain telestial, terrestrial, or celestial glory; rather, they will go with Satan to perdition (outer darkness) after things finish up on earth—see D&C 76:31–48; 88:114*]; and **they who keep their second estate** [*live the gospel on earth or in the spirit world if they didn't get a fair chance on earth*] **shall have glory added upon their heads for ever and ever** [*will attain exaltation*].

In verses 27–28, next, we are given a brief look at the choosing of Jesus Christ to be our Savior and also the rebellion of Lucifer. Additional information can be found in Moses 4:1–4.

27 And **the Lord** [*the Father*] **said: Whom shall I send? And one answered like unto the Son of Man** [*in other words, Jesus Christ—see note after verse 24, above*]: **Here am I, send me. And another** [*Lucifer*] **answered and said: Here am I, send me. And the Lord said: I will send the first** [*Christ*].

28 And **the second** [*Lucifer*] **was angry**, and **kept not his first estate** [*did not remain worthy to come to earth and gain a body*]; and, at that day, **many** [*one-third—see Revelation 12:4*] **followed after him.**

ABRAHAM, CHAPTER 4

Background

Abraham chapters 4 and 5 are accounts of the Creation. There are four major accounts of the Creation available to us. They are:

1. Genesis 1–2.

2. Moses 2–3.

3. Abraham 4–5

4. The account given in the temple.

By looking ahead to Abraham 5:3–4, we are given to understand that Abraham's account of the Creation, up to those verses (in other words, from 4:1–31 through 5:1–2), was primarily an account of the planning stages prior to the actual creation of the earth. This is reflected in the heading to chapter 4 in the Pearl of Great Price, which reads, *"The Gods plan the creation of the earth and all life thereon—Their plans for the six days of creation are set forth."* Therefore, we can easily refer to chapter 4 as a blueprint for the creation of our earth.

If we fail to understand this, we will become confused when we get to chapter 5 and begin reading about the actual Creation. We will likely say, "Wait a minute, I just read that. What's going on here?"

We need to be a bit careful, however, not to consider Abraham 4:1–31 through 5:1–2 to be exclusively a blueprint of creation, since it appears that, occasionally, Abraham refers to the planning and then jumps ahead and says, in effect, "This is what they actually did." It is quite common in ancient writings for the authors not to limit themselves to exact chronological order. Both Isaiah and Revelation are examples of scriptures that do not adhere to strict chronology.

This chapter is a continuation of Abraham 3:22–28, in which plans were being made to create our earth and send us to it. One of the unique contributions of Abraham is the fact that he uses the term "Gods," rather than the singular, "God," in his account. Elder Mark E. Petersen commented on this as follows:

"The account of creation as given in the Book of Abraham is distinctive in that it says that great work was done by 'the Gods' in contrast to the belief that one God—one Almighty Being—made all things by himself, and out of nothing. There was a plurality of Gods engaged in creation. This fact is well corroborated in the Bible, including some passages in Genesis. . . .

"Who were these Gods?

"We believe in a Godhead of Father, Son, and Holy Ghost. Who else would have participated in the Creation?" (*Abraham, Friend of God,* pp. 144–45).

Joseph Fielding Smith taught:

"It is true that Adam helped to form this earth. He labored with our Savior Jesus Christ. I have a strong view or conviction that there were others also who assisted them. Perhaps Noah and Enoch; and why not Joseph Smith, and those who were appointed to be rulers before the earth was formed? We know that Jesus our Savior was a Spirit when this great work was done. He did all of these mighty works before he tabernacled in the flesh" (*Doctrines of Salvation,* Vol. 1:74–75).

We will now proceed with our verse-by-verse study.

1 And then the Lord said: Let us go down. And they went down at the beginning [*of the creation of our earth*], and they, that is **the Gods, organized and formed the heavens** [*the sky, our solar system, and so forth*] **and the earth**.

2 And the earth, after it was formed, was **empty and desolate** [*other accounts say "without form and void"*], because they had not formed anything but the earth; and darkness reigned upon the face of the deep, and the Spirit of the Gods was **brooding** [*what a mother hen does when watching over her eggs and chicks*] upon the face of the waters.

3 And **they (the Gods)** said: Let there be light; and there was light.

4 And **they (the Gods)** comprehended the light, for it was bright; and they divided the light, or caused it to be divided, from the darkness.

5 And **the Gods** called the light **Day**, and the darkness they called **Night**. And it came to pass that from the evening until morning they called night; and from the morning until the evening they called day; and this was the first, or the beginning, of that which they called day and night.

6 And **the Gods** also said: Let there be an expanse [*atmosphere—see Bible Dictionary, under "Firmament"*] in the midst of the waters [*between the earth and the heavens*], and it shall divide the waters [*on earth*] from the waters [*clouds in the sky*].

7 And **the Gods** ordered [*organized, created*] the expanse, so that it divided the waters which were under the expanse from the waters which were above the expanse; and it was so, even as they ordered.

Another unique contribution of Abraham's account of the Creation is that he refers to each "day" of creation as a "time." This leaves it open as to how long each creative period was. In the Gospel Doctrine manual for Old Testament classes, we read:

"The length of time required for the Creation is not known" (*Old Testament Gospel Doctrine Teacher's Manual,* page 11).

Speaking of the "six days" required for creating the earth, President Brigham Young said that it "is a mere term, but it matters not whether it took six days, six months, six years, or six thousand years. The Creation occupied certain periods of time. **We are not authorized to say what the duration** of these days was (**bold** added for emphasis), whether Moses penned these words as we have them, or whether the translators of the Bible have given the words their intended meaning. However, God created the world. God brought forth material out of which he formed this little terra firma upon which we roam. How long had this material been in existence? Forever and forever, in some shape, in some condition" (*Discourses of Brigham Young,* page 100).

Furthermore, Elder Bruce R. McConkie taught that a day, as used in the creation accounts, "is a specified time period; it is an age, an eon, a division of eternity; it is the time between two identifiable events. And each day, of whatever length, has the duration needed for its purposes. . . . There is no revealed recitation specifying that each of the 'six days' involved in the Creation was of the same duration" ("Christ and the Creation," *Ensign,* June 1982, page 11).

We see this use of the word "time" at the end of verse 8, next. We will also see it in verses 13, 19, 23, 31, and in chapter 5, verse 2. We will denote these with **bold** as we go along.

8 And **the Gods** called the expanse, Heaven. And it came to pass that it was from evening until morning that they called night; and it came to pass that it was from morning until evening that they called day; and this was **the second time** that they called night and day.

Next, the water on the earth is separated from the land, and the dry land is organized, preparatory to placing the earth's ecosystem upon it. As you can see, they planned for one ocean and one continent, initially. Later, in the days of Peleg (Genesis 10:25), the continent and ocean will be broken up into several of each.

9 And **the Gods** ordered, saying: **Let the waters under the heaven be gathered together unto one place,** and **let the earth come up dry**; and it was so as they ordered;

10 And **the Gods** pronounced the dry land, Earth; and the gathering together of the waters, pronounced they, Great Waters; and **the Gods saw that they were obeyed.**

The last phrase of verse 9 is interesting. We see a similar thing in verses 12, 18, and 25. It seems that the organization of elements to form the earth was not instantaneous; rather, it took some time for the elements to organize as commanded.

Next, the ecosystem for the "dry land" is planned. The wording here in verses 11 and 12 is important. You will see that Abraham places an emphasis on each plant's reproducing after its "own" kind. The emphasis is especially strong in verse 12, where he says, "Whose seed could only bring forth the same in itself, after his kind." This tends to discredit theories in which God's creations evolve from one major species to another.

11 And **the Gods said: Let us prepare** [*implies that this is the planning stage of creation*] the earth to bring forth grass; the herb yielding seed; the fruit tree yielding fruit, **after his kind, whose seed in itself yieldeth its own likeness** upon the earth; and **it was so** [*it took place just as the Gods had planned it*], **even as they ordered** [*just as they had planned*].

12 And the Gods organized the earth to bring forth **grass from its own seed**, and **the herb to bring forth herb from its own seed**, yielding **seed after his kind**; and the earth to bring forth the tree **from its own seed**, yielding fruit, **whose seed could only bring forth the same in itself, after his kind**; and the Gods saw that they were obeyed.

13 And it came to pass that they numbered the days; from the evening until the morning they called night; and it came to pass, from the morning until the evening they called day; and it was **the third time**.

Next, we see the plan for creating the sun, moon, and stars. Abraham tells us that these will be used for navigation, calendaring, and so forth.

14 And the Gods organized the lights in the expanse of the heaven [*the sky*], and caused them to divide the day from the night; and **organized them to be for signs and for seasons, and for days and for years**;

15 And organized them to be for lights in the expanse of the heaven to give light upon the earth; and it was so.

16 And the Gods organized the two great lights, **the greater light** [*the sun*] to rule the day, and **the lesser light** [*the moon*] to rule the night; with the lesser light they set **the stars** also;

17 And the Gods set them in the expanse of the heavens [*the sky*], to give light upon the earth, and to rule over the day and over the night, and to cause to divide the light from the darkness.

As stated previously, verse 18 is one of Abraham's unique contributions to the story of the Creation. His statement here almost brings a grin to our faces.

18 **And the Gods watched those things which they had ordered until they obeyed.**

19 And it came to pass that it was from evening until morning that it was night; and it came to pass that it was from morning until evening that it was day; and it was **the fourth time**.

20 And the Gods said: **Let us prepare** [*the planning phase continued*] the waters to bring forth abundantly the moving creatures that have life; and the fowl, that they may fly above the earth in the open expanse of heaven [*the sky*].

21 And the Gods prepared the waters that they might bring forth great whales, and every living creature that moveth, which the waters were to bring forth abundantly **after their kind**; and every winged fowl **after their kind**. And the Gods saw that they **would be obeyed** [*in the future, when They implemented the plan*]**, and that their plan was good.**

22 And the Gods said: We will bless them, and cause them to be fruitful and multiply, and fill the waters in the seas or great waters; and cause the fowl to multiply in the earth.

23 And it came to pass that it was from evening until morning that they called night; and it came to pass that it was from morning until evening that they called day; and it was **the fifth time**.

24 And the Gods prepared the earth to bring forth the living creature **after his kind**, cattle and creeping things, and beasts of the earth **after their kind**; and it was so, as they had said [*planned*].

25 And the Gods organized the earth to bring forth the beasts after their kind, and cattle after their kind, and every thing that creepeth upon the earth after its kind; and **the Gods saw they would obey** [*when the plan was implemented*].

Next, plans are made to place Adam and Eve on the earth.

26 **And the Gods took counsel** [*planned*] **among themselves** and said: Let us go down and form man in our image, after our likeness; and we will give them dominion over the fish of the sea, and over the fowl of the air, and over the cattle, and over all the earth, and over every creeping thing that creepeth upon the earth.

It appears that in verse 27, next, Abraham is telling us that the plans made by the Gods were eventually carried out as discussed by Them.

27 **So the Gods went down to organize man** in their own image, in the image of the Gods to form

they him, male and female to form they them.

The wording in verses 28–31, next, indicates that Abraham is once again dealing with the planning, or blueprint, stage here.

28 And the Gods said: **We will bless** them. And the Gods said: **We will cause** them to be fruitful and multiply, and replenish [*"fill"— see Genesis 1:28, footnote c*] the earth, and subdue it, and to have dominion over the fish of the sea, and over the fowl of the air, and over every living thing that moveth upon the earth.

29 And the Gods said: Behold, **we will give** them every herb bearing seed **that shall come** upon the face of all the earth, and every tree **which shall have fruit** upon it; yea, the fruit of the tree yielding seed to them **we will give** it; it shall be for their meat [*food*].

30 And to every beast of the earth, and to every fowl of the air, and to every thing that creepeth upon the earth, behold, **we will give** them life, and also **we will give** to them every green herb for meat, and **all these things shall be thus organized** [*this will be the plan*].

31 And the Gods said: **We will do everything that we have said**, and organize them; and behold, **they shall be** very obedient. And it came to pass that it was from evening until morning they called night; and it came to pass that it was from morning until evening that they called day; and they numbered **the sixth time**.

ABRAHAM, CHAPTER 5

Background

As you can see from the heading to Abraham, chapter 5, in your Pearl of Great Price, the Gods will finish planning the Creation (verses 1–3) and then proceed to carry it out in this chapter. One of the unique contributions of Abraham to our knowledge about the Creation is the fact that it was done on "Kolob standard time" (see verse 13). Abraham was a trained astronomer, taught by the Lord (Abraham 3:1–17); thus, he noticed such things.

We will now proceed with our verse-by-verse study. Verses 1-3 show us that Abraham's account of the Creation in chapter 4 was primarily that of the planning stages before the actual Creation.

1 And **thus** [*according to the plan We have made*] **we** [*the Gods*] **will finish the heavens and the earth, and all the hosts of them.**

2 And **the Gods said among**

ABRAHAM 5

themselves: On **the seventh time we will end our work, which we have counseled** [*planned*]; and **we will rest** on the seventh time from all our work which we have counseled.

3 And the Gods concluded upon the seventh time, because that on the seventh time they would rest from all their works which they (the Gods) counseled among themselves to form [*organize, create*]; and sanctified it [*blessed it and made it holy*]. And **thus were their decisions at the time that they counseled among themselves to form the heavens and the earth.**

Next, the Gods will begin the actual physical creation of the earth, sky, solar system, and so forth. The word "generations," in verse 4, may imply that there was considerable time involved and that there were several series of events leading up to the final preparation of the earth for the placement of man upon it. We will learn more details about the Creation and have all of our questions answered at the beginning of the Millennium, according to the Doctrine and Covenants. We read:

D&C 101:32–34

32 Yea, verily I say unto you, in that day when the Lord shall come, he shall reveal all things—

33 Things which have passed, and hidden things which no man knew, **things of the earth, by which it was made**, and the purpose and the end thereof—

34 Things most precious, things that are above, and things that are beneath, things that are in the earth, and upon the earth, and in heaven.

4 And **the Gods came down and formed these the generations of the heavens and of the earth**, when they were formed in the day that **the Gods formed the earth and the heavens,**

We are reminded in verse 5, next, that all things were created in spirit form before being placed on earth as physical creations. We will point this out with one of the phrases in verse 5.

5 **According to all that which they had said** [*according to their plan*] concerning every **plant of the field** before it was in the earth, and every herb of the field before it grew [*all things were created in spirit form, long before the earth was created physically*]; **for the Gods had not caused it to rain upon the earth when they counseled to do them**, and had not formed a man to till the ground.

6 But there went up a mist from the earth, and watered the whole face of the ground.

We find another one of Abraham's important contributions to our understanding of the Creation in verse 7. Genesis 2:7 and Moses 3:7 say that God "breathed into his [*Adam's*] nostrils the breath of life." Abraham says this also but explains this phrase by saying "took his spirit and put it into him."

7 And the Gods formed man from the dust of the ground [*formed his physical body from the elements of the earth*], **and took his spirit** (that is, the man's spirit), **and put it into him**; and breathed into his nostrils the breath of life, and man became a living soul.

8 And the Gods planted a garden, eastward in Eden, and **there they put the man**, whose spirit they had put into the body which they had formed.

In verse 9, next, we see that the tree of knowledge of good and evil, of which Adam and Eve had been commanded not to partake, was placed in the midst of the garden, in plain sight rather than in an obscure corner of Eden. So, likewise, was the tree of life placed in plain sight.

9 And out of the ground made the Gods to grow every tree that is pleasant to the sight and good for food; the tree of life, also, **in the midst of the garden,** and the tree of knowledge of good and evil.

Elder Bruce R. McConkie explained the symbolic meaning of the two trees mentioned in verse 9, above. He said:

"The scriptures set forth that there were in the Garden of Eden two trees. One was **the tree of life**, which figuratively refers to eternal life; the other was **the tree of knowledge of good and evil**, which figuratively refers to how and why and in what manner mortality and all that appertains to it came into being" (*A New Witness for the Articles of Faith,* page 86).

With this in mind, one possible message for us, in verse 9, is that the Fall of Adam and Eve was absolutely essential in order for us to have eternal life (exaltation) available to us. Another possible message is that agency choices between good and evil are essential for gaining eternal life.

Next, Abraham gives a bit more detail about Eden and then tells us about Adam in the Garden of Eden.

10 There was a river running out of Eden, to water the garden, and from thence it was parted and became into four heads.

11 And **the Gods took the man and put him in the Garden of Eden,** to dress it and to keep it [*to take care of it*].

> Next, Adam is commanded not to partake of the tree of knowledge of good and evil. For more on this, see the notes following Moses 3:17, in this study guide.

12 And **the Gods commanded** the man, saying: **Of every tree of the garden thou mayest freely eat,**

13 **But of the tree of knowledge of good and evil, thou shalt not eat of it;** for in the time that thou eatest thereof, thou shalt surely die. **Now I, Abraham, saw that it was after the Lord's time, which was after the time of Kolob; for as yet the Gods had not appointed unto Adam his reckoning** [*the earth's time system*].

> Based on Abraham's comment in the last half of verse 13, above, we understand that the earth was created in the presence of God and was still on the time system used by Kolob and the planet on which the Father resides. When Adam and Eve "fell," the earth "fell" with them and was brought to its current area of space and placed in this solar system. President Brigham Young explained a bit more about this. He said (**bold** used for emphasis):

"This earth is our home, it was framed expressly for the habitation of those who are faithful to God, and who prove themselves worthy to inherit the earth when the Lord shall have sanctified, purified and glorified it and brought it back into his presence, **from which it fell far into space**. Ask the astronomer how far we are from the nearest of those heavenly bodies that are called the fixed stars. Can he count the miles? It would be a task for him to tell us the distance. **When the earth was framed and brought into existence and man was placed upon it, it was near the throne of our Father in heaven**. And when man fell—though that was designed in the economy, there was nothing about it mysterious or unknown to the Gods, they understood it all, it was all planned—but **when man fell, the earth fell into space, and took up its abode in this planetary system, and the sun became our light**. When the Lord said—"Let there be light," there was light, for the earth was brought near the sun that it might reflect upon it so as to give us light by day, and the moon to give us light by night. This is the glory the earth came from, and **when it is glorified it will return again unto the presence of the Father**, and it will dwell there, and these intelligent beings that I am looking at, if they live worthy of it, will dwell upon this earth" (*Journal of Discourses,* Vol. 7, p. 143).

Joseph Smith taught that this earth will be taken back to where it came from. He said:

"This earth will be rolled back into the presence of God, and crowned with celestial glory" (*Teachings of the Prophet Joseph Smith,* page 181).

Having learned that our earth will be returned to the presence of God—as the celestial kingdom for the worthy who lived on it as mortals (see D&C 130:9–11)—we will take a moment and answer another question that sometimes arises. The question is whether other earths also become celestial planets for their worthy residents and are likewise moved through space into the presence of God. Orson Pratt tells us that the answer is yes. He said (**bold** added for emphasis):

"Inquires one—**'Do you mean to say that other worlds have fallen as well as ours?' Yes**, man is an agent; intelligence cannot exist on any other principle. All beings having intelligence must have their agency. Laws must be given, suited and adapted to this agency; and **when God sends inhabitants on various creations he sends them on the great and grand principle of giving them an opportunity to exercise that agency; and they have exercised it, and have fallen. . . . By and by, when each of these creations has fulfilled the measure and bounds set and the times given for this continuance in a temporal state, it and its inhabitants who are worthy will be made celestial and glorified together . . . they will all be in his presence** (in *Journal of Discourses,* Vol. 17, pp. 332–33; the *Doctrine and Covenants Student Manual,* page 201, gives part of this quote from Elder Pratt).

Next, Abraham teaches us about the creation of Eve. Much ancient cultural symbolism is used to present emotion and feeling with the account.

First, though, we must look at the words "help meet" in verse 14. Many mistakenly read these words as one word, "helpmeet," which implies lesser status for Eve than for Adam. This is not true. The word "meet," as used in this type of context in the scriptures (such as D&C 58:26) means "essential, necessary, vital." Thus, Eve is a vital help for Adam, just as Adam is an essential help for Eve. Neither can attain exaltation and become a god without the other (D&C 131:1–4; 132:20).

14 And the Gods said: **Let us make an help meet for the man**, for **it is not good that the man should be alone**, therefore we will form an help meet for him.

15 **And the Gods caused a deep sleep to fall upon Adam**; and he slept**, and they took one of his ribs,** and closed up the flesh in the stead thereof;

16 **And of the rib which the Gods had taken from man, formed they a woman**, and brought her unto the man.

> President Spencer W. Kimball taught that the Gods did not literally take a rib from Adam and make Eve; rather, the account is symbolical. He said:
>
> "The story of the rib, of course, is figurative" ("The Blessings and Responsibilities of Womanhood," Ensign, March 1976, page 71).
>
> We will read the next two verses and then say a bit more about the symbolism here.

17 And Adam said: **This was bone of my bones, and flesh of my flesh** [*we belong to each other, we are family*]; now she shall be called Woman, because she was taken out of man;

18 **Therefore shall a man leave his father and his mother, and shall cleave unto his wife, and they shall be one flesh**.

> Students often wonder why the account of the "rib" given here sounds so literal if it is just symbolic. Why the details about the "surgery," including putting Adam to sleep and closing up the flesh in place of the rib?
>
> The answer has to do with differences in cultures. Many Westerners are also "literalists." That is, they want the plain facts and don't want them embellished. Most Easterners, meaning people from cultures in the Middle East, tell a story with symbolism that provides the essential facts accompanied by words denoting feeling and emotion. In the case of the creation of Eve, we see descriptive words that provide emotion and tenderness, protectiveness and warmth, belonging and teamwork, unity and purpose, all carefully and tenderly crafted by the Gods, who attend to this union with personal focus. One can feel the caring of the Gods as they introduce Adam and Eve to each other, the culmination of Their creative endeavors, and the final step in carrying out their blueprint of creation.
>
> Some of my male students, thinking that this account of taking

a rib from Adam and creating Eve was literal, have actually counted their ribs on both sides, thinking that they would find one less rib on the one side than on the other.

Next, we are informed that Adam and Eve are innocent, as far as modesty is concerned.

19 And they were both naked, the man and his wife, **and were not ashamed** [*embarrassed*].

Abraham now finishes his account of the Creation with a review of the things that had been done by the Gods in preparation for placing Adam and Eve on the earth. Then he tells us that Adam was given the responsibility to name the living creatures.

Symbolically, this is a reminder that God delegates much to mortals for their growth and development.

20 And **out of the ground** [*the physical creation*] **the Gods formed every beast** of the field, and **every fowl** of the air, and **brought them unto Adam to see what he would call them**; and whatsoever Adam called every living creature, that should be the name thereof.

Abraham finishes with the most important thing of all. Adam now has his eternal companion, Eve; and Eve now has her eternal companion, Adam.

21 **And Adam gave names to all cattle, to the fowl of the air, to every beast of the field; and for Adam, there was found an help meet** [*vital*] **for him** [*Eve*].

The Facsimiles in the Book of Abraham

There is considerable debate among scholars as to the interpretation of these facsimiles. For our purposes here, we will avoid getting caught up in these debates and, instead, feel the witness of the Spirit to the work of the Lord's Prophet as he brought these precious parts of the Book of Abraham to light. As with the gold plates, from which the Book of Mormon was translated "by the gift and power of God" (D&C 135:3; *History of the Church* 4:537), so also the Egyptian papyri, from which Joseph Smith translated the Book of Abraham, were translated by the same gift.

Joseph Smith's explanations follow each facsimile. After each explanation, we will use some questions and observations to draw your attention to a few interesting details in the accompanying facsimile.

A FACSIMILE FROM THE BOOK OF ABRAHAM
No. 1

EXPLANATION

Fig. 1. The Angel of the Lord.
Fig. 2. Abraham fastened upon an altar.
Fig. 3. The idolatrous priest of Elkenah attempting to offer up Abraham as a sacrifice.
Fig. 4. The altar for sacrifice by the idolatrous priests, standing before the gods of Elkenah, Libnah, Mahmackrah, Korash, and Pharaoh.
Fig. 5. The idolatrous god of Elkenah.
Fig. 6. The idolatrous god of Libnah.
Fig. 7. The idolatrous god of Mahmackrah.
Fig. 8. The idolatrous god of Korash.
Fig. 9. The idolatrous god of Pharaoh.
Fig. 10. Abraham in Egypt.
Fig. 11. Designed to represent the pillars of heaven, as understood by the Egyptians.
Fig. 12. Raukeeyang, signifying expanse, or the firmament over our heads; but in this case, in relation to this subject, the Egyptians meant it to signify Shaumau, to be high, or the heavens, answering to the Hebrew word, Shaumahyeem.

Observations and Questions for Facsimile No. 1

1. One of the messages we might draw from this facsimile is that Abraham has put it all on the altar. His loyalty to God and his covenants with Him hold firm no matter what the circumstance.
2. Have you noticed that Abraham's eyes are on figure 1, the Angel of the Lord? According to Abraham 1:15–16, the angel represented Jehovah (the premortal Christ) who came down to deliver Abraham from death.
3. Note that Abraham's legs are apart, which would represent that he is still alive. Also, his right foot is forward, which would signify that he is stepping through the veil and entering the presence of God.
4. It is possible that the clothing depicted on Abraham might represent garments?
5. Have you noticed the crocodile lurking beneath the altar? As you can see from the explanation of figure 9, it represents the god of Pharaoh. It was known as Sobek, the water god, in ancient Egypt. It reminds us that the false religion of Pharaoh in far away Egypt was dominant in Abraham's home country. Abraham 1:7 informs us that figure 3, the priest of Elkenah, "was also the priest of Pharaoh." The worship of crocodiles was common in Egypt.
6. Later in his life, when Abraham is commanded to sacrifice Isaac (Genesis 22), he will no doubt relate even more to what it means to be placed on an altar to be sacrificed because of what he went through here. It appears in this facsimile that the knife in the hand of the priest of Elkenah was on its way down to Abraham when he was rescued by the Lord. In other words, Abraham was rescued at the last moment. So also was the case with Abraham and Isaac. The sacrifice of Isaac was stopped at the last moment (Genesis 22:10–12).
7. Have you noticed that the lotus flower representing Abraham in Egypt, figure 10, also appears in Facsimile No. 3? The lotus flower played a prominent role in ancient Egypt. The pure white lotus flower bore fruit and flowers simultaneously.

A FACSIMILE FROM THE BOOK OF ABRAHAM
No. 2

EXPLANATION

Fig. 1. Kolob, signifying the first creation, nearest to the celestial, or the residence of God. First in government, the last pertaining to the measurement of time. The measurement according to celestial time, which celestial time signifies one day to a cubit. One day in Kolob is equal to a thousand years according to the measurement of this earth, which is called by the Egyptians Jah-oh-eh.

Fig. 2. Stands next to Kolob, called by the Egyptians Oliblish, which is the next grand governing creation near to the celestial or the place where God resides; holding the key of power also, pertaining to other planets; as revealed from God to Abraham, as he offered sacrifice upon an altar, which he had built unto the Lord.

Fig. 3. Is made to represent God, sitting upon his throne, clothed with power and authority; with a crown of eternal light upon his head; representing also the grand Key-words of the Holy Priesthood, as revealed to Adam in the Garden of Eden, as also to Seth, Noah, Melchizedek, Abraham, and all to whom the Priesthood was revealed.

Fig. 4. Answers to the Hebrew word Raukeeyang, signifying expanse, or the firmament of the heavens; also a numerical figure, in Egyptian signifying one thousand; answering to the measuring of the time of Oliblish, which is equal with Kolob in its revolution and in its measuring of time.

Fig. 5. Is called in Egyptian Enish-go-on-dosh; this is one of the governing planets also, and is said by the Egyptians to be the Sun, and to borrow its light from Kolob through the medium of Kae-e-vanrash, which is the grand Key, or, in other words, the governing power, which governs fifteen other fixed planets or stars, as also Floeese or the Moon, the Earth and the Sun in their annual revolutions. This planet receives its power through the medium of Kli-flos-is-es, or Hah-ko-kau-beam, the stars represented by numbers 22 and 23, receiving light from the revolutions of Kolob.

Fig. 6. Represents this earth in its four quarters.

Fig. 7. Represents God sitting upon his throne, revealing through the heavens the grand Key-words of the Priesthood; as, also, the sign of the Holy Ghost unto Abraham, in the form of a dove.

Fig. 8. Contains writings that cannot be revealed unto the world; but is to be had in the Holy Temple of God.

Fig. 9. Ought not to be revealed at the present time.

Fig. 10. Also.

Fig. 11. Also. If the world can find out these numbers, so let it be. Amen.

Figures 12, 13, 14, 15, 16, 17, 18, 19, 20, and 21, will be given in the own due time of the Lord.

The above translation is given as far as we have any right to give at the present time.

Observations and Questions for Facsimile No. 2

1. The type of drawing represented by Facsimile No. 2 is commonly referred to among Egyptian scholars as a hypocephalus. Such drawings were placed under the head of the dead and contained all the dead person needed to know in order to continue in the next life. In fact, it was believed by ancient Egyptians that a hypocephalus placed under the head of the dead would magically make the person divine. It is interesting to note that the ancient Egyptians believed strongly in life after death and that the mortal body would be needed again, in resurrected form, in order to continue the journey in the next life.
2. The student manual used by the Institutes of Religion of the Church for Pearl of Great Price has a helpful quote regarding figure 1 (in the center of the facsimile): "The center of facsimile 2 contains a representation of Kolob. In his explanation for figure 1, the Prophet Joseph Smith said that Kolob is 'first in government, the last pertaining to the measurement of time.' This means that Kolob is the star nearest to the presence of God (see Abraham 3:2–3), is the governing star in all the universe (see v. 3), and that time passes more slowly on Kolob than on any other star in this order (see v. 4). Kolob is also symbolic of Jesus Christ, the central figure in God's plan of salvation" (*Pearl of Great Price Student Manual*, p. 39).
3. Occasionally we hear it said that Heavenly Father lives on Kolob. The explanation of fig. 1, given above, teaches the correct doctrine that Kolob is nearest to the celestial planet (D&C 130:6–11) upon which He lives.
4. Have you noticed the two-headed god in figure 2? The two faces can represent the fact that God sees all.
5. Did you notice the crown of eternal light depicted above God's head in figure 3? (It is mentioned in the explanation for this figure.) It can be a reminder that light and truth emanate to us from God.
6. The boats depicted in figures 3 and 4 can represent the fact that after we die there is yet progress to be made. In other words, we can continue progressing to exaltation, to become gods.
7. Since, in Abraham 3, the Lord compared the stars and planets to the noble and great spirits, the stars discussed in the explanation to figure 5 can easily likewise symbolize the noble and great about whom God

said, "These I will make my rulers" (Abraham 3:23). In the ultimate sense, "rulers" can be symbolic of exaltation.
8. Have you noticed that many of the explanations about the order of governing planets and so forth, given here and in Abraham 3, tie in with what the Savior taught in D&C 88:42–45? We may not be able to even come close to comprehending what is given in these revelations, but we can appreciate the knowledge that Abraham was given about astronomy through revelation and the basic knowledge about astronomy given us by the Savior through the Prophet Joseph Smith. Through the revelation in section 88, we understand that it is the power of God that holds the planets and stars in their proper orbits and thus keeps the universe operating in an orderly fashion. Remember that the day will come, if we continue faithful, when we will understand all these things and "comprehend even God" (D&C 88:49) as we become gods ourselves (D&C 132:20).
9. Did you notice that the explanation of figure 8 indicates that there are some things pertaining to exaltation that we must go to the temple to learn?
10. The *Pearl of Great Price Student Manual* contains a helpful quote for Figures 7 and 8: "Egyptologists suggest that hypocephali contain information to help deceased persons return to the presence of God. Similarly, the Lord has given Latter-day Saints divine help to return to His presence. President Brigham Young taught: 'Your [temple] endowment is, to receive all those ordinances in the house of the Lord, which are necessary for you, after you have departed this life, to enable you to walk back to the presence of the Father, passing the angels who stand as sentinels' (*Discourses of Brigham Young*, 416)" (*Pearl of Great Price Student Manual*, p. 40).

A FACSIMILE FROM THE BOOK OF ABRAHAM
No. 3

EXPLANATION

Fig. 1. Abraham sitting upon Pharaoh's throne, by the politeness of the king, with a crown upon his head, representing the Priesthood, as emblematical of the grand Presidency in Heaven; with the scepter of justice and judgment in his hand.

Fig. 2. King Pharaoh, whose name is given in the characters above his head.

Fig. 3. Signifies Abraham in Egypt as given also in Figure 10 of Facsimile No. 1.

Fig. 4. Prince of Pharaoh, King of Egypt, as written above the hand.

Fig. 5. Shulem, one of the king's principal waiters, as represented by the characters above his hand.

Fig. 6. Olimlah, a slave belonging to the prince.

Abraham is reasoning upon the principles of Astronomy, in the king's court.

Observations and Questions for Facsimile No. 3

1. Concerning Abraham's teaching astronomy to the Egyptians, Joseph Smith taught: "The learning of the Egyptians, and their knowledge of astronomy was no doubt taught them by Abraham and Joseph, as their records testify, who received it from the Lord" (*Teachings of the Prophet Joseph Smith*, p. 251).

2. Can you see the symbolism of exaltation in this facsimile? Consider the following:

    a. Pharaoh was considered by the Egyptians to be a god.

    b. Symbolically, in the facsimile, Abraham is sitting on the throne of God. He is exalted, that is, has become a god "by the politeness of the king," or, in other words, "by the grace of God" (1 Corinthians 15:10).

    c. Symbolically, we, too, can sit upon the throne of God, if we, through the Atonement of Jesus Christ, prove ourselves worthy of exaltation. This clear doctrine is taught by the Savior in Revelation 3:21: "To him that overcometh will I grant to sit with me in my throne, even as I also overcame, and am set down with my Father in his throne."

3. Is there perhaps significant symbolism when you put all three facsimiles together?

    a. In Facsimile No. 1, Abraham is willing to put everything on the altar in order to be loyal and obedient and keep his commitments to God.

    b. In Facsimile No. 2, we see that the gospel of Jesus Christ provides everything necessary for us to continue our journey successfully to exaltation in the presence of God.

c. In Facsimile No. 3, we see Abraham as an example of one who has successfully completed his journey to exaltation. In fact, we know through revelation that he has indeed attained exaltation.

"Abraham received all things, whatsoever he received, by revelation and commandment, by my word, saith the Lord, and hath entered into his exaltation and sitteth upon his throne." (D&C 132:29)

Joseph Smith—Matthew

AN EXTRACT FROM THE TRANSLATION OF THE BIBLE AS REVEALED TO JOSEPH SMITH THE PROPHET IN 1831: MATTHEW 23:39 AND CHAPTER 24.

Background

Joseph Smith—Matthew is the Prophet Joseph Smith's inspired translation of Matthew 24 in the Bible. It consists of additions to the King James Bible version of Matthew 23:39 and Matthew chapter 24. It is a direct result of his work of translating the Bible, now usually referred to as the "Joseph Smith Translation of the Bible" or the "JST." His main work on the JST spanned the time period from June 1830 to July 1833 although he continued to make revisions until his death on June 27, 1844.

The Prophet's work on translating the Bible resulted in many revelations from the Lord. One example is Doctrine and Covenants section 76, which is a revelation on the three degrees of glory and perdition. In this case, while working on the translation of the Bible, Joseph Smith and Sidney Rigdon came to John 5:29, which caused them to have a question about where people go after the resurrection of the dead. (See D&C 76:15.) While they were pondering the question, the revelation known now as section 76 was given.

Matthew 24 is a rather well-known chapter of the Bible, not only to Latter-day Saints but to Christians throughout the world. It deals with many of the signs of the times, prophecies that will be fulfilled in the last days before the Savior's Second Coming and that indicate that His coming is getting close.

The Prophet added about 450 words to Matthew 23:39 and chapter 24 in the Bible and rearranged the order of some of the verses. First, we will study this chapter of the Pearl of Great Price verse by verse, and then we will provide a parallel column comparison of Joseph Smith—Matthew and Matthew 24 from the King James Version of the Bible so that you can readily see the changes and additions made by Joseph Smith.

Joseph Smith—Matthew

At this point in the New Testament, it is still the third day of the last week of the Savior's mortal life (see *New Testament Student Manual, Religion 211*, pp. 136 and 150). The most common thinking is that this is Tuesday. He will be crucified on Friday. After His severe scolding of the hypocritical Jewish leaders in Matthew 23, Jesus speaks a few words to His disciples (Matthew 23:39) and then leaves the Jerusalem temple. He will not teach the public any more; rather, He will spend the rest of the last week of His mortal life teaching the Twelve. As they approach Him now for further instruction, they look back at the temple, and He begins teaching them many things that will occur before His Second Coming.

As mentioned in the background above, Matthew 24 is very well known among Christians because it contains so many prophecies that will be fulfilled before the Second Coming of Christ. These prophecies are known as "the signs of the times." Many of them are being fulfilled in our day and bear witness to us that the gospel is true and that the Second Coming is near. However, since we do not know how close it is, we should plan on living a full lifetime and keeping our lives in order, so that when we meet the Savior, whether at our death, or at His coming, we will be prepared.

Watch now as the Master prophesies about His departure from His mortal mission and His Second Coming.

1 FOR I say unto you, that ye shall not see me henceforth and know that I am he of whom it is written by the prophets, until ye shall say: Blessed is he who cometh in the name of the Lord, in the clouds of heaven, and all the holy angels with him [*the Second Coming will bear witness to all that Jesus Christ is indeed who He claimed to be during His mortal ministry*]. Then understood his disciples that he should come again on the earth [*the Second Coming*], after that he was glorified and crowned on the right hand of God.

2 And Jesus went out, and departed from the temple; and his disciples came to him, for to hear him, saying: Master, show us concerning the buildings of the temple, as thou hast said—They shall be thrown down, and left unto you desolate [*the disciples would like Him to give them more details about the coming destruction of the temple in Jerusalem*].

The Savior's prophecy that the buildings of the temple would be torn down was fulfilled by about AD 70 to 73 as the Romans finally conquered the Jews and destroyed many of their cities.

Next, it appears that the Savior scolds His disciples just a bit because of their apparent hesitancy to believe what He has already told them.

3 And Jesus said unto them: See ye not all these things, and do ye not understand them? Verily [*listen carefully*] I say unto you, there shall not be left here, upon this temple, one stone upon another that shall not be thrown down.

In verse 4, next, the disciples will ask the Savior two questions that will form the background for the rest of the chapter.

Question 1: When will the destruction of the Jerusalem Temple and the Jews take place? **Answer:** Verses 5–21 (through the first phrase of verse 21). These verses deal mainly with the years immediately following the crucifixion of Christ.

Question 2: What signs will precede the Second Coming and the destruction of the wicked? **Answer:** Verse 21 (except for the first phrase) through verse 55. These verses deal mainly with our day, the last days leading up to the coming of the Lord.

4 And Jesus left them, and went upon the Mount of Olives [*located just outside Jerusalem*]. And as he sat upon the Mount of Olives, the disciples came unto him privately, saying: [*question #1*] Tell us when shall these things be which thou hast said concerning the destruction of the temple, and the Jews; and [*question #2*] what is the sign of thy coming, and of the end of the world, or the destruction of the wicked, which is the end of the world?

Did you notice that the end of verse 4, above, gives a doctrinal definition of the meaning of the phrase "end of the world"? If you did not understand that the end of the world is the destruction of the wicked, you might end up thinking that the earth was going to be completely destroyed at that time, which would be false.

Beginning with verse 5, next, Jesus proceeds to answer the question about the destruction of the temple and the destruction and scattering of the Jews, as a nation, in the years and decades following the Lord's crucifixion.

You will see that many of the conditions that led to the destruction and scattering of the Jews in the days of the early Apostles after the Savior's crucifixion are quite similar to the conditions in our day, leading up to the Second Coming. Have you noticed that Satan's tactics for leading people away from God seem to be effective no matter what time period in the world's history?

5 And Jesus answered, and said unto them: Take heed that no man deceive you;

6 For many shall come in my name, saying—I am Christ—and shall deceive many [*we see that there were false christs among the Jews in these former days, whose false teachings helped lead them away from God and to their destruction*];

7 Then shall they deliver you [*the Apostles, disciples, and Jewish people*] up to be afflicted, and shall kill you, and ye shall be hated of all nations, for my name's sake;

Verses 8 and 9, next, are very concentrated summaries of social attitudes and conditions that result when people no longer adhere to the standards of the gospel of Jesus Christ.

8 And then shall many be offended [*can include "victim" mentality, lawsuits, self-centeredness, taking offense at gospel standards, God's commandments, and so forth*] and shall betray one another, and shall hate one another;

9 And many false prophets shall arise, and shall deceive many;

The reference to "false prophets" spoken of in verse 9, above, does not have to necessarily refer only to false religious teachers. It can include anyone who leads people away from God, such as philosophers, media stars, scientists who teach atheism, politicians who sponsor legislation that opposes God's laws and commandments, and so forth.

10 And because iniquity [*wickedness*] shall abound, the love of many shall wax cold;

Next, in verse 11, the Savior tells us how to survive spiritually during such times of intense wickedness.

11 But he that remaineth steadfast and is not overcome, the same shall be saved.

The Lord refers prophetically to the "abomination of desolation" two times in this chapter, once in verse 12, next, and again in verse 32. We will explain the phrase after verse 12.

12 When you, therefore, shall see the abomination of desolation, spoken of by Daniel the prophet [*Daniel 11:31 and 12:11*], concerning the destruction of Jerusalem, then you shall stand in the holy place; whoso readeth let him understand.

The phrase "abomination of desolation" means terrible things which will cause much destruction and misery. The "abomination that maketh desolate" spoken of by Daniel (Daniel 11:31, 12:11) was to have two fulfillments. The first occurred in AD 70 when Titus, with his Roman legions, surrounded Jerusalem and laid siege to conquer the Jews. This siege resulted in much destruction, terrible human misery, and loss of life. In the last days, the "abomination of desolation" will occur again (see Joseph Smith–Matthew 1:31–32), meaning that Jerusalem will again be under siege (see Bible Dictionary, under "Abomination of Desolation").

Verses 13–19 describe conditions in the early Church that came after the Crucifixion and give counsel on how to escape the Roman conquerors and coming devastations.

13 Then let them who are in Judea flee into the mountains [*Many faithful saints heeded this warning and fled to Pella, east of Samaria, and thus escaped the Romans.*];

14 Let him who is on the housetop flee, and not return to take anything out of his house;

15 Neither let him who is in the field return back to take his clothes;

16 And wo unto them that are with child, and unto them that give suck in those days;

17 Therefore, pray ye the Lord that your flight be not in the winter, neither on the Sabbath day [*when city gates are closed, making rapid escape impossible*];

18 For then, in those days, shall be great tribulation on the Jews, and upon the inhabitants of Jerusalem, such as was not before sent upon Israel, of God, since the beginning of their kingdom until this time; no, nor ever shall be sent again upon Israel.

19 All things which have befallen them are only the beginning of the sorrows which shall come upon them.

20 And except those days should be shortened, there should none of their flesh be saved; but for the elect's sake, according to the covenant, those days shall be shortened [*the Lord will hold the devastations and destructions back such that some Jews will survive*].

As mentioned previously, the first phrase of verse 21, next, indicates that the above verses deal mainly with conditions among the Jews in the decades following the Crucifixion. The rest of the verse deals primarily with our day and indicates that the rest of this chapter prophesies of conditions and events in the last days leading up to the Second Coming of Christ. These are often referred to as "signs of the times."

21 Behold, these things I have spoken unto you concerning the Jews; and again, after the tribulation of those days which shall come upon Jerusalem, if any man shall say unto you, Lo, here is Christ, or there, believe him not;

> As indicated in verse 22, next, the devil will use false christs and false prophets very effectively in the last days, just as he did in past dispensations. As mentioned previously, these include anyone whose influence and teachings tend to lead individuals and nations away from the true God.

22 For in those days [*the last days*] there shall also arise false Christs, and false prophets, and shall show great signs and wonders, insomuch, that, if possible, they shall deceive the very elect, who are the elect according to the covenant [*indicating, among other things, that Satan's deceptions and counterfeits in the last days will be so cunningly devised as to lead even some endowed, faithful, and strong Latter-day Saints astray, if they are not careful to maintain their testimonies*].

> Next, in verse 23, Jesus counsels us not to get caught up in panic, gloom, and doom, and so forth, as we see the signs of the times being fulfilled all around us in the last days.

23 Behold, I speak these things unto you for the elect's sake; and you also shall hear of wars, and rumors of wars; see that ye be not troubled, for all I have told you must come to pass; but the end is not yet.

> Did you catch the phrase in verse 23, above, that teaches us to use the fulfillment of prophecies in the last days to strengthen our testimonies, rather than to promote fear and gloom? It is "see that ye be not troubled" plus what follows it.

> In verses 24–25, next, the Lord warns, among other things, against deceivers who claim that Christ has already come, who give the exact timing of His coming, or who claim to know things about the Savior's coming that the Brethren either don't know or are reluctant to tell us. Sometimes such individuals are referred to as "gatherers." They attempt to convince people that they have received special revelation and are authorized to lead them to safety, preying on their fears of the last days.

24 Behold, I have told you before;

25 Wherefore, if they shall say unto you: Behold, he is in the desert; go not forth: Behold, he is in the secret chambers; believe it not;

> Next, in verse 26, the Savior

assures us that His coming will not be a low key or secret event. Rather, it will be a spectacular manifestation, impossible to miss. All will see Him coming, just as all can see the light of the day coming on the eastern horizon as the sun rises.

26 For as the light of the morning cometh out of the east, and shineth even unto the west, and covereth the whole earth, so shall also the coming of the Son of Man be.

The Prophet Joseph Smith made significant changes in the Bible version of verse 26, above, clearing up some confusion that arises from mistranslation here in the King James Version of the Bible. We will give it here so you can see the importance of the Prophet's inspired work.

Matthew 24:27
27 For as the lightning [*"lightning" is a mistake in the translation of the Bible, since lightning can come from any direction.*] cometh out of the east, and shineth even unto the west; so shall also the coming of the Son of man be.

27 And now I show unto you a parable. Behold, wheresoever the carcass is, there will the eagles be gathered together; so likewise shall mine elect be gathered from the four quarters of the earth.

This is an unusual use of the word "carcass." Symbolically, in this context, it means "the body of the Church." In other words, the true Church with the true gospel. The "eagles" are converts, faithful members of the Church who will be gathered to the Church for nourishment in all parts of the world. In short, this verse prophesies of the gathering of Israel in the last days prior to the Second Coming (see Bruce R. McConkie, *Doctrinal New Testament Commentary, Vol. 1*, pp. 648–49.)

Several specific signs of the times in the last days are given in the next verses.

28 And they shall hear of wars, and rumors of wars.

29 Behold I speak for mine elect's sake [*those who believe in and pay attention to the word of the Lord, including those who make and keep covenants with Him*]; for nation shall rise against nation, and kingdom against kingdom; there shall be famines, and pestilences, and earthquakes, in divers [*various*] places.

30 And again [*just as was the case in the decades after the Crucifixion—see verse 10*], because iniquity shall abound, the love of men shall wax [*grow*] cold; but he that shall not be overcome [*if they*

remain steadfast in the gospel—see verse 11], the same shall be saved.

A major "sign of the times" is that the gospel will be preached throughout the world before the Second Coming. This is an exciting prophecy that is obviously underway in our day.

31 And again, this Gospel of the Kingdom shall be preached in all the world, for a witness unto all nations, and then shall the end come, or the destruction of the wicked;

32 And again shall the abomination of desolation, spoken of by Daniel the prophet, be fulfilled [*a second fulfillment of this prophecy—see verse 12*].

As mentioned in the note accompanying verse 12, the terrible devastations prophesied by Daniel, and described by him as "the abomination that maketh desolate" (Daniel 11:31, 12:11) were to have two fulfillments. One took place in AD 70 when the Romans laid siege against Jerusalem (see Bible Dictionary, under "Abomination of Desolation") and the fulfillment of this prophecy in the last days will take place when Jerusalem is again under siege (Bible Dictionary, under "Abomination of Desolation").

More signs of the times are given in verse 33, next.

33 And immediately after the tribulation of those days, the sun shall be darkened, and the moon shall not give her light, and the stars shall fall from heaven, and the powers of heaven shall be shaken.

The word "generation," as used in verse 34, next, can sometimes mean "dispensation" or "era." Such seems to be the case here.

34 Verily, I say unto you, this generation, in which these things shall be shown forth, shall not pass away until all I have told you shall be fulfilled.

Next, the Master assures His disciples that everything He has taught and prophesied will come to pass.

35 Although, the days will come, that heaven and earth shall pass away; yet my words shall not pass away, but all shall be fulfilled.

36 And, as I said before, after the tribulation of those days, and the powers of the heavens shall be shaken, then shall appear the sign of the Son of Man in heaven, and then shall all the tribes of the earth mourn; and they shall see the Son of Man coming in the clouds of heaven, with power and great glory [*the Second Coming*];

Joseph Smith gave some information about "the sign of the

Son of Man in heaven" referred to in verse 36, above. He taught, "Judah must return, Jerusalem must be rebuilt, and the temple, and water come out from under the temple, and the waters of the Dead Sea be healed. It will take some time to rebuild the walls of the city and the temple, etc.; and all this must be done before the Son of Man will make His appearance. There will be wars and rumors of wars, signs in the heavens above and on the earth beneath, the sun turned into darkness and the moon to blood, earthquakes in divers places, the seas heaving beyond their bounds; then will appear one grand sign of the Son of Man in heaven. But what will the world do? They will say it is a planet, a comet, etc. But the Son of man will come as the sign of the coming of the Son of Man, which will be as the light of the morning cometh out of the east." (April 6, 1843. See *History of the Church* 5:336–37, also *Teachings of the Prophet Joseph Smith*, p. 286–87)

Next, we see that one of the significant ways to prepare for the last days and to avoid being deceived by the rampant wiles of the devil and his armies is to study and treasure up the gospel of Jesus Christ.

37 And whoso treasureth up my word, shall not be deceived, for the Son of Man shall come, and he shall send his angels before him with the great sound of a trumpet, and they shall gather together the remainder of his elect from the four winds, from one end of heaven to the other.

As also taught in verse 37, above, we see that ultimately no worthy person will miss out on being gathered to Christ, even if they are temporarily missed because of sincere but imperfect work on the part of missionaries before the Second Coming (see *Doctrinal New Testament Commentary*, Vol. 1, p. 662–63).

Next, Jesus compares the signs of the times to a fig tree as it begins to show signs of life again in the springtime. Just as when we see the buds and leaves on a fruit tree begin to shoot forth in the springtime, we know that summer is approaching, so also when we see the signs of the times being fulfilled, we will know that His coming is getting relatively near.

38 Now learn a parable of the fig-tree—When its branches are yet tender, and it begins to put forth leaves, you know that summer is nigh at hand;

39 So likewise, mine elect, when they shall see all these things [*prophecies that will be fulfilled*

relatively shortly before the Second Coming], they shall know that he is near, even at the doors;

> Next, in verse 40, Jesus clearly states that no one except His Father knows the time of Jesus' coming. This is certainly fair warning for us against any who claim to know or claim that others know.

40 But of that day, and hour, no one knoweth; no, not the angels of God in heaven, but my Father only.

> Mark 13:32 is even more explicit as far as the message in verse 40, above, is concerned.
>
> **Mark 13:32**
> 32 But of that day and *that* hour knoweth no man, no, not the angels which are in heaven, neither the Son, but the Father.
>
> Elder M. Russell Ballard addressed this topic when he spoke at a Brigham Young University devotional on March 12, 1996. He said:
>
> "I am called as one of the apostles to be a special witness of Christ in these exciting, trying times, and I do not know when He is going to come again. As far as I know, none of my brethren in the Council of the Twelve or even in the First Presidency knows. And I would humbly suggest to you, my young brothers and sisters, that if we do not know, then nobody knows, no matter how compelling their arguments or how reasonable their calculations."
>
> Next, the Savior explains that most people in the last days will not be expecting the Second Coming, just as the wicked in the days before the Flood did not expect it or believe Noah and his warnings about their coming destruction if they did not repent.

41 But as it was in the days of Noah, so it shall be also at the coming of the Son of Man;

42 For it shall be with them, as it was in the days which were before the flood; for until the day that Noah entered into the ark they were eating and drinking, marrying and giving in marriage [*they went right on living life as usual*];

43 And knew not until the flood came, and took them all away; so shall also the coming of the Son of Man be.

> According to JST Luke 17:36–40, verses 44–45 are parables that deal with the gathering of the righteous in the last days. First, we will read verses 44 and 45. Then we will read the JST explanation.

44 Then shall be fulfilled that which is written, that in the last days, two shall be in the field, the one shall be taken, and the other left;

45 Two shall be grinding at the mill, the one shall be taken, and the other left;

JST Luke 17:36–40
36 And they answered and said unto him, Where, Lord, shall they be taken.

37 And he said unto them, Wheresoever the body is gathered; or, in other words, whithersoever the saints are gathered, thither will the eagles be gathered together; or, thither will the remainder be gathered together.

38 This he spake, signifying the gathering of his saints; and of angels descending and gathering the remainder unto them; the one from the bed, the other from the grinding, and the other from the field, whithersoever he listeth.

39 For verily there shall be new heavens, and a new earth, wherein dwelleth righteousness.

40 And there shall be no unclean thing; for the earth becoming old, even as a garment, having waxed in corruption, wherefore it vanisheth away, and the footstool remaineth sanctified, cleansed from all sin.

President Heber C. Kimball (who served as a counselor to Brigham Young in the First Presidency) gave an explanation of these parables as follows:

"The servants of God are angels in one sense, sent forth to gather the house of Israel from the four corners of the earth; and the Elders of this Church in their labors have fulfilled, partly, the sayings of the Savior, when they have found two working in the field, one has received the Gospel and been gathered, and the other left; two working in a mill, one has been taken and the other left; two lying in a bed, the one has been taken and the other left. But no doubt these sayings will have their final and complete fulfilment about the time of the second coming of the Savior" (*Journal of Discourses*, Vol. 10, p. 103).

Next, in verses 46–48, we see the Lord's counsel to live worthily so that it doesn't make any difference when the Second Coming takes place, as far as personal worthiness is concerned.

46 And what I say unto one, I say unto all men; watch, therefore, for you know not at what hour your Lord doth come.

47 But know this, if the good man [*the owner*] of the house [*the owner is symbolic of people who are not*

ready and will be caught off guard by the Second Coming] had known in what watch [*the Jews divided the night into "watches" of about four hours each—see Bible Dictionary, under "Watches"*] the thief would come, he would have watched, and would not have suffered his house to have been broken up, but would have been ready.

48 Therefore be ye also ready, for in such an hour as ye think not, the Son of Man cometh.

> Next, in verses 49–54, the Master Teacher poses a question to His disciples, asking them who they think the people are who will be saved at His Second Coming. He then answers His own question and basically says that it will be those who are faithful to the gospel and serve others with kindness and wisdom.

49 Who, then, is a faithful and wise servant, whom his lord hath made ruler over his household, to give them meat in due season?

50 Blessed is that servant whom his lord, when he cometh, shall find so doing; and verily I say unto you, he shall make him ruler over all his goods [*in other words, they will be exalted and will become gods. See D&C 84:38, 132:20*].

51 But if that evil servant [*symbolic of the wicked in the last days*] shall say in his heart: My lord delayeth his coming,

52 And shall begin to smite his fellow-servants, and to eat and drink with the drunken,

53 The lord [*Jesus Christ*] of that servant shall come in a day when he looketh not for him, and in an hour that he is not aware of,

54 And shall cut him asunder [*will be destroyed at the time of the Second Coming*], and shall appoint him his portion with the hypocrites [*will be turned over to Satan with the rest of the wicked to be punished for their sins*]; there shall be weeping and gnashing of teeth.

> Verse 55, next, was left out of Matthew 24 in the Bible and restored by Joseph Smith here. Except for the last two phrases, it serves as a summary of the last verses of this chapter dealing with the destruction of the wicked at the Second Coming.

55 And thus cometh the end of the wicked, according to the prophecy of Moses, saying: They shall be cut off from among the people; but the end of the earth is not yet, but by and by.

> Sometimes confusion arises between the phrases "end of the wicked" and "end of the earth," as found in verse 55, above. As explained in verse 4 of this

chapter, the end of the world is the end of wickedness.

However, "the end of the earth" takes place when this earth is transformed into the celestial kingdom for its worthy inhabitants as taught in D&C 130:9–11. President Brigham Young explained: "When the Savior has completed the work, when the faithful Saints have preached the Gospel to the last of the spirits who have lived here and who are designed to come to this earth; when the thousand years of rest shall come and thousands and thousands of Temples shall be built, and the servants and handmaids of the Lord shall have entered therein and officiated for themselves, and for their dead friends back to the days of Adam; when the last of the spirits in prison who will receive the Gospel has received it; when the Savior comes and receives his ready bride, and all who can be are saved in the various kingdoms of God—celestial, terrestrial and telestial, according to their several capacities and opportunities; when sin and iniquity are driven from the earth, and the spirits that now float in this atmosphere are driven into the place prepared for them; and when the earth is sanctified from the effects of the fall, and baptized, cleansed, and purified by fire, and returns to its paradisiacal state, and has become like a sea of glass, a urim and thummim; when all this is done, and the Savior has presented the earth to his Father, and it is placed in the cluster of the celestial kingdoms, and the Son and all his faithful brethren and sisters have received the welcome plaudit—'Enter ye into the joy of your Lord,' and the Savior is crowned, then and not till then, will the Saints receive their everlasting inheritances" (*Journal of Discourses*, Vol. 17, p. 117; see also the *Pearl of Great Price Student Manual*, Religion 327, 2000, [used by Institutes of Religion], p. 51).

JOSEPH SMITH–MATTHEW AND MATTHEW 24
PARALLEL COLUMN COMPARISON

Joseph Smith—Matthew	King James Version
(With Joseph Smith's changes in **bold**)	Matthew 24

1 For I say unto you, that ye shall not see me henceforth **and know that I am he of whom it is written by the prophets,** until ye shall say: Blessed is he who cometh in the name of the Lord, **in the clouds of heaven, and all the holy angels with him. Then understood his disciples that he should come again on the earth, after that he was glorified and crowned on the right hand of God.**

2 And Jesus went out, and departed from the temple; and his disciples came to him, for to **hear him, saying: Master,** show **us concerning** the buildings of the temple, **as thou hast said—They shall be thrown down, and left unto you desolate.**

3 And Jesus said unto them: See ye not all these things, **and do ye not understand them?** Verily I say unto you, there shall not be left here, **upon this temple,** one stone upon another that shall not be thrown down.

Matthew 23:39 For I say unto you, Ye shall not see me henceforth, till ye shall say, Blessed *is* he that cometh in the name of the Lord.

1 And Jesus went out, and departed from the temple: and his disciples came to *him* for to shew him the buildings of the temple.

2 And Jesus said unto them, See ye not all these things? verily I say unto you, There shall not be left here one stone upon another, that shall not be thrown down.

Joseph Smith—Matthew & Matthew 24 Comparison

Joseph Smith—Matthew	Matthew 24

4 **And Jesus left them, and went upon the Mount of Olives.** And as he sat upon the Mount of Olives, the disciples came unto him privately, saying: Tell us when shall these things be **which thou hast said concerning the destruction of the temple, and the Jews;** and what is the sign of thy coming, and of the end of the world, **or the destruction of the wicked, which is the end of the world?**

5 And Jesus answered, and said unto them: Take heed that no man deceive you;

6 For many shall come in my name, saying—I am Christ—and shall deceive many;

7 Then shall they deliver you up to be afflicted, and shall kill you, and ye shall be hated of all nations, for my name's sake;

8 And then shall many be offended, and shall betray one another, and shall hate one another;

9 And many false prophets shall arise, and shall deceive many;

10 And because iniquity shall abound, the love of many shall wax cold;

11 But he that **remaineth steadfast and is not overcome,** the same shall be saved.

---

3 And as he sat upon the mount of Olives, the disciples came unto him privately, saying, Tell us, when shall these things be? and what *shall be* the sign of thy coming, and of the end of the world?

4 And Jesus answered and said unto them, Take heed that no man deceive you.

5 For many shall come in my name, saying, I am Christ; and shall deceive many.

9 Then shall they deliver you up to be afflicted, and shall kill you: and ye shall be hated of all nations for my name's sake.

10 And then shall many be offended, and shall betray one another, and shall hate one another.

11 And many false prophets shall rise, and shall deceive many.

12 And because iniquity shall abound, the love of many shall wax cold.

13 But he that shall endure unto the end, the same shall be saved.

14 And this gospel of the kingdom shall be preached in all the world for a witness unto all nations; and then shall the end come.

Joseph Smith—Matthew	Matthew 24
12 When you, therefore, shall see the abomination of desolation, spoken of by Daniel the prophet, **concerning the destruction of Jerusalem, then** you shall stand in the holy place; whoso readeth let him understand.	15 When ye therefore shall see the abomination of desolation, spoken of by Daniel the prophet, stand in the holy place, (whoso readeth, let him understand:)
13 Then let them **who are** in Judea flee into the mountains;	16 Then let them which be in Judaea flee into the mountains:
14 Let him who is on the housetop **flee, and not return** to take anything out of his house;	17 Let him which is on the housetop not come down to take any thing out of his house:
15 Neither let him who is in the field return back to take his clothes;	18 Neither let him which is in the field return back to take his clothes.
16 And wo unto them that are with child, and unto them that give suck in those days;	19 And woe unto them that are with child, and to them that give suck in those days!
17 **Therefore,** pray ye **the Lord** that your flight be not in the winter, neither on the Sabbath day;	20 But pray ye that your flight be not in the winter, neither on the sabbath day:
18 For then, **in those days,** shall be great tribulation **on the Jews, and upon the inhabitants of Jerusalem,** such as was not **before sent upon Israel, of God,** since the beginning of **their kingdom until** this time; no, nor ever shall be **sent again upon Israel.**	21 For then shall be great tribulation, such as was not since the beginning of the world to this time, no, nor ever shall be.
19 **All things which have befallen them** are **only** the beginning of **the** sorrows **which shall come upon them.**	8 All these *are* the beginning of sorrows.
20 And except those days should be shortened, there should none of their flesh be saved; but for the elect's sake, **according to the covenant,** those days shall be shortened.	22 And except those days should be shortened, there should no flesh be saved: but for the elect's sake those days shall be shortened.

Joseph Smith—Matthew	Matthew 24
21 **Behold, these things I have spoken unto you concerning the Jews; and again, after the tribulation of those days which shall come upon Jerusalem,** if any man shall say unto you, Lo, here is Christ, or there, believe him not;	23 Then if any man shall say unto you, Lo, here is Christ, or there; believe *it* not.
22 For **in those days** there shall **also** arise false Christs, and false prophets, and shall show great signs and wonders, insomuch, that, if possible, they shall deceive the very elect, **who are the elect according to the covenant.**	24 For there shall arise false Christs, and false prophets, and shall shew great signs and wonders; insomuch that, if it *were* possible, they shall deceive the very elect.
23 **Behold, I speak these things unto you for the elect's sake;** and you also shall hear of wars, and rumors of wars; see that ye be not troubled, for all **I have told you** must come to pass; but the end is not yet.	6 And ye shall hear of wars and rumours of wars: see that ye be not troubled: for all *these things* must come to pass, but the end is not yet.
24 Behold, I have told you before;	25 Behold, I have told you before.
25 Wherefore, if they shall say unto you: Behold, he is in the desert; go not forth: Behold, he is in the secret chambers; believe it not;	26 Wherefore if they shall say unto you, Behold, he is in the desert; go not forth: behold, *he* is in the secret chambers; believe *it* not.
26 For as the **light of the morning** cometh out of the east, and shineth even unto the west, **and covereth the whole earth,** so shall also the coming of the Son of Man be.	27 For as the lightning cometh out of the east, and shineth even unto the west; so shall also the coming of the Son of man be.
27 **And now I show unto you a parable. Behold,** wheresoever the carcass is, there will the eagles be gathered together; **so likewise shall mine elect be gathered from the four quarters of the earth.**	28 For wheresoever the carcase is, there will the eagles be gathered together.

Joseph Smith—Matthew	Matthew 24
28 **And they shall hear of wars and rumors of wars.**	
29 **Behold I speak for mine elect's sake;** for nation shall rise against nation, and kingdom against kingdom; there shall be famines, and pestilences, and earthquakes, in divers places.	7 For nation shall rise against nation, and kingdom against kingdom: and there shall be famines, and pestilences, and earthquakes, in divers places.
30 **And again, because iniquity shall abound, the love of men shall wax cold; but he that shall not be overcome, the same shall be saved.**	
31 And **again,** this Gospel of the Kingdom shall be preached in all the world, for a witness unto all nations, and then shall the end come, **or the destruction of the wicked;**	14 And this gospel of the kingdom shall be preached in all the world for a witness unto all nations; and then shall the end come.
32 **(This is <u>not</u> the same as verse 15 in Matthew 24.) And again shall the abomination of desolation, spoken of by Daniel the prophet, be fulfilled.**	
33 **And** immediately after the tribulation of those days, **the sun shall be darkened,** and the moon shall not give her light, and the stars shall fall from heaven, and the powers of heaven shall be shaken.	29 Immediately after the tribulation of those days shall the sun be darkened, and the moon shall not give her light, and the stars shall fall from heaven, and the powers of the heavens shall be shaken:
34 Verily, I say unto you, this generation, **in which these things shall be shown forth,** shall not pass away **un**til all **I have told you shall** be fulfilled.	34 Verily I say unto you, This generation shall not pass, till all these things be fulfilled.

Joseph Smith—Matthew

35 **Although, the days will come, that** heaven and earth shall pass away; yet my words shall not pass away, **but all shall be fulfilled.**

36 And, **as I said before, after the tribulation of those days, and the powers of the heavens shall be shaken,** then shall appear the sign of the Son of Man in heaven, and then shall all the tribes of the earth mourn; and they shall see the Son of Man coming in the clouds of heaven, with power and great glory;

37 **And whoso treasureth up my word, shall not be deceived, for the Son of Man shall come,** and he shall send his angels **before him** with **the** great sound of a trumpet, and they shall gather together **the remainder of** his elect **from the four winds,** from one end of heaven to the other.

38 Now learn a parable of the fig-tree—When its branches are yet tender, and **it begins to** put forth leaves, **you** know that summer is nigh **at hand;**

39 So likewise, **mine elect,** when **they** shall see all these things, **they** shall know that **he** is near, even at the doors;

40 But of that day, and hour, no **one** knoweth; no, not the angels of **God in** heaven, but my Father only.

Matthew 24

35 Heaven and earth shall pass away, but my words shall not pass away.

30 And then shall appear the sign of the Son of man in heaven: and then shall all the tribes of the earth mourn, and they shall see the Son of man coming in the clouds of heaven with power and great glory.

31 And he shall send his angels with a great sound of a trumpet, and they shall gather together his elect from the four winds, from one end of heaven to the other.

32 Now learn a parable of the fig tree; When his branch is yet tender, and putteth forth leaves, ye know that summer *is* nigh:

33 So likewise ye, when ye shall see all these things, know that it is near, *even* at the doors

36 But of that day and hour knoweth no *man*, no, not the angels of heaven, but my Father only.

Joseph Smith—Matthew	Matthew 24
41 But as **it was in** the days of Noah, so **it** shall **be** also **at** the coming of the Son of Man;	37 But as the days of Noe *were*, so shall also the coming of the Son of man be.
42 For **it shall be with them,** as **it was** in the days **which** were before the flood; **for until the day that Noah entered into the ark** they were eating and drinking, marrying and giving in marriage;	38 For as in the days that were before the flood they were eating and drinking, marrying and giving in marriage, until the day that Noe entered into the ark,
43 And knew not until the flood came, and took them all away; so shall also the coming of the Son of Man be.	39 And knew not until the flood came, and took them all away; so shall also the coming of the Son of man be.
44 Then **shall be fulfilled that which is written, that in the last days,** two shall be in the field, the one shall be taken, and the other left;	40 Then shall two be in the field; the one shall be taken, and the other left.
45 Two shall be grinding at the mill, the one shall be taken, and the other left;	41 Two *women shall* be grinding at the mill; the one shall be taken, and the other left
46 **And what I say unto one, I say unto all men;** watch, therefore, for **you** know not at what hour your Lord doth come.	42 Watch therefore: for ye know not what hour your Lord doth come.
47 But know this, if the good man of the house had known in what watch the thief would come, he would have watched, and would not have suffered his house to have been broken up, **but would have been ready.**	43 But know this, that if the goodman of the house had known in what watch the thief would come, he would have watched, and would not have suffered his house to be broken up.
48 Therefore be ye also ready, for in such an hour as ye think not, the Son of Man cometh.	44 Therefore be ye also ready: for in such an hour as ye think not the Son of man cometh.

Joseph Smith—Matthew	Matthew 24
49 Who, then, is a faithful and wise servant, whom his lord hath made ruler over his household, to give them meat in due season?	45 Who then is a faithful and wise servant, whom his lord hath made ruler over his household, to give them meat in due season?
50 Blessed is that servant whom his lord, when he cometh, shall find so doing; **and** verily I say unto you, he shall make him ruler over all his goods.	46 Blessed *is* that servant, whom his lord when he cometh shall find so doing. 47 Verily I say unto you, That he shall make him ruler over all his goods.
51 But if that evil servant shall say in his heart: My lord delayeth his coming,	48 But and if that evil servant shall say in his heart, My lord delayeth his coming;
52 And shall begin to smite his fellow-servants, and to eat and drink with the drunken,	49 And shall begin to smite *his* fellowservants, and to eat and drink with the drunken;
53 The lord of that servant shall come in a day when he looketh not for him, and in an hour that he is not aware of,	50 The lord of that servant shall come in a day when he looketh not for *him*, and in an hour that he is not aware of,
54 And shall cut him asunder, and **shall** appoint him his portion with the hypocrites; there shall be weeping and gnashing of teeth.	51 And shall cut him asunder, and appoint *him* his portion with the hypocrites: there shall be weeping and gnashing of teeth.
55 And thus cometh the end of the wicked, according to the prophecy of Moses, saying: They shall be cut off from among the people; but the end of the earth is not yet, but by and by.	

Joseph Smith History

EXTRACTS FROM THE HISTORY OF
JOSEPH SMITH, THE PROPHET

History of the Church, Volume 1, Chapters 1–5

Background

As you can see in verses 1 and 2, this is the Prophet Joseph Smith's 1838 account of his early history and the history of the early days in the Church. It gives a brief account through the restoration of the Aaronic Priesthood in May 1829.

Preparation of Joseph Smith's Parents

Before we begin our verse-by-verse study of this chapter, we will take time to briefly review the preparation of Joseph Smith's parents to be the parents of the Prophet of the Restoration.

Have you ever thought how unusual it was that Joseph Smith Sr. and Lucy Mack Smith were so completely supportive of their son? Under normal circumstances, one would expect the parents of a young teenager who made such claims as Joseph Smith did to be very upset and to attempt to control him and avoid the inevitable embarrassment and humiliation that such would bring to the family. But this was not the case with the Prophet's parents. They accepted his accounts of heavenly manifestations and went through extreme trials and hardships as a result, remaining faithful until the end of their own lives.

Can you think of other parents in the scriptures who were especially prepared by God to be the parents of prophets? Some examples are: Abraham and Sarah (to be the parents of Isaac), Elizabeth and Zacharias (to be the parents of John the Baptist), Mary (to be the mother of the Son of God) and Joseph (to be the husband of Mary and help her in raising Jesus). Special visions and manifestations attended the preparation of these parents. So also, visions and dreams attended the preparation of Joseph Smith Sr. and Lucy Mack Smith to be Joseph's parents.

For example, in about 1802, roughly three years before Joseph's birth, Lucy Mack Smith became deathly sick as a result of a "heavy cold," a "severe cough," and a "hectic fever . . . which threatened to prove fatal" (see *History of Joseph Smith By His Mother, Lucy Mack Smith*, p. 33). As the illness continued to take her toward death's door, all hope of her survival was given up by the doctors, her husband, and her family, including her mother who had faithfully ministered to her needs as the sickness continued to take its toll. During the night, she "begged and pleaded" with God to spare her life so that she could raise her two young children, Alvin and Hyrum, and continue to be a companion for her husband (ibid., p. 34). According to Lucy's account, that night, she "made a solemn covenant with God that if He would let me live I would endeavor to serve him according to the best of my abilities. Shortly after this I heard a voice say to me, 'Seek, and ye shall find; knock, and it shall be opened unto you. Let your heart be comforted; ye believe in God, believe also in me.' (ibid., p. 34). Lucy's mother came into her room shortly after this manifestation and said "Lucy, you are better." To which Lucy replied, "Yes, mother, the Lord will let me live, if I am faithful to the promise which I made to him" (ibid., pp. 34–35).

Mother Smith recovered rapidly and because of the spiritual manifestation from the Lord, made a concerted effort to become involved in organized religion in order to get help in carrying out her commitment to God. She talked with ministers of various religions and attended various churches, hoping to find the guidance and help she desired, but found only disappointment. Finally, "I said in my heart that there was not then upon earth the religion which I sought." (Ibid, p. 36.) Thus, Mother Smith was prepared for her son Joseph's First Vision, in which he was told that the true church was not on earth at that time (*Joseph Smith—History* 1:18–20).

In about 1803, Lucy had a dream in which she was shown that her husband would "hear and receive with his whole heart" the "pure and undefiled gospel of the Son of God . . . when he was more advanced in life" (ibid., p. 45). Thus, she was prepared for the restoration of the pure gospel of Jesus Christ when her son Joseph Smith Jr. was called by God to restore it.

Now, let's look briefly at the preparation of Father Smith that enabled him, among other things, to respond to Joseph's account of Moroni's visit (as recorded by Joseph). "He replied to me that it was of God, and told me to go and do as commanded by the messenger." (*Joseph Smith—History* 1:50.) Again we will refer to *History of Joseph Smith by His Mother, Lucy Mack Smith*, as our source for the preparation of Joseph Smith Sr. to be the father of the Prophet of the Restoration.

Lucy writes that about five or six years after the birth of Joseph Smith Jr., which would make the time about 1811, her "husband's mind became much excited upon the subject of religion; yet he would not subscribe to any particular system of faith, but contended for the ancient order, as established by our Lord and Savior Jesus Christ and His Apostles" (ibid., p. 46). Thus, long before the First Vision, the Prophet's father had already decided that the Church, as established by the Savior during His mortal ministry, was no longer on earth.

Additionally, according to Lucy Mack Smith's account, her husband had at least seven visions from 1811 to 1819 (ibid., pp 47–50, 64–66, 68), all of which we can see as wonderful preparation for him to be the father of the Prophet. We will briefly mention two of these dreams, both of which came to Father Smith in 1811.

The first of the seven dreams or visions came "the next month after William was born" (see heading in preliminary manuscript of Lucy's book). This would make the time of this dream or vision sometime in April 1811. In it, Brother Smith found himself "traveling in an open, barren field" and in all directions he could "see nothing save dead, fallen timber" (ibid., p. 47).

As he continued traveling, he could see absolutely no life, "either animal or vegetable," and furthermore, "the most death-like silence prevailed" (ibid., p. 47). He was completely alone except for a guide, "an attendant spirit, who kept constantly by my side" (ibid., p. 47). When he asked his guide why he was traveling in such a "dismal place," he answered, "This field is the world, which now lieth inanimate and dumb, in regard to the true religion, of plan of salvation; but travel on, and by the wayside you will find on a certain log a box, the contents of which, if you eat thereof, will make you wise, and give unto you wisdom and understanding" (ibid., p. 47).

Can you see in your mind's eye the relationship between the contents of this box and the contents of the Book of Mormon plates found by young Joseph in the stone box on Hill Cumorah, as directed by Moroni? Let's see what happened after Father Smith partook of the contents of the box and see how that might relate to what happened to the Smith family after Joseph Smith Jr. brought the gold plates home and began translating them.

Continuing with Lucy Mack Smith's account of her husband's vision, "proceeding a short distance, I came to the box. I immediately took it up, and placed it under my left arm; then with eagerness I raised the lid, and began to taste of its contents; upon which all manner of beasts, horned cattle, and roaring animals, rose up on every side in the most threatening manner possible, tearing the earth, tossing their horns, and bellowing most terrifically all around me, and they finally came so close upon me, that I was compelled to drop the box and fly for my life. Yet, in the midst of all this I was perfectly happy, though I awoke trembling" (ibid., p. 47).

Certainly, Father Smith was prepared in advance through this vision for the intense persecutions that arose after Joseph brought the plates home from the stone "box" on the Hill Cumorah to begin translating them. He knew that the persecution could not take away the happiness that became available to him and his family through the contents of the box.

The next vision likewise was no doubt a great blessing and help to Joseph Smith Sr. by way of preparing him to support and sustain his prophet son. It, too, was given him in 1811. If you have read the Book of Mormon, you will quite likely find it to be rather familiar. He again found himself traveling in a desolate field, again accompanied by a guide. The guide told him, "This is the desolate world; but travel on" (ibid., p. 48). Soon he came to a "narrow path" (ibid., p. 48). Following it, he soon saw "a beautiful stream of water, which ran from the east to the west" (ibid., p. 48). He saw "a rope, running along the bank of it, about as high as a man could reach . . . a low, but very pleasant valley, in which stood a tree such as I had never seen before" (ibid., p. 48.) He said that the tree "bore a kind of fruit . . . of dazzling whiteness" and "delicious beyond description" (ibid., p. 49). As he was partaking of the fruit of the tree, he said in his heart, "I cannot eat this alone, I must bring my wife and children, that they may partake with me" (ibid., p. 49). According to his description of the vision, recorded by Lucy Mack Smith, his wife and all seven children came and began partaking of the fruit, which brought them great happiness. He continued, "While thus engaged, I beheld a spacious building standing opposite the valley which we were in . . . full of doors and windows . . . all filled with people, who were very finely dressed. When these people observed us in the low valley, under the tree, they pointed the finger of scorn at us, and treated us with all manner of disrespect and contempt. But their contumely we utterly disregarded" (ibid., p. 49).

Can you imagine the feeling and testimony Father Smith experienced when he first read First Nephi chapter 8 in the Book of Mormon, which contains the account of Lehi's vision of the tree of life! It will be interesting to hear him talk about this someday when we see him in the next life. By the way, in Father Smith's vision, all of his children came when invited to partake of the fruit of the tree (whereas, in Lehi's dream, Laman and Lemuel refused to come) and the guide told him that the fruit "was the pure love of God, shed abroad in the hearts of all those who love him, and keep his commandments" (ibid., p. 49). Furthermore, in the vision received by Joseph Smith Sr., the guide commanded him to bring the rest of his children to partake of the fruit of the tree. Brother Smith replied that they were already all there. The guide said, "No ... look yonder, you have two more, and you must bring them also" (ibid., p. 49). Thus, Father and Mother Smith knew that they had two more children to bring into the world, which they did (Don Carlos on March 25, 1816 and Lucy on July 18, 1821).

Joseph's Early History

We will now proceed with Joseph Smith—History, which, as you can see from the heading at the beginning of Joseph Smith—History in your Pearl of Great Price, consists of extracts from *History of the Church*, Vol. 1, Chapters 1–5. By the way, this brief history was first published in England in 1851 as part of the first Pearl of Great Price pamphlet, which was compiled and circulated by Elder Franklin D. Richards, a member of the Council of the Twelve Apostles, then serving as president of the British Mission. The Pearl of Great Price was accepted as scripture by the Church in a general conference held in Salt Lake City, Utah, on October 10, 1880 (see Introductory Note at the beginning of your Pearl of Great Price).

One of Joseph Smith's clear objectives in writing this history was to set the record straight because of many false rumors and opinions then being spread about him and the establishment of the Church through him.

1 OWING to the many reports which have been put in circulation by evil-disposed and designing persons, in relation to the rise and progress of the Church of Jesus Christ of Latter-day Saints, all of which have been designed by the authors thereof to militate against its character as a Church and its progress in the world—I have been induced to write this history, to

disabuse the public mind, and put all inquirers after truth in possession of the facts, as they have transpired, in relation both to myself and the Church, so far as I have such facts in my possession.

2 In this history I shall present the various events in relation to this Church, in truth and righteousness, as they have transpired, or as they at present exist, being now [1838] the eighth year since the organization of the said Church [*on April 6, 1830*].

3 I was born in the year of our Lord one thousand eight hundred and five, on the twenty-third day of December, in the town of Sharon, Windsor county, State of Vermont . . . My father, Joseph Smith, Sen., left the State of Vermont, and moved to Palmyra, Ontario (now Wayne) county, in the State of New York, when I was in my tenth year, or thereabouts. In about four years after my father's arrival in Palmyra, he moved with his family into Manchester [*located just south of Palmyra*] in the same county of Ontario—

4 His family consisting of eleven souls, namely, my father, Joseph Smith; my mother, Lucy Smith (whose name, previous to her marriage, was Mack, daughter of Solomon Mack); my brothers, Alvin (who died November 19th, 1823, in the 26th year of his age), Hyrum, myself, Samuel Harrison, William, Don Carlos; and my sisters, Sophronia, Catherine, and Lucy.

5 Some time in the second year after our removal to Manchester, there was in the place where we lived an unusual excitement on the subject of religion. It commenced with the Methodists, but soon became general among all the sects in that region of country. Indeed, the whole district of country seemed affected by it, and great multitudes united themselves to the different religious parties, which created no small stir and division amongst the people, some crying, "Lo, here!" and others, "Lo, there!" Some were contending for the Methodist faith, some for the Presbyterian, and some for the Baptist.

It is interesting to note that historians have referred to central and western New York State during this period as the "burned-over district" because of the great number of revivals and the numerous preachers who warned the inhabitants of the fires of hell that awaited them if they did not join their congregations and churches.

The "Burned-Over District"

To shed additional light on this aspect of young Joseph Smith's environment, we will quote from the Church history manual used by the Institutes of Religion of the Church:

"As more and more Americans crossed the Catskill and Adirondack mountains to settle in the Finger Lakes area of western New York, they tended to lose contact with established churches in their former homes. These 'unchurched' settlers worried religious leaders of the main denominations, principally the Baptists, Methodists, and Presbyterians, who established proselyting programs for their disadvantaged brothers in the West.

"The Methodists and Baptists were particularly zealous in their efforts to bring religion to those without its benefits. The Methodists employed circuit riders. These were traveling ministers who rode horseback from town to town throughout a given region, or circuit, ministering to the religious needs of the people. The Baptists used the farmer-preacher system. In this system a local man earned his living by farming but occupied a nearby pulpit on the Sabbath.

"These efforts were bolstered by the enthusiasm of the Second Great Awakening which was then sweeping the United States. Nearly all churches in upstate New York conducted revivals. These were evangelistic gatherings designed to awaken the religiously inert. Revivals were often in the form of camp meetings held on the edge of a grove of trees or in a small clearing in the forest. Participants often traveled many miles over dusty or rut-filled roads to pitch their tents or park their wagons on the outskirts of the encampment. Camp meetings frequently lasted several days with some sessions lasting nearly all day and into the night. Ministers rotated, but it was not uncommon to find two or three ministers exhorting their listeners simultaneously. So fervent and enthusiastic was the religious zeal in western New York in the early 1800s that the region came to be known as the Burned-Over District. Because the Finger Lakes area was set figuratively ablaze with evangelistic fire, it is not surprising that young Joseph Smith and his family were caught up in the fervor" (*Church History in the Fulness of Times*, p. 30).

We continue now with Joseph Smith—History.

6 For, notwithstanding the great love which the converts to these different faiths expressed at the time of their conversion, and the great zeal manifested by the respective clergy, who were active

in getting up and promoting this extraordinary scene of religious feeling, in order to have everybody converted, as they were pleased to call it, let them join what sect they pleased; yet when the converts began to file off, some to one party and some to another, it was seen that the seemingly good feelings of both the priests and the converts were more pretended than real; for a scene of great confusion and bad feeling ensued—priest contending against priest, and convert against convert; so that all their good feelings one for another, if they ever had any, were entirely lost in a strife of words and a contest about opinions.

> We learn additional details from other writings of Joseph Smith about this period of his young life, including that he spent about two years, from ages twelve to fourteen, actively investigating different churches. He wrote that "at about the age of twelve years, my mind became seriously impressed with regard to the all important concerns for the welfare of my immortal soul" (Jessee, *Personal Writings of Joseph Smith*, p. 4, quoted in *Church History in the Fulness of Times*, p. 31).
>
> By the time he was in his fifteenth year (in other words, age 14) he was still undecided as to which church to join.

7 I was at this time in my fifteenth year. My father's family was proselyted to the Presbyterian faith, and four of them joined that church, namely, my mother, Lucy; my brothers Hyrum and Samuel Harrison; and my sister Sophronia.

8 During this time of great excitement my mind was called up to serious reflection and great uneasiness; but though my feelings were deep and often poignant [*very painful—see 1828 Noah Webster Dictionary*], still I kept myself aloof from all these parties, though I attended their several meetings as often as occasion would permit. In process of time my mind became somewhat partial to the Methodist sect, and I felt some desire to be united with them; but so great were the confusion and strife among the different denominations, that it was impossible for a person young as I was, and so unacquainted with men and things, to come to any certain conclusion who was right and who was wrong.

9 My mind at times was greatly excited, the cry and tumult were so great and incessant. The Presbyterians were most decided against the Baptists and Methodists, and used all the powers of both reason and sophistry to prove their errors, or, at least, to make the people think they were in error. On the other

hand, the Baptists and Methodists in their turn were equally zealous in endeavoring to establish their own tenets and disprove all others.

10 In the midst of this war of words and tumult of opinions, I often said to myself: What is to be done? Who of all these parties are right; or, are they all wrong together? If any one of them be right, which is it, and how shall I know it?

> Next, in verse 11, we see a simple and beautiful example of the value of scripture reading to set the stage for personal inspiration and revelation to us from God.

The First Vision

11 While I was laboring under the extreme difficulties caused by the contests of these parties of religionists, I was one day reading the Epistle of James, first chapter and fifth verse, which reads: *If any of you lack wisdom, let him ask of God, that giveth to all men liberally, and upbraideth not; and it shall be given him.*

> The word "upbraideth" in verse 11, above, means "to scold." It comes from the practice in some cultures in times past of disciplining or scolding a young girl by jerking her braids upward.
>
> As the Prophet reflects back some eighteen years to the impact of this verse of scripture in his young life (remember, he is writing this history in 1838) we feel the witness of the Spirit that he was indeed being guided and inspired to pray, in preparation for the visit of the Father and the Son. It is a prime example of how the Spirit can communicate with our heart and mind (see D&C 8:2–3) and move us to action.

12 Never did any passage of scripture come with more power to the heart of man than this did at this time to mine. It seemed to enter with great force into every feeling of my heart. I reflected on it again and again, knowing that if any person needed wisdom from God, I did; for how to act I did not know, and unless I could get more wisdom than I then had, I would never know; for the teachers of religion of the different sects understood the same passages of scripture so differently as to destroy all confidence in settling the question by an appeal to the Bible.

13 At length I came to the conclusion that I must either remain in darkness and confusion, or else I must do as James directs, that is, ask of God. I at length came to the determination to "ask of God," concluding that if he gave wisdom to them that lacked wisdom, and would give liberally, and not upbraid, I might venture.

Have you noticed that some of the most momentous events in the history of the Lord's dealings with His children on earth have had very humble beginnings? For example, Adam and Eve humbly and obediently offered the firstlings of their flocks, not knowing any more other than that they were so commanded, which led to great revelation and an outpouring of the Holy Ghost (Moses 5:5–12). Abraham quietly and humbly "sought for the blessings of the fathers" (Abraham 1:2), which opened up vast revelations to him (Abraham 2, 3). Moses, as a humble shepherd, walked tentatively toward the burning bush (Exodus 3:1–3), which was the beginning of tremendous revelation to him and which set the stage for a call to serve as a prophet for the rest of his life.

So also, as young Joseph Smith walked into the grove of trees not far from his parent's home, another choice son of our Heavenly Father was about to be taken from humble obscurity into a life of revelation and service as a mighty prophet of the Living God.

14 So, in accordance with this, my determination to ask of God, I retired to the woods to make the attempt. It was on the morning of a beautiful, clear day, early in the spring of eighteen hundred and twenty. It was the first time in my life that I had made such an attempt, for amidst all my anxieties I had never as yet made the attempt to pray vocally.

15 After I had retired to the place where I had previously designed to go, having looked around me, and finding myself alone, I kneeled down and began to offer up the desires of my heart to God. I had scarcely done so, when immediately I was seized upon by some power which entirely overcame me, and had such an astonishing influence over me as to bind my tongue so that I could not speak. Thick darkness gathered around me, and it seemed to me for a time as if I were doomed to sudden destruction.

> Moses likewise experienced intense direct opposition from Satan in conjunction with his call as a prophet (Moses 1:12–22). In both cases, the devil did not depart until compelled to do so by the power of God.

16 But, exerting all my powers to call upon God to deliver me out of the power of this enemy which had seized upon me, and at the very moment when I was ready to sink into despair and abandon myself to destruction—not to an imaginary ruin, but to the power of

some actual being from the unseen world, who had such marvelous power as I had never before felt in any being—just at this moment of great alarm, I saw a pillar of light exactly over my head, above the brightness of the sun, which descended gradually until it fell upon me.

17 It no sooner appeared than I found myself delivered from the enemy which held me bound. When the light rested upon me I saw two Personages, whose brightness and glory defy all description, standing above me in the air. One of them spake unto me, calling me by name and said, pointing to the other—*This is My Beloved Son. Hear Him!*

18 My object in going to inquire of the Lord was to know which of all the sects was right, that I might know which to join. No sooner, therefore, did I get possession of myself, so as to be able to speak, than I asked the Personages who stood above me in the light, which of all the sects was right (for at this time it had never entered into my heart that all were wrong)—and which I should join.

> On occasions, my students have asked why Joseph said "it had never entered into my heart that all were wrong," in verse 18, above, whereas, in verse 10, describing the confusion in his mind before the First Vision, he posed the question, "Who of all these parties are right; or, are they all wrong together?"
>
> My response has been that it would make perfect sense that, in verse 10, he was simply making a list of possible answers in his mind (he did not consider "all wrong" as a viable choice but was trying to list all possible answers to his dilemma.) In verse 18, he explains that he was truly startled by the answer, since he had never considered that to be a valid possibility.

19 I was answered that I must join none of them, for they were all wrong; and the Personage who addressed me said that all their creeds were an abomination in his sight; that those professors were all corrupt; that: "they draw near to me with their lips, but their hearts are far from me, they teach for doctrines the commandments of men, having a form of godliness, but they deny the power thereof."

> Elder Boyd K. Packer of the Quorum of the Twelve gave us counsel regarding the phrase "they were all wrong," as we attempt to share the gospel with others. He taught:
>
> "Now this is not to say that the churches, all of them, are

without some truth. They have some truth—some of them very much of it. They have a form of godliness. Often the clergy and adherents are not without dedication, and many of them practice remarkably well the virtues of Christianity. They are nonetheless, incomplete" (Conference Report, Oct. 1971, p. 8; see also *Ensign*, Dec. 1971, p. 40).

In the Doctrine and Covenants, the Lord explains that the restored gospel is not designed to destroy the good that others have, rather, to fill in the gaps and build upon what they already have. He said:

D&C 10:52
And now, behold, according to their faith in their prayers will I bring this part of my gospel to the knowledge of my people. Behold, I do not bring it to destroy that which they have received, but to build it up.

We see from the first sentence in verse 20, next, that Joseph Smith learned much more from the First Vision than he recorded here.

20 He again forbade me to join with any of them; and many other things did he say unto me, which I cannot write at this time. When I came to myself again, I found myself lying on my back, looking up into heaven. When the light had departed, I had no strength [*similar to Moses, after he saw the Savior and was instructed by Him—see Moses 1:10*]; but soon recovering in some degree, I went home. And as I leaned up to the fireplace, mother inquired what the matter was. I replied, "Never mind, all is well—I am well enough off." I then said to my mother, "I have learned for myself that Presbyterianism is not true." It seems as though the adversary was aware, at a very early period of my life, that I was destined to prove a disturber and an annoyer of his kingdom; else why should the powers of darkness combine against me? Why the opposition and persecution that arose against me, almost in my infancy?

As suggested in the background to Joseph Smith—History, given at the beginning of this section, Joseph Smith's mother was well prepared to hear what her son told her as he came home after seeing the Father and Son, leaned against the fireplace, and said what he said about other religions in verse 20, above.

As indicated in verse 20, above, as well as in verses 21–26, next, the young Prophet was saddened and indeed startled by the hostility of others as he shared with them the glorious truths he had learned in the First Vision.

21 Some few days after I had this vision, I happened to be in company with one of the Methodist preachers, who was very active in the before mentioned religious excitement; and, conversing with him on the subject of religion, I took occasion to give him an account of the vision which I had had. I was greatly surprised at his behavior; he treated my communication not only lightly, but with great contempt, saying it was all of the devil, that there were no such things as visions or revelations in these days; that all such things had ceased with the apostles, and that there would never be any more of them.

22 I soon found, however, that my telling the story had excited a great deal of prejudice against me among professors of religion, and was the cause of great persecution, which continued to increase; and though I was an obscure boy, only between fourteen and fifteen years of age, and my circumstances in life such as to make a boy of no consequence in the world, yet men of high standing would take notice sufficient to excite the public mind against me, and create a bitter persecution; and this was common among all the sects—all united to persecute me.

23 It caused me serious reflection then, and often has since, how very strange it was that an obscure boy, of a little over fourteen years of age, and one, too, who was doomed to the necessity of obtaining a scanty maintenance by his daily labor, should be thought a character of sufficient importance to attract the attention of the great ones of the most popular sects of the day, and in a manner to create in them a spirit of the most bitter persecution and reviling. But strange or not, so it was, and it was often the cause of great sorrow to myself.

24 However, it was nevertheless a fact that I had beheld a vision. I have thought since, that I felt much like Paul, when he made his defense before King Agrippa [*Acts 26:1–32*], and related the account of the vision he had when he saw a light, and heard a voice; but still there were but few who believed him; some said he was dishonest, others said he was mad; and he was ridiculed and reviled. But all this did not destroy the reality of his vision. He had seen a vision, he knew he had, and all the persecution under heaven could not make it otherwise; and though they should persecute him unto death, yet he knew, and would know to his latest breath, that he had both seen a light and heard a voice speaking unto him, and all the world could not make him think or believe otherwise.

25 So it was with me. I had actually

seen a light, and in the midst of that light I saw two Personages, and they did in reality speak to me; and though I was hated and persecuted for saying that I had seen a vision, yet it was true; and while they were persecuting me, reviling me, and speaking all manner of evil against me falsely for so saying, I was led to say in my heart: Why persecute me for telling the truth? I have actually seen a vision; and who am I that I can withstand God, or why does the world think to make me deny what I have actually seen? For I had seen a vision; I knew it, and I knew that God knew it, and I could not deny it, neither dared I do it; at least I knew that by so doing I would offend God, and come under condemnation.

26 I had now got my mind satisfied so far as the sectarian world [*the other churches of the day*] was concerned—that it was not my duty to join with any of them, but to continue as I was until further directed. I had found the testimony of James to be true—that a man who lacked wisdom might ask of God, and obtain, and not be upbraided.

Moroni Comes

Next, in verses 27–54, the Prophet gives an account of the appearance of Moroni to him when he was seventeen and tells of the angel's prophecy that his name would be known for good and evil among all nations. He is told about the gold plates and shown in vision their hiding place. Moroni continues to give him instructions over the course of the next four years.

27 I continued to pursue my common vocations in life until the twenty-first of September, one thousand eight hundred and twenty-three, all the time suffering severe persecution at the hands of all classes of men, both religious and irreligious, because I continued to affirm that I had seen a vision.

28 During the space of time which intervened between the time I had the vision and the year eighteen hundred and twenty-three—having been forbidden to join any of the religious sects of the day, and being of very tender years, and persecuted by those who ought to have been my friends and to have treated me kindly, and if they supposed me to be deluded to have endeavored in a proper and affectionate manner to have reclaimed me—I was left to all kinds of temptations; and, mingling with all kinds of society, I frequently fell into many foolish errors, and displayed the weakness of youth, and the foibles of human nature; which, I am sorry to say, led me into divers [*various*] temptations, offensive in the sight

of God. In making this confession, no one need suppose me guilty of any great or malignant sins. A disposition to commit such was never in my nature. But I was guilty of levity, and sometimes associated with jovial company, etc., not consistent with that character which ought to be maintained by one who was called of God as I had been. But this will not seem very strange to any one who recollects my youth, and is acquainted with my native cheery temperament.

> Joseph Smith's mother described Joseph Smith Jr. as "a remarkably quiet, well-disposed child . . . He seemed much less inclined to the perusal of books than any of the rest of our children, but far more given to meditation and deep study" (Backman, *The Heavens Resound*, p. 51. See also *History of Joseph Smith, By His Mother, Lucy Mack Smith*, p. 82).

29 In consequence of these things, I often felt condemned for my weakness and imperfections; when, on the evening of the above-mentioned twenty-first of September, after I had retired to my bed for the night, I betook myself to prayer and supplication to Almighty God for forgiveness of all my sins and follies, and also for a manifestation to me, that I might know of my state and standing before him; for I had full confidence in obtaining a divine manifestation, as I previously had one.

30 While I was thus in the act of calling upon God, I discovered a light appearing in my room, which continued to increase until the room was lighter than at noonday, when immediately a personage appeared at my bedside, standing in the air, for his feet did not touch the floor.

31 He had on a loose robe of most exquisite whiteness. It was a whiteness beyond anything earthly I had ever seen; nor do I believe that any earthly thing could be made to appear so exceedingly white and brilliant. His hands were naked, and his arms also, a little above the wrist; so, also, were his feet naked, as were his legs, a little above the ankles. His head and neck were also bare. I could discover that he had no other clothing on but this robe, as it was open, so that I could see into his bosom.

32 Not only was his robe exceedingly white, but his whole person was glorious beyond description, and his countenance truly like lightning. The room was exceedingly light, but not so very bright as immediately around his person. When I first looked upon him, I was afraid; but the fear soon left me.

> Can you imagine Moroni's feelings, after over 1,400 years of waiting, as he prepared to

appear to Joseph Smith and teach him about the gold plates and his role in translating the Book of Mormon!

Moroni was the last prophet in the Book of Mormon. He had witnessed the entire destruction of his people, either through war or apostasy (Moroni 1:2). After having engraved a few more words of counsel to those who would later read the Book of Mormon, he buried the plates (Mormon 8:14, Moroni 10:1–2) in a stone box on the hill where they would await the calling of Joseph Smith to be the prophet of the Restoration.

Now that time had arrived. Joseph Smith Jr. had retired to bed and was fervently praying about his standing before God. Moroni, as a resurrected being (*Encyclopedia of Mormonism*, under "Moroni, Angel," and under "Moroni 2,") was sent in answer to that prayer. We sense that Moroni was a gentle and kind man, since young Joseph tells us "the fear soon left me" (verse 32, above). He further put Joseph at ease by calling him by name, then introducing himself and beginning to describe Joseph's mission.

33 He called me by name, and said unto me that he was a messenger sent from the presence of God to me, and that his name was Moroni; that God had a work for me to do; and that my name should be had for good and evil among all nations, kindreds, and tongues, or that it should be both good and evil spoken of among all people.

Can you imagine the impact Moroni's words that Joseph's "name should be had for good and evil among all nations" would have had on this seventeen-year-old back woods farm boy? This mighty prophecy has come true and continues to be fulfilled today throughout the world as groups and individuals either praise him and bear witness of Joseph Smith's calling as the prophet of the Restoration, or vilify and ridicule him and the work he accomplished under the direction of the Lord.

34 He said there was a book deposited, written upon gold plates, giving an account of the former inhabitants of this continent, and the source from whence they sprang. He also said that the fulness of the everlasting Gospel was contained in it, as delivered by the Savior to the ancient inhabitants;

Have you ever wondered how the Book of Mormon can have the "fulness of the everlasting Gospel," as stated in verse 34, above, when it does not mention things such as celestial marriage, the three degrees of glory, or work for the dead?

Since Joseph Smith translated only the portion of the gold plates that was not sealed, it is highly likely that the sealed portion contained those things. But the Doctrine and Covenants confirms that the Book of Mormon that we have contains "the fulness of the gospel (D&C 20:9)."

In fact, no details are given about a number of doctrines contained in the Doctrine and Covenants. Since we know that the Book of Mormon is true, whenever we see something which appears on the surface to be a contradiction, we know that it is our understanding that is flawed, rather than the word of God. Therefore, whenever we come to a word or phrase we may not understand, there is wisdom in looking at other possible meanings for it, especially paying attention to the context in which it is found.

When we do this, we find a number of possibilities. For instance, "fulness" in this context, could easily mean the gospel of faith, repentance, baptism, and the gift of the Holy Ghost followed by the lifestyle of living the gospel with Christlike charity and humility which will lead to exaltation.

Charles W. Penrose, who served as a counselor in the First Presidency of the Church, explained "fulness of the gospel" as follows:

"We are told that the Book of Mormon contains the fulness of the gospel, that those who like to get up a dispute, say that the Book of Mormon does not contain any reference to the work of salvation for the dead, and there are many other things pertaining to the gospel that are not developed in that book, and yet we are told that book contains 'the fulness of the everlasting gospel.' Well, what is the fulness of the gospel? You read carefully the revelation in regard to the three glories, section 76, in the Doctrine and Covenants, and you find there defined what the gospel is [76:40–43]. There God, the Eternal Father, and Jesus Christ, his Son, and the Holy Ghost, are held up as the three persons in the Trinity—the one God, the Father, the Word and the Holy Ghost, all three being united and being one God. When people believe in that doctrine and obey the ordinances which are spoken of in the same list of principles [20:17–28], you get the fulness of the gospel for this reason: If you really believe so as to have faith in our Eternal Father and in his Son, Jesus Christ, the Redeemer, and will hear him, you will learn all about what is needed to be done for the salvation of the living and the redemption of the dead.

"When people believe and repent and are baptized by Divine authority and the Holy Ghost is conferred upon them as a gift, they receive the everlasting gospel . . . and when the Holy Ghost as a gift is conferred upon people, young or old, as an 'abiding witness,' as a continuous gift, as a revelating spirit, they have the beginning, and I would not say the end, but they have the substance of the gospel of Jesus Christ. They have that which will bring salvation, for the gift of the Holy Ghost is such that it will highly enliven everyone who receives it." (Conference Report, April 1922, pp. 27–28)

As we continue now, we are given a brief description of the Urim and Thummim that the Prophet will use in translating the gold plates. We are informed in the Bible Dictionary that the Urim and Thummim used by the Prophet Joseph Smith were the same ones that the brother of Jared used in ancient times (Bible Dictionary, under "Urim and Thummim").

35 Also, that there were two stones in silver bows—and these stones, fastened to a breastplate, constituted what is called the Urim and Thummim—deposited with the plates; and the possession and use of these stones were what constituted "seers" in ancient or former times; and that God had prepared them for the purpose of translating the book.

David Whitmer, one of the Three Witnesses to the Book of Mormon, was shown the Urim and Thummim by an angel, as promised in D&C 17:1. He described it, saying "I saw the Interpreters in the holy vision; they looked like whitish stones put in the rim of a bow—looked like spectacles, only much larger." (*Investigating the Book of Mormon Witnesses*, p. 81.)

As we continue with this brief summary of his history, by the Prophet himself, you will see that a major part of young Joseph's instruction and orientation by Moroni for his mission to translate the gold plates consisted of quotes from the scriptures. This is a reminder of the importance of the scriptures in preparing us and enabling us to fulfill our callings in the Church.

As we proceed, we will include the scriptures quoted by Moroni so that you can see how they relate to the work to which Joseph Smith is being called. In cases where Moroni made corrections to the verses as they stand in the King James Version of the Bible, we will include the Bible version so that you can compare it with Moroni's rendition and see what he changed.

In verse 36, next, Moroni quotes part of Malachi 3 and Malachi 4. Since we don't know what part of chapter 3 he quoted (see *Joseph Smith—History* 1:36), we will include the whole chapter here.

As you can see, many verses in this chapter deal with the last days and the coming of Christ. Thus, they would, among other things, teach Joseph Smith the context and setting in which he would serve as the prophet of the Restoration, including the pride, wickedness, and rebelliousness of people in the last days.

Malachi 3
1 BEHOLD, I will send my messenger, and he shall prepare the way before me: and the Lord, whom ye seek, shall suddenly come to his temple, even the messenger of the covenant, whom ye delight in: behold, he shall come, saith the LORD of hosts.

2 But who may abide the day of his coming? and who shall stand when he appeareth? for he *is* like a refiner's fire, and like fullers' soap:

3 And he shall sit *as* a refiner and purifer of silver: and he shall purify the sons of Levi, and purge them as gold and silver, that they may offer unto the LORD an offering in righteousness.

4 Then shall the offering of Judah and Jerusalem be pleasant unto the LORD, as in the days of old, and as in former years.

5 And I will come near to you to judgment; and I will be a swift witness against the sorcerers, and against the adulterers, and against false swearers, and against those that oppress the hireling in *his* wages, the widow, and the fatherless, and that turn aside the stranger *from his right,* and fear not me, saith the LORD of hosts.

6 For I *am* the LORD, I change not; therefore ye sons of Jacob are not consumed.

7 Even from the days of your fathers ye are gone away from mine ordinances, and have not kept *them.* Return unto me, and I will return unto you, saith the LORD of hosts. But ye said, Wherein shall we return?

8 Will a man rob God? Yet ye have robbed me. But ye say, Wherein have we robbed thee? In tithes and offerings.

9 Ye *are* cursed with a curse: for ye have robbed me, *even* this whole nation.

10 Bring ye all the tithes into the storehouse, that there may be meat in mine house, and prove me now herewith, saith the LORD of hosts, if I will not open you the windows of heaven, and pour you out a blessing, that *there shall* not *be room* enough *to receive it.*

11 And I will rebuke the devourer for your sakes, and he shall not destroy the fruits of your ground; neither shall your vine cast her fruit before the time in the field, saith the LORD of hosts.

12 And all nations shall call you blessed: for ye shall be a delightsome land, saith the LORD of hosts.

13 Your words have been stout against me, saith the LORD. Yet ye say, What have we spoken *so much* against thee?

14 Ye have said, It *is* vain to serve God: and what profit *is it* that we have kept his ordinance, and that we have walked mournfully before the LORD of hosts?

15 And now we call the proud happy; yea, they that work wickedness are set up; yea, *they that* tempt God are even delivered.

16 Then they that feared the LORD spake often one to another: and the LORD hearkened, and heard *it,* and a book of remembrance was written before him for them that feared the LORD, and that thought upon his name.

17 And they shall be mine, saith the LORD of hosts, in that day when I make up my jewels; and I will spare them, as a man spareth his own son that serveth him.

18 Then shall ye return, and discern between the righteous and the wicked, between him that serveth God and him that serveth him not.

36 After telling me these things, he commenced quoting the prophecies of the Old Testament. He first quoted part of the third chapter of Malachi; and he quoted also the fourth or last chapter of the same prophecy, though with a little variation from the way it reads in our Bibles. Instead of quoting the first verse as it reads in our books, he quoted it thus:

37 *For behold, the day cometh that shall burn as an oven, and all the proud, yea, and all that do wickedly shall burn as stubble; for they that come shall burn them, saith the Lord of Hosts, that it shall leave them neither root nor branch.*

Malachi 4:1 (from the Bible)

1 FOR, behold, the day cometh, that shall burn as an oven; and all the proud, yea, and all that do wickedly, shall be stubble:

and the day that cometh shall burn them up, saith the LORD of hosts, that it shall leave them neither root nor branch.

We will include verses 2–4 here so you can see how they might help Joseph understand the import of his mission as the prophet of the Restoration. We will add brief notes of explanation. Moroni apparently quoted these verses without any changes.

Malachi 4:2–4
2 But unto you that fear [*respect and honor*] my name shall the Sun of righteousness [*"Son of Righteousness, see 3 Nephi 25:2*"] arise with healing in his wings [*you will be blessed by the full powers of the Atonement*]; and ye shall go forth, and grow up as calves of the stall [*you will be protected from evil, like calves are protected from the elements by their individual stalls in the barn*].

3 And ye shall tread down the wicked [*you will triumph over all your former enemies, physical and spiritual, at the time of the Second Coming*]; for they shall be ashes under the soles of your feet in the day that I shall do *this*, saith the LORD of hosts.

4 Remember ye [*keep, obey*] the law of Moses my servant, which I commanded unto him in Horeb [*another name for Sinai—see Bible Dictionary, under "Horeb"*] for all Israel, *with* the statutes and judgments.

38 And again, he quoted the fifth verse thus: *Behold, I will reveal unto you the Priesthood, by the hand of Elijah the prophet, before the coming of the great and dreadful day of the Lord.*

Malachi 4:5 (from the Bible)
5 Behold, I will send you Elijah the prophet before the coming of the great and dreadful day of the LORD:

39 He also quoted the next verse differently: *And he shall plant in the hearts of the children the promises made to the fathers, and the hearts of the children shall turn to their fathers. If it were not so, the whole earth would be utterly wasted at his coming.*

Malachi 4:6 (from the Bible)
6 And he shall turn the heart of the fathers to the children, and the heart of the children to their fathers, lest I come and smite the earth with a curse.

40 In addition to these, he quoted the eleventh chapter of Isaiah, saying that it was about to be fulfilled. He quoted also the third chapter of Acts, twenty-second and twenty-third verses, precisely as they stand in our New Testament. He said that that prophet

was Christ; but the day had not yet come when "they who would not hear his voice should be cut off from among the people," but soon would come.

Through Isaiah, chapter 11, Joseph was taught, among other things, that powerful leaders will come forth in the last days to lead the gathering of Israel. He was instructed in Christlike qualities of leadership and shown the peace that will abound during the Millennium. We will add a few notes of explanation as we review these verses of Isaiah quoted by Moroni.

Isaiah 11
1 And there shall come forth a rod [*Hebrew: twig or branch; D&C 113:3–4 defines this "rod" as "a servant in the hands of Christ"*] out of the stem [*root*] of Jesse [*Christ—see heading to this chapter in your Bible*], and a Branch shall grow out of his roots:

Perhaps, the imagery here in verse one grows out of the last two verses of the previous chapter of Isaiah, chapter 10, where the wicked leaders end up, in effect, as "stumps" and have been destroyed. In the last days, new, righteous, powerful leaders will be brought forth to replace the apostate "stumps" of the past and will have their origins in the "roots" of Christ. "Roots" can symbolically represent being solid and firmly rooted in God.

Next, we see a description of Christlike qualities of leadership.

2 And the spirit of the Lord shall rest upon him, the spirit of wisdom and understanding, the spirit of counsel and might, the spirit of knowledge and of the fear of [*respect, honoring of*] the Lord;

3 And shall make him of quick understanding in the fear of the Lord: and he shall not judge after the sight of his eyes, neither reprove after the hearing of his ears:

Verse 4, next, makes a transition into describing powers held by the Savior.

4 But with righteousness shall he judge the poor, and reprove with equity for the meek of the earth: and he shall smite the earth with the rod of his mouth, and with the breath of his lips shall he slay the wicked.

5 And righteousness shall be the girdle of his loins [*He will be clothed in righteousness*], and faithfulness the girdle of his reins [*desires, thoughts*].

Next, we are taken into the Millennium, where we are shown conditions of peace. One thing this could show Joseph Smith is that the dispensation of the fulness of the gospel restored through him would usher in the Second Coming and millennial reign of the Savior.

6 The wolf also shall dwell with the lamb and the leopard shall lie down with the kid [*young goat*]; and the calf and the young lion and the fatling together; and a little child shall lead [*herd*] them [*peaceful conditions during the Millennium*].

7 And the cow and the bear shall feed [*graze*]; their young ones shall lie down together: and the lion shall eat straw like the ox.

8 And the sucking [*nursing*] child shall play on the hole of the asp [*viper*], and the weaned child shall put his hand on the cockatrice's [*venomous serpent's*] den [*more emphasis on the peace that will exist during the Millennium*].

9 They shall not hurt nor destroy in all my holy mountain [*throughout the earth*]: for the earth shall be full of the knowledge of [*Hebrew: devotion to*] the Lord, as the waters cover the sea.

10 And in that day there shall be a root of Jesse [*probably Joseph Smith; see* Doctrine and Covenants Student Manual*, p. 284*], which shall stand for an ensign [*a rallying point for gathering*] of the people; to it shall the Gentiles seek: and his rest shall be glorious.

11 And it shall come to pass in that day, that the Lord shall set his hand again the second time to recover [*gather*] the remnant of his people, which shall be left, from Assyria [*modern Iraq*], and from Egypt, and from Pathros [*upper Egypt; Bible Dictionary, under "Pathros"*], and from Cush [*Ethiopia; Bible Dictionary, under "Cush"*], and from Elam [*Iran*], and from Shinar [*the area between the Tigris and Euphrates rivers—Bible Dictionary, under "Shinar, Plain of"*], and from Hamath [*a city in Syria; Bible Dictionary, under "Hamath"*], and from the islands of the sea [*all other nations and peoples of the earth; in other words, Israel will be gathered from throughout the earth*].

12 And he shall set up an ensign [*the Church in the last days*] for the nations, and shall assemble the outcasts of Israel, and gather together the dispersed of Judah from the four corners of the earth.

13 The envy also of Ephraim shall depart, and the adversaries of Judah shall be cut off: Ephraim shall not envy Judah, and Judah shall not vex Ephraim [*the US and others who will work with the Jews*].

14 But they [*the Jews with Ephraim's help*] shall fly upon the shoulders of the Philistines toward the west [*they will attack the western slopes that were Philistine territory*]; they shall spoil them of the east together: they shall lay their hand upon Edom and Moab; and the children of Ammon shall obey them [*the Jews will be powerful in the last days rather than easy prey for their enemies*].

15 And the Lord shall utterly destroy the tongue of the Egyptian sea [*perhaps meaning that the productivity of the Nile River will be ruined; see Isaiah 19:5–10*]; and with his mighty wind shall he shake his hand over the river [*perhaps the river referred to in Revelation 16:12; symbolically, the Euphrates represents preparation for the Battle of Armageddon*], and shall smite it in the seven streams, and make men go over dryshod.

16 And there shall be an highway [*God will prepare a way for Israel to return; the gathering*] for the remnant of his people, which shall be left, from Assyria; like as it was to Israel in the day that he came up out of the land of Egypt [*just like He gathered Israel out of Egyptian bondage through Moses*].

As mentioned in *Joseph Smith— History* 1:40, Moroni also quoted the following verses from Acts:

Acts 3:22–23
22 For Moses truly said unto the fathers, A prophet [*Christ*] shall the Lord your God raise up unto you of your brethren, like unto me; him shall ye hear in all things whatsoever he shall say unto you.

23 And it shall come to pass, *that* every soul, which will not hear that prophet, shall be destroyed from among the people.

41 He also quoted the second chapter of Joel, from the twenty-eighth verse to the last. He also said that this was not yet fulfilled, but was soon to be. And he further stated that the fulness of the Gentiles was soon to come in. He quoted many other passages of scripture, and offered many explanations which cannot be mentioned here.

Joel 2:28–32
28 And it shall come to pass afterward, *that* I will pour out my spirit upon all flesh; and your sons and your daughters shall prophesy, your old men shall dream dreams, your young men shall see visions:

29 And also upon the servants and upon the handmaids in those days will I pour out my spirit.

30 And I will shew wonders in the heavens and in the earth,

blood, and fire, and pillars of smoke.

31 The sun shall be turned into darkness, and the moon into blood, before the great and the terrible day of the LORD come.

32 And it shall come to pass, *that* whosoever shall call on the name of the LORD shall be delivered: for in mount Zion and in Jerusalem shall be deliverance, as the LORD hath said, and in the remnant whom the LORD shall call.

It is interesting to note that Moroni told Joseph Smith that these verses of Joel were not yet fulfilled but soon would be (verse 41, above). President Gordon B. Hinckley, in the October 2001 general conference of the Church, Saturday morning session, stated that these words of Joel are now fulfilled. He said:

"The era in which we live is the fulness of times spoken of in the scriptures, when God has brought together all of the elements of previous dispensations. From the day that He and His Beloved Son manifested themselves to the boy Joseph, there has been a tremendous cascade of enlightenment poured out upon the world. The hearts of men have turned to their fathers in fulfillment of the words of Malachi. The vision of Joel has been fulfilled wherein he declared: (President Hinckley then read Joel 2:28–32.)"

Thus, we see that Moroni was quoting scripture showing Joseph that his work as a prophet of God would usher in the day when the Spirit of the Lord would be poured out upon all flesh and many other prophecies would be fulfilled.

We understand that the "fulness of the Gentiles" spoken of in verse 41, above, refers to the missionary work that will go forth to the Gentiles (meaning everyone except the Jews, in this context) in all the world in the last days, before it is finally taken to the Jews as a people. You may recall that the scriptures say that the last shall be first and the first shall be last (Ether 13:12), referring to the fact that, during the Savior's mortal mission, the gospel was taken to the Jews first, and then, after His Crucifixion and Resurrection, it was taken to the Gentiles (Mark 16:15). In the last days, the order will be reversed. The gospel will be first taken to the Gentiles and then it will be taken to the Jews. We live in the day when it is being taken to the Gentiles.

42 Again, he told me, that when I got those plates of which he had spoken—for the time that they

should be obtained was not yet fulfilled—I should not show them to any person; neither the breastplate with the Urim and Thummim; only to those to whom I should be commanded to show them [*the three witnesses and the eight witnesses to the Book of Mormon*]; if I did I should be destroyed. While he was conversing with me about the plates, the vision was opened to my mind that I could see the place where the plates were deposited, and that so clearly and distinctly that I knew the place again when I visited it.

> Joseph was required to wait four years, until September 22, 1827, to receive the gold plates and take them home to begin translating the unsealed portion.

43 After this communication, I saw the light in the room begin to gather immediately around the person of him who had been speaking to me, and it continued to do so until the room was again left dark, except just around him; when, instantly I saw, as it were, a conduit open right up into heaven, and he ascended till he entirely disappeared, and the room was left as it had been before this heavenly light had made its appearance.

44 I lay musing on the singularity of the scene, and marveling greatly at what had been told to me by this extraordinary messenger; when, in the midst of my meditation, I suddenly discovered that my room was again beginning to get lighted, and in an instant, as it were, the same heavenly messenger was again by my bedside.

45 He commenced, and again related the very same things which he had done at his first visit, without the least variation; which having done, he informed me of great judgments which were coming upon the earth, with great desolations by famine, sword, and pestilence; and that these grievous judgments would come on the earth in this generation. Having related these things, he again ascended as he had done before.

> One of the things we can learn here from the Prophet's account is the value of repetition, including in our gospel classes and in our reading of the scriptures, as we continually prepare ourselves for more effective service in the kingdom of God.

> Moroni will appear once more during this night and twice the next day, making a total of five appearances during this roughly twenty-four hour period, repeating much and giving additional counsel and instruction.

46 By this time, so deep were the impressions made on my mind, that

sleep had fled from my eyes, and I lay overwhelmed in astonishment at what I had both seen and heard. But what was my surprise when again I beheld the same messenger at my bedside, and heard him rehearse or repeat over again to me the same things as before; and added a caution to me, telling me that Satan would try to tempt me (in consequence of the indigent circumstances of my father's family), to get the plates for the purpose of getting rich. This he forbade me, saying that I must have no other object in view in getting the plates but to glorify God, and must not be influenced by any other motive than that of building his kingdom; otherwise I could not get them.

47 After this third visit, he again ascended into heaven as before, and I was again left to ponder on the strangeness of what I had just experienced; when almost immediately after the heavenly messenger had ascended from me for the third time, the cock crowed, and I found that day was approaching, so that our interviews must have occupied the whole of that night.

48 I shortly after arose from my bed, and, as usual, went to the necessary labors of the day; but, in attempting to work as at other times, I found my strength so exhausted as to render me entirely unable. My father, who was laboring along with me, discovered something to be wrong with me, and told me to go home. I started with the intention of going to the house; but, in attempting to cross the fence out of the field where we were, my strength entirely failed me, and I fell helpless on the ground, and for a time was quite unconscious of anything.

> Watch now as Moroni honors Joseph Smith's father when he instructs Joseph to go tell his father about the vision and commandments he has received. Remember, also, that his father has already been prepared to be supportive to his son in the great latter-day work to which he has been called (see background for Joseph Smith—History in this study guide).

49 The first thing that I can recollect was a voice speaking unto me, calling me by name. I looked up, and beheld the same messenger standing over my head, surrounded by light as before. He then again related unto me all that he had related to me the previous night, and commanded me to go to my father and tell him of the vision and commandments which I had received.

50 I obeyed; I returned to my father in the field, and rehearsed the whole matter to him. He replied to me that it was of God, and told me to go and do as commanded by the messenger. I left the field, and

went to the place where the messenger had told me the plates were deposited; and owing to the distinctness of the vision which I had had concerning it, I knew the place the instant that I arrived there.

> Joseph will now describe the Hill Cumorah, located about three miles from his parent's home in upstate New York, and the contents of the stone box on the hill where Moroni had buried the gold plates and other items some 1,400 years ago.

51 Convenient to the village of Manchester, Ontario county, New York, stands a hill of considerable size, and the most elevated of any in the neighborhood. On the west side of this hill, not far from the top, under a stone of considerable size, lay the plates, deposited in a stone box. This stone was thick and rounding in the middle on the upper side, and thinner towards the edges, so that the middle part of it was visible above the ground, but the edge all around was covered with earth.

52 Having removed the earth, I obtained a lever, which I got fixed under the edge of the stone, and with a little exertion raised it up. I looked in, and there indeed did I behold the plates, the Urim and Thummim, and the breastplate, as stated by the messenger. The box in which they lay was formed by laying stones together in some kind of cement. In the bottom of the box were laid two stones crossways of the box, and on these stones lay the plates and the other things with them.

53 I made an attempt to take them out, but was forbidden by the messenger, and was again informed that the time for bringing them forth had not yet arrived, neither would it, until four years from that time; but he told me that I should come to that place precisely in one year from that time [*September 22, 1823*], and that he would there meet with me, and that I should continue to do so until the time should come for obtaining the plates.

> Moroni first appeared to Joseph Smith on the evening of September 21, 1823, appearing twice more that night and twice the next day (once in the morning to Joseph after he became unconscious by the fence and again on the Hill Cumorah by the stone box). Thus, it was September 22, 1823 when Joseph Smith was instructed to return "precisely in one year from that time" to the location of the plates. Therefore, he will return to the place on September 22nd of 1824, 1825, 1826, and 1827, when he will be allowed to take the plates home.

54 Accordingly, as I had been commanded, I went at the end of each year, and at each time I

found the same messenger there, and received instruction and intelligence from him at each of our interviews, respecting what the Lord was going to do, and how and in what manner his kingdom was to be conducted in the last days.

Joseph Smith's Mother, Lucy Mack Smith, gives fascinating details of these years while her son, Joseph, was continuing his instruction and preparation at the hands of Moroni.

"During our evening conversations, Joseph would occasionally give us some of the most amusing recitals that could be imagined. He would describe the ancient inhabitants of this continent, their dress, mode of traveling, and the animals upon which they rode; their cities, their buildings, with every particular; their mode of warfare; and also their religious worship. This he would do with as much ease, seemingly, as if he had spent his whole life among them." (*History of Joseph Smith by His Mother, Lucy Mack Smith*, p. 83)

In her writings, Mother Smith included an account of a rather severe lesson that Joseph received from Moroni during these preparation years regarding the gold plates.

"On the twenty-second of September, 1824, Joseph again visited the place where he found the plates the year previous; and supposing at this time that the only thing required, in order to possess them until the time for their translation, was to be able to keep the commandments of God—and he firmly believed he could keep every commandment which had been given him—he fully expected to carry them home with him. Therefore, having arrived at the place, and uncovering the plates, he put forth his hand and took them up, but, as he was taking them hence, the unhappy thought darted through his mind that probably there was something else in the box besides the plates, which would be of some pecuniary [*monetary*] advantage to him. So, in the moment of excitement, he laid them down very carefully, for the purpose of covering the box, lest some one might happen to pass that way and get whatever there might be remaining in it. After covering it, he turned round to take the Record again, but behold it was gone, and where, he knew not, neither did he know the means by which it had been taken from him.

"At this, as a natural consequence, he was much alarmed. He kneeled down and asked the Lord why the Record had been taken from him; upon which the angel of the Lord appeared to him, and told him that he had not done as he had been commanded, for in a former revelation he had been commanded not to lay the plates down, or put them for a moment out of his hands, until he got into the house and deposited them in a chest or trunk, having a good lock and key, and, contrary to this, he had laid them down with the view of securing some fancied or imaginary treasure that remained.

"In the moment of excitement, Joseph was overcome by the powers of darkness, and forgot the injunction that was laid upon him.

"Having some further conversation with the angel, on this occasion, Joseph was permitted to raise the stone again, when he beheld the plates as he had done before. He immediately reached forth his hand to take them, but instead of getting them, as he anticipated, he was hurled back upon the ground with great violence. When he recovered, the angel was gone, and he arose and returned to the house, weeping for grief and disappointment.

"As he was aware that we would expect him to bring the plates home with him, he was greatly troubled, fearing that we might doubt his having seen them. As soon as he entered the house, my husband asked if he had obtained the plates. The answer was, 'No, father, I could not get them.'

"His father then said, 'Did you see them?'

" 'Yes,' replied Joseph, 'I saw them, but could not take them.' " (*History of Joseph Smith by His Mother, Lucy Mack Smith*, pp. 83–85).

As the prophet of the Restoration, it was not unusual for Joseph Smith to be taught by beings from beyond the veil. In addition to Moroni's visits during these four years, throughout his lifetime Joseph Smith was taught by many other beings from the past. President John Taylor, in various talks, mentioned many of these "teachers" of the Prophet. The following quotes from some of his talks help us realize how many personages were involved. We have underlined and bolded these Heavenly messengers from the past who taught Joseph Smith. Some of the names are repeated.

"When God selected Joseph Smith to open up the last dispensation . . . the **Father** and the **Son** appeared to him . . . **Moroni** came to Joseph . . . Then comes another personage, whose name is **John the Baptist** . . . Afterwards came **Peter,**

James and John ... Then we read again of **Elias or Elijah** ... who committed to him the powers and authority associated with his position. Then **Abraham**, who had the Gospel, the Priesthood and Patriarchal powers in his day; and **Moses** who stood at the head of the gathering dispensation in his day ... We are informed that **Noah**, who was a Patriarch, and all in the line of the Priesthood, in every generation back to **Adam**, who was the first man, possessed the same. Why was it that all these people ... could communicate with Joseph Smith? Because he stood at the head of the dispensation of the fullness of times ... If you were to ask Joseph what sort of a looking man **Adam** was, he would tell you at once; he would tell you his size and appearance and all about him. You might have asked him what sort of men **Peter, James and John** were, and he could have told you. Why? Because he had seen them" (*Journal of Discourses*, Vol. 18, pp. 325–26).

"And when Joseph Smith was raised up as a Prophet of God, **Mormon, Moroni, Nephi, and others of the ancient Prophets who formerly lived on this Continent, and Peter and John and others who lived on the Asiatic Continent**, came to him and communicated to him certain principles pertaining to the gospel of the Son of God" (*Journal of Discourses*, Vol. 17, p. 374).

"I know of what I speak for I was very well acquainted with him [Joseph Smith] and was with him a great deal during his life, and was with him when he died. The principles which he had, placed him in communication with the Lord, and not only with the Lord, but with the ancient apostles and prophets, such men, for instance, as **Abraham, Isaac, Jacob, Noah, Adam, Seth, Enoch, and Jesus and the Father, and the apostles that lived on this continent as well as those who lived on the Asiatic Continent**. He seemed to be as familiar with these people as we are with one another" (*Journal of Discourses*, Vol. 21, p. 94).

The Prophet Joseph Smith also gave the following description of the **Apostle Paul**: "He is about five feet high; very dark hair; dark complexion; dark skin; large Roman nose; sharp face; small black eyes, penetrating as eternity; round shoulders; a whining voice, except when elevated, and then it almost resembled the roaring of a lion. He was a good orator, active and diligent, always employing himself in doing good to his fellow man" (*Teachings of the Prophet Joseph Smith*, p. 180).

Next, in verses 55–65, the Prophet Joseph Smith briefly summarizes events during the four years from 1823–27, when he finally received the gold plates, including his marriage to Emma Hale. In addition, he informs us that Martin Harris, who became one of the three witnesses to the Book of Mormon, took copies of some characters from the plates which Joseph had copied for him, and showed them to Professor Charles Anthon in New York City. The professor fulfilled a prophecy by Isaiah when he said, "I cannot read a sealed book" (Isaiah 29:11).

Joseph and Emma

55 As my father's worldly circumstances were very limited, we were under the necessity of laboring with our hands, hiring out by day's work and otherwise, as we could get opportunity. Sometimes we were at home, and sometimes abroad, and by continuous labor were enabled to get a comfortable maintenance.

56 In the year 1823 my father's family met with a great affliction by the death of my eldest brother, Alvin. In the month of October, 1825, I hired with an old gentleman by the name of Josiah Stoal, who lived in Chenango county, State of New York. He had heard something of a silver mine having been opened by the Spaniards in Harmony, Susquehanna county, State of Pennsylvania; and had, previous to my hiring to him, been digging, in order, if possible, to discover the mine. After I went to live with him, he took me, with the rest of his hands, to dig for the silver mine, at which I continued to work for nearly a month, without success in our undertaking, and finally I prevailed with the old gentleman to cease digging after it. Hence arose the very prevalent story of my having been a money-digger.

57 During the time that I was thus employed, I was put to board with a Mr. Isaac Hale, of that place; it was there I first saw my wife (his daughter), Emma Hale. On the 18th of January, 1827, we were married, while I was yet employed in the service of Mr. Stoal.

Emma Hale was the seventh of nine children. She was born on July 10, 1804, to Isaac and Elizabeth Hale. She was about a year and a half older than Joseph Smith and is described in the *Doctrine and Covenants Student Manual* as follows:

"Emma was a beautiful woman with an attractive personality, and she had the reputation of being a refined and dignified woman who was an excellent housekeeper and cook. Her Methodist upbringing had helped her develop a great love of music" (*Doctrine and Covenants Student Manual*, p. 50).

We will add a few additional details about Emma Hale Smith. She was about five feet, nine inches tall, used excellent English grammar, had dark hair and brown eyes, and was a schoolteacher in the area. Joseph continued to court her over time and eventually asked her father for permission to marry her. He refused to give it, expressing concerns about Joseph's lack of education and involvement with "gold digging." As a result, Joseph and Emma eloped and were married in South Bainbridge, New York, on January 18, 1827, after which they lived for a time with Joseph's parents in Manchester, New York.

They stayed in Manchester until after Moroni delivered the gold plates to Joseph, on September 22, 1827. In fact, Emma accompanied her husband to the Hill Cumorah on that occasion and waited at the bottom of the hill while Joseph climbed up the hill to his meeting place with Moroni.

58 Owing to my continuing to assert that I had seen a vision, persecution still followed me, and my wife's father's family were very much opposed to our being married. I was, therefore, under the necessity of taking her elsewhere; so we went and were married at the house of Squire Tarbill, in South Bainbridge, Chenango county, New York. Immediately after my marriage, I left Mr. Stoal's, and went to my father's, and farmed with him that season.

> Next, Joseph recounts the day when he was permitted to take the plates home.

Joseph Obtains the Plates

59 At length the time arrived for obtaining the plates, the Urim and Thummim, and the breastplate. On the twenty-second day of September, one thousand eight hundred and twenty-seven, having gone as usual at the end of another year to the place where they were deposited, the same heavenly messenger delivered them up to me with this charge: that I should be responsible for them; that if I should let them go carelessly, or through any neglect of mine, I should be cut off; but that if I would use all my endeavors to preserve them, until he, the messenger, should call for them, they should be protected.

60 I soon found out the reason why I had received such strict charges to keep them safe, and why it was that the messenger had said that when I had done what was required at my hand, he would call for them. For no sooner was it known that I

had them, than the most strenuous exertions were used to get them from me. Every stratagem that could be invented was resorted to for that purpose. The persecution became more bitter and severe than before, and multitudes were on the alert continually to get them from me if possible. But by the wisdom of God, they remained safe in my hands, until I had accomplished by them what was required at my hand. When, according to arrangements, the messenger called for them, I delivered them up to him; and he has them in his charge until this day, being the second day of May, one thousand eight hundred and thirty-eight.

As a side note here, we will mention that Brigham Young indicated that there were many other records kept in the Hill Cumorah. He said:

"I lived right in the country where the plates were found from which the Book of Mormon was translated, and I know a great many things pertaining to that country. I believe I will take the liberty to tell you of another circumstance that will be as marvelous as anything can be. This is an incident in the life of Oliver Cowdery, but he did not take the liberty of telling such things in meeting as I take. I tell these things to you, and I have a motive for doing so. I want to carry them to the ears of my brethren and sisters, and to the children also, that they may grow to an understanding of some things that seem to be entirely hidden from the human family. Oliver Cowdery went with the Prophet Joseph when he deposited these plates. Joseph did not translate all of the plates; there was a portion of them sealed, which you can learn from the Book of Doctrine and Covenants. When Joseph got the plates, the angel instructed him to carry them back to the hill Cumorah, which he did. Oliver says that when Joseph and Oliver went there, the hill opened, and they walked into a cave, in which there was a large and spacious room. He says he did not think, at the time, whether they had the light of the sun or artificial light; but that it was just as light as day. They laid the plates on a table; it was a large table that stood in the room. Under this table there was a pile of plates as much as two feet high, and there were altogether in this room more plates than probably many wagon loads; they were piled up in the corners and along the walls. The first time they went there the sword of Laban hung upon the wall; but when they went again it had been taken down and laid upon the table across the gold plates; it was unsheathed, and on it was written these words: "This sword will never be sheathed again until the kingdoms of this world become the kingdom of our God and his Christ" (*Journal of Discourses*, Vol. 19, p. 38).

Next, Joseph tells us that because of persecution in and around Palmyra and Manchester, he and his wife, Emma, found it necessary to move to Harmony, Pennsylvania, to live with her parents for a time. We see the kindness of Martin Harris as he provided money to enable them to make the move.

61 The excitement, however, still continued, and rumor with her thousand tongues was all the time employed in circulating falsehoods about my father's family, and about myself. If I were to relate a thousandth part of them, it would fill up volumes. The persecution, however, became so intolerable that I was under the necessity of leaving Manchester, and going with my wife to Susquehanna county, in the State of Pennsylvania. While preparing to start—being very poor, and the persecution so heavy upon us that there was no probability that we would ever be otherwise—in the midst of our afflictions we found a friend in a gentleman by the name of Martin Harris, who came to us and gave me fifty dollars to assist us on our journey. Mr. Harris was a resident of Palmyra township, Wayne county, in the State of New York, and a farmer of respectability.

Just a note about Martin Harris. He was a farmer, a weaver, and a successful businessman in Palmyra, New York. Known for his honesty and integrity, he was active and respected in local government and community affairs.

He was born May 18, 1783, which made him about 22 years older than Joseph Smith. He was about five feet, eight inches tall, had blue eyes and brown hair. He married his first cousin, Lucy Harris, and they had at least six children.

Sometime after the Smith family moved to the Palmyra area, in 1816, Martin Harris became acquainted with young Joseph Smith Jr. By 1824, Joseph had told Martin about the angel Moroni's visits to him. Later, Martin agreed to finance the publication of the Book of Mormon.

Joseph and Emma made the 135 mile journey to her parents' home in Harmony, Pennsylvania in December 1827. At the time, Emma was in her first three months of pregnancy with their first child. At some point after Joseph and Emma moved in with her parents, her father, Isaac

Hale, became angry because Joseph would not show him the plates. This made it necessary for Joseph and Emma to move out. Eventually, they purchased a small cabin on 13½ acres on the Hale family farm for two hundred dollars, and they moved into it.

We continue now with Joseph Smith's account of the move to Harmony.

62 By this timely aid was I enabled to reach the place of my destination in Pennsylvania; and immediately after my arrival there I commenced copying the characters off the plates. I copied a considerable number of them, and by means of the Urim and Thummim I translated some of them, which I did between the time I arrived at the house of my wife's father, in the month of December, and the February following.

Martin Harris was a very careful man and protective of his reputation in the community. We see this in the fact that, in verse 63, next, he traveled to New York City in the dead of winter cold to seek verification that the characters drawn from the gold plates by Joseph Smith were authentic.

63 Sometime in this month of February, the aforementioned Mr. Martin Harris came to our place, got the characters which I had drawn off the plates, and started with them to the city of New York. For what took place relative to him and the characters, I refer to his own account of the circumstances, as he related them to me after his return, which was as follows:

64 "I went to the city of New York, and presented the characters which had been translated, with the translation thereof, to Professor Charles Anthon, a gentleman celebrated for his literary attainments. Professor Anthon stated that the translation was correct, more so than any he had before seen translated from the Egyptian. I then showed him those which were not yet translated, and he said that they were Egyptian, Chaldaic, Assyriac, and Arabic; and he said they were true characters. He gave me a certificate, certifying to the people of Palmyra that they were true characters, and that the translation of such of them as had been translated was also correct. I took the certificate and put it into my pocket, and was just leaving the house, when Mr. Anthon called me back, and asked me how the young man found out that there were gold plates in the place where he found them. I answered that an angel of God had revealed it unto him.

65 "He then said to me, 'Let me see

that certificate.' I accordingly took it out of my pocket and gave it to him, when he took it and tore it to pieces, saying that there was no such thing now as ministering of angels, and that if I would bring the plates to him he would translate them. I informed him that part of the plates were sealed, and that I was forbidden to bring them. He replied, 'I cannot read a sealed book.' I left him and went to Dr. Mitchell, who sanctioned what Professor Anthon had said respecting both the characters and the translation."

In verses 64 and 65, above, we see the fulfillment of a prophecy given by Isaiah in which he foretold the conversation of Martin Harris with Professor Anthon. We will review this prophecy in Isaiah, which he gave over 2,500 years before it was fulfilled by Martin Harris and Charles Anthon, adding some explanatory notes.

Isaiah 29:11–12

11 And the vision of all [*German Bible says, "the vision of all the prophets;" in other words, the scriptures*] is become unto you [*Israelites who are spiritually dead*] as the words of a book [*Book of Mormon—see footnote 11a, in your Bible*] that is sealed [*because you refuse to hearken to the scriptures, they might just as well be sealed and unreadable to you like the copy of characters from the Book of Mormon plates*], which men [*Martin Harris, with the help of Joseph Smith*] deliver to one that is learned [*Professor Charles Anthon of Colombia College in New York City, Feb. 1828*], saying, Read this, I pray thee: and he [*Charles Anthon*] saith, I cannot; for it is sealed:

12 And the book [*the gold plates*] is delivered to him [*Joseph Smith*] that is not learned [*not educated like Professor Anthon*], saying, Read this, I pray thee: and he saith, I am not learned [*I can't translate it without God's help*].

From the *Church History in the Fulness of Times* manual, we read additional details regarding Martin Harris' trip to New York.

"According to previous arrangement, Martin Harris visited Joseph in Harmony sometime in February of 1828. By then the Lord had prepared Martin to assist Joseph in his mission. According to his own testimony, Martin was instructed by the Lord in 1818 not to join any church until the words of Isaiah were fulfilled. Sometime later, it was revealed to Martin that the Lord had a work for him to do. In 1827 several manifestations convinced Martin Harris that Joseph Smith was a prophet and that he should assist Joseph in bringing the Book of Mormon to this generation. Therefore, Martin went to Harmony to obtain a copy of some of the characters from the plates to show several noted linguists of the time, which fulfilled the prophecy of Isaiah 29:11–12 to help convince an unbelieving world.

"Martin visited at least three men with reputations as able linguists. In Albany, New York, he talked with Luther Bradish, a diplomat, statesman, world traveler, and student of languages. In New York City he visited Dr. Samuel Mitchell (sometimes spelled "Mitchill"), vice president of Rutgers Medical College. He also visited a man who knew several languages including Hebrew and Babylonian. This was Professor Charles Anthon of Columbia College in New York City, who was perhaps the most qualified of Martin's contacts to judge the characters on the document. He was among the leading classical scholars of his day. At the time of Martin Harris's visit, Charles Anthon was adjunct professor of Greek and Latin. He knew French, German, Greek, and Latin, and was familiar, if books in his library are evidence, with the latest discoveries pertaining to the Egyptian language including the early work of Champollion.

"Charles Anthon was a professor of classical studies at Columbia College (now Columbia University) in New York for forty-seven years. According to Martin Harris, Professor Anthon examined the characters and their translation and willingly gave him a certificate stating to the citizens of Palmyra that the writings were authentic. Anthon further told Martin the characters resembled Egyptian, Chaldean, Assyrian, and Arabic, and expressed his opinion that the translation was correct. Martin put the certificate in his pocket and was about to leave when Anthon called him back and asked how Joseph Smith found the gold plates in the hill. Martin explained that an angel of God revealed the location to Joseph, whereupon Charles Anthon asked for the certificate, which Martin gave to him. 'He took it and tore it to pieces, saying, that there was no such thing now as ministering of angels, and that if I [Martin] would bring the plates to him, he would translate them. I informed him that part of the plates were sealed, and that I was forbidden to bring them. He replied, 'I cannot read a sealed book.'"

"Martin Harris's trip was significant for several reasons. First, it showed that scholars had an interest in the characters and were willing to give them serious consideration as long as an angel was not part of their story. Second, it was, in the view of Martin and Joseph, the direct fulfillment of prophecy relative to the Book of Mormon. Third, it was a demonstration that translating the record would require the assistance of God; intellect alone was insufficient (see Isaiah 29:11–12; 2 Nephi 27:15–20). Finally, it built up Martin's own faith. He returned home confident that he had evidence to convince his neighbors of Joseph Smith's work. He was now ready to wholeheartedly commit himself and his means to the bringing forth of the Book of Mormon" (*Church History in the Fulness of Times*, p. 46).

After Martin Harris returned from New York, he eventually volunteered to serve as a scribe for Joseph Smith as he translated the Book of Mormon. He served from April 12 to June 14, 1828, during which time 116 manuscript pages were produced. At that point, Martin asked Joseph to ask the Lord if he could take the 116 pages back home to Palmyra to show his wife and others what he was doing with Joseph Smith in Pennsylvania. After being turned down twice by the Lord, Martin had Joseph request a third time and the Lord gave permission (*History of Joseph Smith by His Mother, Lucy Mack Smith*, p. 124) on condition that Martin only show the 116 manuscript pages to his wife, his brother, his mother and father, and his wife's sister. As you know, Martin was not true to his oath to show the pages only to the five the Lord specified, and the 116 pages were lost (see D&C 3 and 10 for the consequences).

Since Martin could no longer serve as a scribe, Joseph Smith was left for several months without one, and the work of translation was severely curtailed.

Martin eventually left the Church, in 1837, but never did deny his testimony. He returned to the Church and was rebaptized on November 7, 1842. In 1870, he joined the Saints in Utah, arriving by train in Salt Lake City, on August 30, 1870. He died, faithful to his testimony and faithful to the Church on July 10, 1875, in Clarkston, Utah, at age 92.

In verses 66–75, Joseph Smith reports that Oliver Cowdery came and served as a scribe for the translation of the Book of Mormon, and also tells of the appearance of John the Baptist, who conferred the Aaronic Priesthood upon Joseph and Oliver.

In order for you to feel what a relief it was for Joseph to have Oliver come to help with the translation of the Book of Mormon, we will fill in a little more history.

It had been almost 10 months since Martin Harris had lost the 116 manuscript pages. He had taken them on June 15, 1828, and headed out for Palmyra. That same day, Emma had given birth to their first child, a baby boy, who died after three hours. Emma almost died and was not out of danger for another two weeks' time. After three weeks, Emma insisted that her husband go to Palmyra, find Martin Harris, and check on the 116 pages. Joseph did. Martin could not find them. Joseph returned to Harmony in deep anguish because of the loss and because he had gone against the Lord's counsel in pursuing permission for Martin to take them in the first place.

Shortly after Joseph returned to Harmony, Moroni appeared, chastised him for what he had done, and took the gold plates and the Urim and Thummim (*Church History in the Fulness of Times*, pp. 48–49). Before he left, however, he said, "If you are very humble and penitent, it may be you will receive them again; if so, it will be on the twenty-second of next September." (*History of Joseph Smith by His Mother*, pp. 133–34.)

Lucy Mack Smith wrote what Joseph told her later that year:

"After the angel left me," said he, "I continued my supplications to God, without cessation, and on the twenty-second of September, I had the joy and satisfaction of again receiving the Urim and Thummim, with which I have again commenced translating, and Emma writes for me, but the angel said that the Lord would send me a scribe, and I trust his promise will be verified. The angel seemed pleased with me when he gave me back the Urim and Thummim, and he told me that the Lord loved me, for my faithfulness and humility." (*History of Joseph Smith by His Mother Lucy Mack Smith*, p. 135.)

Joseph continues now with his account of the arrival of Oliver Cowdery.

66 On the 5th day of April, 1829, Oliver Cowdery came to my house, until which time I had never seen him. He stated to me that having been teaching school in the neighborhood where my father resided, and my father being one of those who sent to the school, he went to board for a season at his house, and while there the family related to him the circumstances of my having received the plates, and accordingly he had come to make inquiries of me.

67 Two days after the arrival of Mr. Cowdery (being the 7th of April) I commenced to translate the Book of Mormon, and he began to write for me.

The work of translating will now move along much faster than heretofore. Over the next three months, Joseph Smith, with Oliver Cowdery as scribe, will translate what will become approximately 500 printed pages of the Book of Mormon.

Restoration of the Aaronic Priesthood

Next, beginning with verse 68, we are given brief details of the restoration of the Aaronic Priesthood by John the Baptist. Can you sense what a special occasion this would have been for him? He had ministered during his mortal mission by virtue of the Aaronic Priesthood, preaching to large throngs of people. He had prepared the way for Christ and had baptized Him. John was beheaded by Herod, after almost a year in prison (see Mark 6:17–29), and was resurrected with the Savior (see D&C 133:55).

Imagine how the resurrected John the Baptist must have felt now, as Joseph and Oliver walked to the banks of the Susquehanna River near Joseph's home, to pray about baptism, knowing that the time had finally arrived when he could restore the Aaronic Priesthood. And imagine what feelings must have swelled up in his heart as he actually laid his hands upon their heads and conferred upon Joseph and Oliver this sacred Aaronic Priesthood. Having performed many baptisms himself, he must have thrilled as he instructed them in the mode of proper baptism, so that they could baptize each other and begin the work of baptizing for the remission of sins in this, the dispensation of the fulness of times.

We will now continue with Joseph Smith's account of this monumental event in the restoration of the gospel of Jesus Christ.

68 We still continued the work of translation, when, in the ensuing month (May, 1829), we on a certain day [*May 15—see verse 72; see also D&C 13, heading*] went into the woods to pray and inquire of the Lord respecting baptism for the remission of sins, that we found mentioned in the translation of the plates. While we were thus employed, praying and calling upon the Lord, a messenger from heaven descended in a cloud of light, and having laid his hands upon us, he ordained us, saying:

69 *Upon you my fellow servants, in the name of Messiah, I confer the Priesthood of Aaron, which holds the keys of the ministering of angels, and of the gospel of repentance, and of baptism by immersion for the remission of sins; and this shall never be taken again from the*

earth until the sons of Levi do offer again an offering unto the Lord in righteousness.

Oliver Cowdery spoke of this visitation by John the Baptist as follows:

"On a sudden, as from the midst of eternity, the voice of the Redeemer spake peace to us, while the veil was parted and the angel of God came down clothed with glory, and delivered the anxiously looked for message, and the keys of the gospel of repentance!—What joy! what wonder! what amazement! While the world were racked and distracted . . . our eyes beheld—our ears heard." (*Messenger and Advocate*, Oct. 1834, p. 15; see also *Church History in the Fulness of Times*, p. 55.)

A clarification for the phrase *"until the sons of Levi do offer again an offering unto the Lord in righteousness,"* in verse 69, above, is found at the end of Joseph Smith—History where Oliver Cowdery gives a brief account of these events in his own words. If you look at the last phrase of paragraph five of Oliver's account, you will see a different word used in his rendition of this phrase. He said, *"that the Sons of Levi may yet offer an offering unto the Lord in righteousness!"*

Oliver used *"that"* rather than *"until."* It could be that the phrase means, in effect, that the Aaronic Priesthood is being restored and "shall never be taken again from the earth" (verse 69) in order that authorized Aaronic Priesthood ordinances such as baptism and the sacrament can once again be offered before the Lord by sincere saints. 3 Nephi 24:3 also uses the word, "that," in this phrase, as does D&C 128:24.

The question also comes up as to who the "sons of Levi" are. One possibility is that modern priesthood holders could be considered, symbolically, to be the "sons of Levi." In the days of Moses, the sons of Levi were the ones who held the Aaronic Priesthood and officiated in the Aaronic Priesthood ordinances among the Children of Israel. This seems to be the meaning of "sons of Moses and Aaron," who were of the tribe of Levi, as referred to in D&C 84:31–32. In that revelation, the Lord addressed a number of elders who had gathered in Kirtland, Ohio, after returning from their missions in the eastern states. He used the phrase "sons of Moses and also the sons of Aaron" as a synonym for "sons of Levi." We will quote these two verses here and add some notes of explanation.

JOSEPH SMITH HISTORY

D&C 84:31–32

31 Therefore, as I said concerning the sons of Moses—for the sons of Moses and also the sons of Aaron [*sons of Levi*] shall offer an acceptable offering and sacrifice in the house of the Lord, which house [*the Kirtland Temple*] shall be built unto the Lord in this generation, upon the consecrated spot as I have appointed—

32 And the sons of Moses and of Aaron shall be filled with the glory of the Lord, upon Mount Zion in the Lord's house, whose sons are ye [*you are the "sons of Moses and of Aaron"*]; and also many whom I have called and sent forth to build up my church.

Continuing now with Joseph's account, we see that John the Baptist explained to Joseph and Oliver that the Aaronic Priesthood does not have the power to confer the gift of the Holy Ghost.

70 He said this Aaronic Priesthood had not the power of laying on hands for the gift of the Holy Ghost, but that this should be conferred on us hereafter; and he commanded us to go and be baptized, and gave us directions that I should baptize Oliver Cowdery, and that afterwards he should baptize me.

71 Accordingly we went and were baptized. I baptized him first, and afterwards he baptized me—after which I laid my hands upon his head and ordained him to the Aaronic Priesthood, and afterwards he laid his hands on me and ordained me to the same Priesthood—for so we were commanded.

72 The messenger who visited us on this occasion and conferred this Priesthood upon us, said that his name was John, the same that is called John the Baptist in the New Testament, and that he acted under the direction of Peter, James and John, who held the keys of the Priesthood of Melchizedek, which Priesthood, he said, would in due time be conferred on us, and that I should be called the first Elder of the Church, and he (Oliver Cowdery) the second. It was on the fifteenth day of May, 1829, that we were ordained under the hand of this messenger, and baptized.

As promised by John the Baptist in verse 72, above, Peter, James, and John appeared and conferred the Melchizedek Priesthood upon Joseph and Oliver on the banks of the Susquehanna River (D&C 128:20) and gave them the keys of the apostleship (D&C 27:12). The exact date of this event was not recorded, but appears to have taken place in the spring of 1829 (Bible Dictionary, "Melchizedek Priesthood").

Additional evidence suggests that Peter, James, and John

conferred the Melchizedek Priesthood on Joseph Smith and Oliver Cowdery before the end of May 1829. We quote from a 1996 *Ensign* article: "factors point to the visitation of Peter, James, and John to restore the Melchizedek Priesthood as occurring within the 13-day period of 16 to 28 May 1829" (*Ensign*, December 1996, Larry C. Porter, "The Restoration of the Aaronic and Melchizedek Priesthoods," pp. 33–47).

Joseph continues his account, describing the spiritual manifestations which followed their baptism.

73 Immediately on our coming up out of the water after we had been baptized, we experienced great and glorious blessings from our Heavenly Father. No sooner had I baptized Oliver Cowdery, than the Holy Ghost fell upon him, and he stood up and prophesied many things which should shortly come to pass. And again, so soon as I had been baptized by him, I also had the spirit of prophecy, when, standing up, I prophesied concerning the rise of this Church, and many other things connected with the Church, and this generation of the children of men. We were filled with the Holy Ghost, and rejoiced in the God of our salvation.

Verse 74, next, is a simple, yet powerful reminder of the blessing of having the Holy Ghost upon us. Through the power of the Holy Ghost, Joseph and Oliver were now able to understand the scriptures as never before.

74 Our minds being now enlightened, we began to have the scriptures laid open to our understandings, and the true meaning and intention of their more mysterious passages revealed unto us in a manner which we never could attain to previously, nor ever before had thought of. In the meantime we were forced to keep secret the circumstances of having received the Priesthood and our having been baptized, owing to a spirit of persecution which had already manifested itself in the neighborhood.

It is gratifying to see, in verse 75, next, that Emma's father, Isaac Hale, and his family had by now become friendly to Joseph and exerted their influence to protect him as best they could from those who desired to destroy his work.

75 We had been threatened with being mobbed, from time to time, and this, too, by professors of religion. And their intentions of mobbing us were only counteracted by the influence of my wife's father's family (under Divine providence),

who had become very friendly to me, and who were opposed to mobs, and were willing that I should be allowed to continue the work of translation without interruption; and therefore offered and promised us protection from all unlawful proceedings, as far as in them lay.

Oliver Cowdery's Account

A brief account by Oliver Cowdery of the translation of the Book of Mormon and the restoration of the Aaronic Priesthood by John the Baptist is included in the Pearl of Great Price at the end of Joseph Smith—History. The account is taken from an article written by him for the *Messenger and Advocate*, which was a periodical published by the Church in Kirtland, Ohio, from October 1834 until September 1837. It was published once a month and consisted of sixteen pages per issue.

Not only does this account provide feeling and testimony of the "marvelous work and a wonder" (Isaiah 29:14), which came to pass with the restoration of the gospel of Jesus Christ, it also acquaints us with Oliver Cowdery's great gift of teaching and writing. He is articulate and passionate as he recounts the unforgettable days spent with Joseph Smith as the Book of Mormon was brought forth and the Aaronic Priesthood was restored. His account follows, as contained in the Pearl of Great Price.

Oliver Cowdery describes these events thus: "These were days never to be forgotten—to sit under the sound of a voice dictated by the inspiration of heaven, awakened the utmost gratitude of this bosom! Day after day I continued, uninterrupted, to write from his mouth, as he translated with the Urim and Thummim, or, as the Nephites would have said, 'Interpreters,' the history or record called 'The Book of Mormon.'

"To notice, in even few words, the interesting account given by Mormon and his faithful son, Moroni, of a people once beloved and favored of heaven, would supersede my present design; I shall therefore defer this to a future period, and, as I said in the introduction, pass more directly to some few incidents immediately connected with the rise of this Church, which may be entertaining to some thousands who have stepped forward, amid the frowns of bigots and the calumny of hypocrites, and embraced the Gospel of Christ.

"No men, in their sober senses, could translate and write the directions given to the Nephites from the mouth of the Savior, of the precise manner in which men should build up His Church, and especially when corruption had spread an uncertainty over all forms and systems practiced among men, without desiring a privilege of showing the willingness of the heart by being buried in the liquid grave, to answer a 'good conscience by the resurrection of Jesus Christ.'

"After writing the account given of the Savior's ministry to the remnant of the seed of Jacob, upon this continent, it was easy to be seen, as the prophet said it would be, that darkness covered the earth and gross darkness the minds of the people. On reflecting further it was as easy to be seen that amid the great strife and noise concerning religion, none had authority from God to administer the ordinances of the Gospel. For the question might be asked, have men authority to administer in the name of Christ, who deny revelations, when His testimony is no less than the spirit of prophecy, and His religion based, built, and sustained by immediate revelations, in all ages of the world when He has had a people on earth? If these facts were buried, and carefully concealed by men whose craft would have been in danger if once permitted to shine in the faces of men, they were no longer to us; and we only waited for the commandment to be given 'Arise and be baptized.'

"This was not long desired before it was realized. The Lord, who is rich in mercy, and ever willing to answer the consistent prayer of the humble, after we had called upon Him in a fervent manner, aside from the abodes of men, condescended to manifest to us His will. On a sudden, as from the midst of eternity, the voice of the Redeemer spake peace to us, while the veil was parted and the angel of God came down clothed with glory, and delivered the anxiously looked for message, and the keys of the Gospel of repentance. What joy! what wonder! what amazement! While the world was racked and distracted—while millions were groping as the blind for the wall, and while all men were resting upon uncertainty, as a general mass, our eyes beheld, our ears heard, as in the 'blaze of day'; yes, more—above the glitter of the May sunbeam, which then shed its brilliancy over the face of nature! Then his voice, though mild, pierced to the center, and his words, 'I am thy fellow-servant,' dispelled every fear. We listened, we gazed, we admired! 'Twas the voice of an angel from glory, 'twas a message from the Most High! And as we heard we rejoiced, while His love enkindled upon our souls, and we were wrapped in the vision of the Almighty! Where was room for doubt? Nowhere; uncertainty had fled, doubt had sunk no more to rise, while fiction and deception had fled forever!

"But, dear brother, think, further think for a moment, what joy filled our hearts, and with what surprise we must have bowed, (for who would not have bowed the knee for such a blessing?) when we received under his hand the Holy Priesthood as he said, 'Upon you my fellow-servants, in the name of Messiah, I confer this Priesthood and this authority, which shall remain upon earth, that the Sons of Levi may yet offer an offering unto the Lord in righteousness!'

"I shall not attempt to paint to you the feelings of this heart, nor the majestic beauty and glory which surrounded us on this occasion; but you will believe me when I say, that earth, nor men, with the eloquence of time, cannot begin to clothe language in as interesting and sublime a manner as this holy personage. No; nor has this earth power to give the joy, to bestow the peace, or comprehend the wisdom which was contained in each sentence as they were delivered by the power of the Holy Spirit! Man may deceive his fellow-men, deception may follow deception, and the children of the wicked one may have power to seduce the foolish and untaught, till naught but fiction feeds the many, and the fruit of falsehood carries in its current the giddy to the grave; but one touch with the finger of his love, yes, one ray of glory from the upper world, or one word from the mouth of the Savior, from the bosom of eternity, strikes it all into insignificance, and blots it forever from the mind. The assurance that we were in the presence of an angel, the certainty that we heard the voice of Jesus, and the truth unsullied as it flowed from a pure personage, dictated by the will of God, is to me past description, and I shall ever look upon this expression of the Savior's goodness with wonder and thanksgiving while I am permitted to tarry; and in those mansions where perfection dwells and sin never comes, I hope to adore in that day which shall never cease" (*Messenger and Advocate,* Vol. 1, October 1834, pp. 14–16).

Articles of Faith

THE CHURCH OF JESUS CHRIST OF LATTER-DAY SAINTS

History of the Church, Vol. 4, pp. 535–541

Background

The Articles of Faith originally appeared in a letter, now known as The Wentworth Letter. In the spring of 1842, the editor of the *Chicago Democrat*, John Wentworth, asked Joseph Smith to provide him with a brief history of the rise of the Church. The Prophet responded and the result was a several-page document containing the early history of the Church, including the First Vision and the coming forth of the Book of Mormon. We have included this letter in its entirety at the end of the Articles of Faith, in this study guide. The document included thirteen brief statements of the teachings of the Church on some issues and doctrines commonly discussed and often debated by churches of the day. Thus, these statements, now known as The Articles of Faith, do not cover all of the doctrines and teachings of the Church. Rather, they are brief and inspired statements of belief that, in Joseph Smith's day and in our day as well, provide a concise summary of our beliefs on a number of important topics.

John Wentworth did not publish this letter in his newspaper, but it was published in the Church's newspaper, the *Times and Seasons*, in March 1842, in Nauvoo.

1 WE believe in God, the Eternal Father, and in His Son, Jesus Christ, and in the Holy Ghost.

2 We believe that men will be punished for their own sins, and not for Adam's transgression.

3 We believe that through the Atonement of Christ, all mankind may be saved, by obedience to the laws and ordinances of the Gospel.

4 We believe that the first principles and ordinances of the Gospel are: first, Faith in the Lord Jesus Christ; second, Repentance; third, Baptism by immersion for the remission of sins; fourth, Laying on of hands for the gift of the Holy Ghost.

243

5 We believe that a man must be called of God, by prophecy, and by the laying on of hands by those who are in authority, to preach the Gospel and administer in the ordinances thereof.

6 We believe in the same organization that existed in the Primitive Church, namely, apostles, prophets, pastors, teachers, evangelists, and so forth.

7 We believe in the gift of tongues, prophecy, revelation, visions, healing, interpretation of tongues, and so forth.

8 We believe the Bible to be the word of God as far as it is translated correctly; we also believe the Book of Mormon to be the word of God.

9 We believe all that God has revealed, all that He does now reveal, and we believe that He will yet reveal many great and important things pertaining to the Kingdom of God.

10 We believe in the literal gathering of Israel and in the restoration of the Ten Tribes; that Zion (the New Jerusalem) will be built upon the American continent; that Christ will reign personally upon the earth; and, that the earth will be renewed and receive its paradisiacal glory.

11 We claim the privilege of worshiping Almighty God according to the dictates of our own conscience, and allow all men the same privilege, let them worship how, where, or what they may.

12 We believe in being subject to kings, presidents, rulers, and magistrates, in obeying, honoring, and sustaining the law.

13 We believe in being honest, true, chaste, benevolent, virtuous, and in doing good to all men; indeed, we may say that we follow the admonition of Paul—We believe all things, we hope all things, we have endured many things, and hope to be able to endure all things. If there is anything virtuous, lovely, or of good report or praiseworthy, we seek after these things.

JOSEPH SMITH

For your further study, the Wentworth Letter is included here. You will see the Articles of Faith at the end of the letter.

The Wentworth Letter

Following is the complete text of the Wentworth Letter, as written by the Prophet Joseph Smith:

"I was born in the town of Sharon, Windsor County, Vermont, on the 23rd of December, AD 1805. When ten years old, my parents removed to Palmyra, New York, where we resided about four years, and from thence we removed to the town of Manchester. My father was a farmer and taught me the art of husbandry. When about fourteen years of age, I began to reflect upon the importance of being prepared for a future state, and upon inquiring [about] the plan of salvation, I found that there was a great clash in religious sentiment; if I went to one society they referred me to one plan, and another to another; each one pointing to his own particular creed as the summum bonum of perfection. Considering that all could not be right, and that God could not be the author of so much confusion, I determined to investigate the subject more fully, believing that if God had a Church it would not be split up into factions, and that if He taught one society to worship one way, and administer in one set of ordinances, He would not teach another, principles which were diametrically opposed.

"Believing the word of God, I had confidence in the declaration of James—'If any of you lack wisdom, let him ask of God, that giveth to all men liberally, and upbraideth not; and it shall be given him.' I retired to a secret place in a grove, and began to call upon the Lord; while fervently engaged in supplication, my mind was taken away from the objects with which I was surrounded, and I was enwrapped in a heavenly vision, and saw two glorious personages, who exactly resembled each other in features and likeness, surrounded with a brilliant light which eclipsed the sun at noon day. They told me that all religious denominations were believing in incorrect doctrines, and that none of them was acknowledged of God as His Church and kingdom: and I was expressly commanded 'to go not after them,' at the same time receiving a promise that the fullness of the Gospel should at some future time be made known unto me.

"On the evening of the 21st of September, AD 1823, while I was praying unto God, and endeavoring to exercise faith in the precious promises of Scripture, on a sudden a light like that of day, only of a far purer and more glorious appearance and brightness, burst into the room, indeed the first sight was as though the house was filled with consuming fire; the appearance produced a shock that affected the whole body; in a moment a personage stood before me surrounded with a glory yet greater than that with which I was already surrounded. This messenger proclaimed himself to be an angel of God, sent to bring the joyful tidings that the covenant which God made with ancient Israel was at hand to be fulfilled, that the preparatory work for the second coming of the Messiah was speedily to commence; that the time was at hand for the Gospel in all its fullness to be preached in power, unto all nations that a people might be prepared for the Millennial reign. I was informed that I was chosen to be an instrument in the hands of God to bring about some of His purposes in this glorious dispensation.

"I was also informed concerning the aboriginal inhabitants of this country and shown who they were, and from whence they came; a brief sketch of their origin, progress, civilization, laws, governments, of their righteousness and iniquity, and the blessings of God being finally withdrawn from them as a people, was made known unto me; I was also told where were deposited some plates on which were engraven an abridgment of the records of the ancient Prophets that had existed on this continent. The angel appeared to me three times the same night and unfolded the same things. After having received many visits from the angels of God unfolding the majesty and glory of the events that should transpire in the last days, on the morning of the 22nd of September, AD 1827, the angel of the Lord delivered the records into my hands.

"These records were engraven on plates which had the appearance of gold, each plate was six inches wide and eight inches long, and not quite so thick as common tin. They were filled with engravings, in Egyptian characters, and bound together in a volume as the leaves of a book, with three rings running through the whole. The volume was something near six inches in thickness, a part of which was sealed. The characters on the unsealed part were small, and beautifully engraved. The whole book exhibited many marks of antiquity in its construction, and much skill in the art of engraving. With the records was found a curious instrument, which the ancients called 'Urim and Thummim,' which consisted of two transparent stones set in the rim of a bow fastened to a breast plate. Through the medium of the Urim and Thummim I translated the record by the gift and power of God.

"In this important and interesting book the history of ancient America is unfolded, from its first settlement by a colony that came from the Tower of Babel, at the confusion of languages to the beginning of the fifth century of the Christian Era. We are informed by these records that America in ancient times has been inhabited by two distinct races of people. The first were called Jaredites, and came directly from the Tower of Babel. The second race came directly from the city of Jerusalem, about six hundred years before Christ. They were principally Israelites, of the descendants of Joseph. The Jaredites were destroyed about the time that the Israelites came from Jerusalem, who succeeded them in the inheritance of the country. The principal nation of the second race fell in battle towards the close of the fourth century. The remnant are the Indians that now inhabit this country. This book also tells us that our Savior made His appearance upon this continent after His resurrection; that He planted the Gospel here in all its fulness, and richness, and power, and blessing; that they had Apostles, Prophets, Pastors, Teachers, and Evangelists; the same order, the same priesthood, the same ordinances, gifts, powers, and blessings, as were enjoyed on the eastern continent, that the people were cut off in consequence of their transgressions, that the last of their prophets who existed among them was commanded to write an abridgment of their prophecies, history, &c, and to hide it up in the earth, and that it should come forth and be united with the Bible for the accomplishment of the purposes of God in the last days. For a more particular account I would refer to the Book of Mormon, which can be purchased at Nauvoo, or from any of our Traveling Elders.

"As soon as the news of this discovery was made known, false reports, misrepresentation and slander flew, as on the wings of the wind, in every direction; the house was frequently beset by mobs and evil designing persons. Several times I was shot at, and very narrowly escaped, and every device was made use of to get the plates away from me; but the power and blessing of God attended me, and several began to believe my testimony.

"On the 6th of April, 1830, the 'Church of Jesus Christ of Latter-day Saints' was first organized in the town of Fayette, Seneca county, state of New York. Some few were called and ordained by the Spirit of revelation and prophecy, and began to preach as the Spirit gave them utterance, and though weak, yet were they strengthened by the power of God, and many were brought to repentance, were immersed in the water, and were filled with the Holy Ghost by the laying on of hands. They saw visions and prophesied, devils were cast out, and the sick healed by the laying on of hands. From that time the work rolled forth with astonishing rapidity, and churches were soon formed in the states of New York, Pennsylvania[,]

Ohio, Indiana, Illinois, and Missouri; in the last named state a considerable settlement was formed in Jackson county: numbers joined the Church and we were increasing rapidly; we made large purchases of land, our farms teemed with plenty, and peace and happiness were enjoyed in our domestic circle, and throughout our neighborhood; but as we could not associate with our neighbors (who were, many of them, of the basest of men, and had fled from the face of civilized society, to the frontier country to escape the hand of justice,) in their midnight revels, their Sabbath breaking, horse racing and gambling; they commenced at first to ridicule, then to persecute, and finally an organized mob assembled and burned our houses, tarred and feathered and whipped many of our brethren, and finally, contrary to law, justice and humanity, drove them from their habitations; who, houseless and homeless, had to wander on the bleak prairies till the children left the tracks of their blood on the prairie. This took place in the month of November, and they had no other covering but the canopy of heaven, in this inclement season of the year; this proceeding was winked at by the government, and although we had warantee deeds for our land, and had violated no law, we could obtain no redress.

"There were many sick, who were thus inhumanly driven from their houses, and had to endure all this abuse and to seek homes where they could be found. The result was, that a great many of them being deprived of the comforts of life, and the necessary attendances, died; many children were left orphans, wives, widows and husbands, widowers; our farms were taken possession of by the mob, many thousands of cattle, sheep, horses and hogs were taken, and our household goods, store goods, and printing press and type were broken, taken, or otherwise destroyed.

"Many of our brethren removed to Clay county, where they continued until 1836, three years; there was no violence offered, but there were threatenings of violence. But in the summer of 1836 these threatenings began to assume a more serious form, from threats, public meetings were called, resolutions were passed, vengeance and destruction were threatened, and affairs again assumed a fearful attitude, Jackson county was a sufficient precedent, and as the authorities in that county did not interfere they boasted that they would not in this; which on application to the authorities we found to be too true, and after much privation and loss of property, we were again driven from our homes.

"We next settled in Caldwell and Daviess counties, where we made large and extensive settlements, thinking to free ourselves from the power of oppression, by settling in new counties, with very few inhabitants in them; but here we were not allowed to live in peace, but in 1838 we were again attacked by mobs, an exterminating order was issued by Governor Boggs, and under the sanction of law, an organized banditti ranged through the country, robbed us of our cattle, sheep, hogs, &c., many of our people were murdered in cold blood, the chastity of our women was violated, and we were forced to sign away our property at the point of the sword; and after enduring every indignity that could be heaped upon us by an inhuman, ungodly band of marauders, from twelve to fifteen thousand souls, men[,] women, and children were driven from their own firesides, and from lands to which they had warantee deeds, houseless, friendless, and homeless (in the depths of winter) to wander as exiles on the earth, or to seek an asylum in a more genial clime, and among a less barbarous people. Many sickened and died in consequence of the cold and hardships they had to endure; many wives were left widows, and children, orphans, and destitute. It would take more time than is allotted me here to describe the injustice, the wrongs, the murders the bloodshed, the theft, misery and woe that have been caused by the barbarous, inhuman, and lawless proceedings of the state of Missouri.

"In the situation before alluded to, we arrived in the state of Illinois in 1839, where we found a hospitable people and a friendly home: a people who were willing to be governed by the principles of law and humanity. We have commenced to build a city called 'Nauvoo,' in Hancock county. We number from six to eight thousand here, besides vast numbers in the county around, and in almost every county of the state. We have a city charter granted us, and charter for a Legion, the troops of which now number 1,500. We have also a charter for a University, for an Agricultural and Manufacturing Society, have our own laws and administrators, and possess all the privileges that other free and enlightened citizens enjoy.

"Persecution has not stopped the progress of truth, but has only added fuel to the flame, it has spread with increasing rapidity. Proud of the cause which they have espoused, and conscious of our innocence, and of the truth of their system, amidst calumny and reproach, have the Elders of this Church gone forth, and planted the Gospel in almost every state in the Union; it has penetrated our cities, it has spread over our villages, and has caused thousands of our intelligent, noble, and patriotic citizens to obey its divine mandates, and be governed by its sacred truths. It has also spread into England, Ireland, Scotland, and Wales, where, in the year 1840, a few of our missionaries were sent, and over five thousand joined the Standard of Truth; there are numbers now joining in every land.

"Our missionaries are going forth to different nations, and in Germany, Palestine, New Holland, Australia, the East Indies, and other places, the Standard of Truth has been erected; no unhallowed hand can stop the work from progressing; persecutions may rage, mobs may combine, armies may assemble, calumny may defame, but the truth of God will go forth boldly, nobly, and independent, till it has penetrated every continent, visited every clime, swept every country, and sounded in every ear, till the purposes of God shall be accomplished, and the Great Jehovah shall say the work is done.

"We believe in God the eternal Father, and in His Son Jesus Christ, and in the Holy Ghost.

"We believe that men will be punished for their own sins, and not for Adam's transgression.

"We believe that through the atonement of Christ all mankind may be saved by obedience to the laws and ordinances of the Gospel.

"We believe that the first principle[s] and ordinances of the Gospel are: (1) Faith in the Lord Jesus Christ; (2) Repentance; (3) Baptism by immersion for the remission of sins; (4) Laying on of hands for the gift of the Holy Ghost.

"We believe that a man must be called of God by prophecy and by the laying on hands, by those who are in authority, to preach the Gospel and administer in the ordinances thereof.

"We believe in the same organization that existed in the primitive Church, viz: apostles, prophets, pastors, teachers, evangelists, etc.

"We believe in the gift of tongues, prophecy, revelation, visions, healing, interpretation of tongues, etc.

"We believe the Bible to be the word of God, as far as it is translated correctly; we also believe the Book of Mormon to be the word of God.

"We believe all that God has revealed, all that He does now reveal, and we believe that He will yet reveal many great and important things pertaining to the kingdom of God.

"We believe in the literal gathering of Israel and in the restoration of the Ten Tribes; that Zion will be built upon this [the American] continent; that Christ will reign personally upon the earth; and that the earth will be renewed and receive its paradisiacal glory.

"We claim the privilege of worshiping Almighty God according to the dictates of our own conscience, and allow all men the same privilege, let them worship how, where, or what they may.

"We believe in being subject to kings, presidents, rulers and magistrates, in obeying[,] honoring, and sustaining the law.

"We believe in being honest, true, chaste, benevolent, virtuous, and in doing good to all men; indeed we may say that we follow the admonition of Paul, 'We believe all thing[s], we hope all things, we have endured many things, and hope to be able to endure all things. If there is anything virtuous, lovely, or of good report, or praiseworthy, we seek after these things.

"Respectfully, &c., Joseph Smith" (*History of the Church*, 4:536–41).

SOURCES

Anderson, Richard Lloyd. *Investigating the Book of Mormon Witnesses.* Salt Lake City: Deseret Book, 1981.

Backman, Milton V. Jr. *The Heavens Resound, A History of the Latter-day Saints in Ohio, 1830–38.* Salt Lake City: Deseret Book, 1983.

Bible Dictionary, Authorized King James Version of the Bible. Salt Lake City: The Church of Jesus Christ of Latter-day Saints, 1979.

Church History in the Fulness of Times, Religion 341–343. Salt Lake City: The Church of Jesus Christ of Latter-day Saints (Institutes of Religion), 1989.

Clark, James R., comp. *Messages of the First Presidency of The Church of Jesus Christ of Latter-day Saints.* 6 vols. Salt Lake City: Bookcraft, 1965–75

Doctrine and Covenants Student Manual, Religion 324–325. Salt Lake City: The Church of Jesus Christ of Latter-day Saints (Institutes of Religion), 1981.

Doctrines of the Gospel Student Manual. Salt Lake City: The Church of Jesus Christ of Latter-day Saints (Institutes of Religion), 2000.

Encyclopedia of Mormonism. Edited by Daniel H. Ludlow. 5 vols. New York: Macmillan, 1992.

Journal of Discourses, 26 vols. London: Latter-day Saints' Book Depot, 1854–86.

McConkie, Bruce R. *A New Witness for the Articles of Faith.* Salt Lake City: Deseret Book, 1985.

McConkie, Bruce R. *Doctrinal New Testament Commentary,* 3 vols. Salt Lake City: Bookcraft, 1965–73, Vol. 1.

McConkie, Bruce R. *Mormon Doctrine.* 2d ed. Salt Lake City: Bookcraft, 1966.

New Testament Student Manual, Religion 211: The Life and Teachings of Jesus and His Apostles. Salt Lake City: The Church of Jesus Christ of Latter-day Saints, 1979.

Old Testament Gospel Doctrine Teacher's Manual. Salt Lake City: The Church of

Jesus Christ of Latter-day Saints (Institutes of Religion), 2001.

Old Testament Student Manual: Genesis–2 Samuel. Salt Lake City: The Church of Jesus Christ of Latter-day Saints (Institutes of Religion), 1981.

Pratt, Parley P. *Key to the Science of Theology/A Voice of Warning.* Salt Lake City: Deseret Book, 2002.

Pearl of Great Price Student Manual. Salt Lake City: The Church of Jesus Christ of Latter-day Saints (Institutes of Religion), 2000.

Petersen, Mark E. *Noah and the Flood.* Salt Lake City: Deseret Book, 1982.

Smith, Joseph. *History of The Church of Jesus Christ of Latter-day Saints.* Edited by B. H. Roberts. 2d ed. rev., 7 vols. Salt Lake City: The Church of Jesus Christ of Latter-day Saints, 1932–51.

Smith, Joseph. *Teachings of the Prophet Joseph Smith,* selected and arranged by Joseph Fielding Smith. Salt Lake City: Deseret Book, 1977.

Smith, Joseph Fielding. *Answers to Gospel Questions.* Compiled by Joseph Fielding Smith Jr. 5 vols. Salt Lake City: Deseret Book, 1957–66

Smith, Joseph Fielding. *Church History and Modern Revelation: A Course of Study for the Melchizedek Priesthood Quorums.* 4 vols. Salt Lake City: The Council of the Twelve Apostles, 1947–50.

Smith, Joseph Fielding. *Doctrines of Salvation,* 3 vols., edited by Bruce R. McConkie. Salt Lake City: Bookcraft, 1954–56.

Smith, Lucy Mack. *History of Joseph Smith by His Mother.* Salt Lake City: Bookcraft, 1958.

Widtsoe, John A. *Evidences and Reconciliations.* Salt Lake City: Bookcraft, 1943.

Young, Brigham. *Discourses of Brigham Young,* selected and arranged by John A. Widtsoe. Salt Lake City: Deseret Book, 1954.

About the Author

David J. Ridges taught for the Church Educational System for thirty-five years and has taught for several years at BYU Campus Education Week. He taught adult religion classes and Know Your Religion classes for BYU Continuing Education for many years. He has also served as a curriculum writer for Sunday School, seminary, and institute of religion manuals.

He has served in many callings in the Church, including Gospel Doctrine teacher, bishop, stake president, and patriarch. He and Sister Ridges served a full-time eighteen-month mission, training senior CES missionaries and helping coordinate their assignments throughout the world.

Brother Ridges and his wife, Janette, are the parents of six children and make their home in Springville, Utah.